1973

THE
IMPRINT OF ROMAN
INSTITUTIONS

Western Man *An Interdisciplinary Introduction to the History of Western Civilization*

THE
IMPRINT OF ROMAN
INSTITUTIONS

Edited by

David W. Savage
Clark University

HOLT, RINEHART AND WINSTON, INC.

New York   Chicago   San Francisco   Atlanta   Dallas   Montreal   Toronto

Cover illustration: The praetorian guard—from the period of Hadrian. (Giraudon)

Art research editor: Enid Klass

Copyright © 1971 by Holt, Rinehart and Winston, Inc.
All Rights Reserved
Library of Congress Catalog Card Number: 78–126800
SBN: 03-084674-9
Printed in the United States of America
1234   17   9 8 7 6 5 4 3 2 1

Preface

"What is history for?" [History is] "for" human self-knowledge, . . . [and knowing] yourself means knowing, first, what it is to be a man; secondly, knowing what it is to be the kind of man you are; and thirdly, knowing what it is to be the man *you* are and nobody else is. Knowing yourself means knowing what you can do; and since nobody knows what he can do until he tries, the only clue to what man can do is what man has done. The value of history, then, is that it teaches us what man has done and thus what man is.

R. G. Collingwood, The Idea of History *(New York: Oxford University Press, 1957), p. 10*

For more than a decade there has been a great deal of discussion about the relation between history and the social sciences. Many historians have wanted to make use of those disciplines which are chiefly concerned with man's psychological makeup and with his physical and social environments. To date, however, there has been a wide gap between this wish and visible accomplishments, especially in the content of university and college courses. The series "Western Man" is the product of several years of experimentation with a number of ways of organizing such an interdisciplinary course in the history of Western civilization. We had tried various combinations of texts, books of readings, paperbacks, and offprints in an attempt to reach this goal, but each combination created as many pedagogical problems as it solved. What we seemed to need in order to present exciting material in manageable and teachable form was a carefully edited integration of primary historical materials, interpretative works, and the analytical tools of sociologists, anthropologists, psychologists, and other social scientists. The result—after several years of selecting, editing, and trial in the classroom—is this series of volumes.

We have constructed these volumes in the belief that the study of one's personal and cultural history is an indispensable means by which experience is organized. We considered it desirable, therefore, that students know something about the historical development of the concept of the

v

psyche, soul, personality, or self so that they might understand the relationship between the accomplishments made by Western man and the view of the self at a given moment in history. Likewise it is important to understand the unique historical circumstances which were the source of, and gave a particular stamp to, the institutions which comprise Western society and the values which in large part structure our individual and collective behavior. The goal of this series, then, is to give the student some insight into the concept of self, social institutions, and values as they have developed in the West from ancient to modern times.

This particular purpose has made it necessary to treat the various stages in the history of Western civilization selectively. In *The Contribution of Ancient Greece,* for example, the focus is on the emergence of self-awareness and the concomitant development of natural philosophy, abstract mathematics, rhetoric, moral philosophy, epistemology, metaphysics, political theory, formal logic, and the concept of natural law. In *The Judeo-Christian Heritage,* on the other hand, emphasis is placed primarily on the development of the religious concepts and moral values of West-

ern society. *The Imprint of Roman Institutions* provides the student with an understanding of the early stages in the evolution of Western political and legal institutions, and the transformation of classical culture in that institutional matrix. Each period in Western history emerges as one in which a lasting dimension was given to the concept of self, social institutions, or values or to any combination of these three.

We have attempted to create a series of volumes which, with the addition of a few readily available paperbacks, can be used as the full reading assignment in a course in the history of Western civilization. Individual volumes can of course be used separately and in upper level courses. It is hoped that instructors and students will find that conceptual materials introduced in each volume will be useful in considering other historical problems.

We would like to express our deep appreciation to the students, friends, editors, and spouses who gave either support or active assistance while we were at work on this project. We would also like to thank those colleagues in the Western civilization program at Stanford University who tested our materials in the classroom and gave us both criticism and suggestions.

Donald E. Buck   William J. Courtenay   David W. Savage   Jacqueline Strain
Cupertino, Calif.   *Madison, Wis.*   *Worcester, Mass.*   *Rohnert Park, Calif.*

Fall 1970

Contents

Maps

Introduction

Political problems took on the dimension which is familiar to the Western tradition when the Hellenistic and Roman empires replaced the small communities of the tribe and the polis. It was in this historical context that the "state" first became a meaningful concept. The Greeks during most of their history did not draw a distinction between the social community and the political community. The polis was at once society and state. For the Hebrews and early Christians the words "kingdom," "nation," "tribe," and "people" all referred to small, closely-knit communities. It is not possible to say precisely when the distinction between society and state was first made. We can only say that the state emerged in recognizable form when the size of the territory ruled by a single government became larger than the polis or the tribe. At that point it became evident that the Greek and Hebrew assumptions about a homogeneous sociopolitical community were no longer applicable. The necessity of governing diverse peoples called forth a set of political institutions that possessed a monopoly of power within a larger social order and can be recognized as the state. In this historical setting, where political institutions are clearly distinguished from other basic institutions of society, we can analyze them and examine their function in the social system.

In this volume we will explore the origins and development of Roman political and legal institutions and examine their imprint on the Western tradition. Rome was not the first great empire known to history. It was preceded by Egypt, Assyria, Persia, and the Hellenistic monarchies. But it was Rome that most directly affected the Western tradition. Rome first brought Western and Central Europe within the reach of the civilization of the Mediterranean basin. Rome absorbed the philosophy of Greece and the Judeo-Christian religion and transmitted both to the West. But she first adapted these cultural elements to her own society and gave them an institutional setting which changed their original character before they became the foundations of Western civilization. Rome is also worth examining for her own sake, as perhaps the most spectacular example of the ways in which political and legal institutions perform their basic task of maintaining social cohesion in the face of continuous conflict among the members and groups of a complex society.

Each chapter is headed by quotations which indicate the more important themes in the readings. Careful attention should be given to them, for they give structure to the information provided by the selections. It should also be noted that the final chapter, Chapter 6, is twice the length of other chapters and should be assigned accordingly.

THE
IMPRINT OF ROMAN
INSTITUTIONS

CHAPTER 1

THE KINSHIP BASIS OF AUTHORITY AND VALUES:
The Roman Aristocratic Family

The family, in its essential meaning, must be considered as an example for imitation, constituting a fundamental category in human life and thought. It is the essence of ethics and morality; it is implicit in education. The concept of the Good is transmitted through the family and is derived from the ontological, indigenous needs of man's nature, which are actualized in the family structure.

Ruth Nanda Anshen, The Family: Its Function and Destiny

It was the ancient custom that we should learn from our elders not only by hearing but also by seeing what we ourselves in due course do and then hand down in turn to our successors. Thus the young were early taught by service in the camp so that they should learn to command by obeying, to be leaders by following; thus too when entering on a political career they stood at the doors of the senate house and watched the conduct of public business before they took part in it. Each had his father for master or if he had no father, a man of distinction and ripe age took the father's place.

Pliny the Younger, Letters

[The Roman's] house is for him what a church is for us; there he finds his worship and his gods. His hearth is a god; the walls, the doors, the threshold are gods; the posts which mark off his field are also gods. The tomb is an altar, and his ancestors are divine beings.

Fustel de Coulanges, in Albert Grenier, The Roman Spirit

The three main fields within which *pietas* might be exercised were the family, the state, and the divine purpose. Ultimately the three were the same. The loyalty owed to the state was only an extended form of the loyalty owed within the family. The loyalty to the gods was only an extended form of the loyalty to the state.

John Ferguson, Moral Values in the Ancient World.

1

Fundamental to the study of any society is the study of institutions. In our examination of Rome we will be dealing primarily with political institutions, and in this chapter, with kinship institutions. But these are only two of the major groupings which constitute the building blocks of society.

The number of institutions and the degree of their specialization varies from society to society. High civilizations and modern large-scale industrial societies are characterized by the intensive specialization of institutions organized around delimited problems of social life, and by the extensive internal elaboration of sub-systems within the larger institutions.

We must, therefore, think in terms of small-scale and large-scale institutions, and of complexes of institutions which form sub-systems within the larger society. At least four major sets or complexes of important institutions are recognized by most sociologists. It will be evident, however, that each group could readily be broken up into several still categories.

First, are the *political institutions*, concerned with the exercise of power and which have a monopoly on the legitimate use of force. Institutions involving relations with other societies, including war, are also considered to fall into the political category. Second, there are the *economic institutions*, concerned with the production and distribution of goods and services. *Expressive-integrative institutions*, including those dealing with the arts, drama, and recreation, represent a third set. This group also includes institutions which deal with ideas, and with the transmission of received values. We may, therefore, include scientific, religious, philosophical, and educational organizations within this category. *Kinship institutions*, the fourth main category, are principally focused around the problem of regulating sex and providing a stable and secure framework for the care and rearing of the young.

Although it is helpful and to a degree accurate to think of institutions as organized mainly around *one* central problem of social existence, it is misleading to assume that each institution's contribution to social life is limited to that main concern. Each major institutional complex participates in and contributes in a number of ways to the life of the community. The family, for example, may be, and often is, itself a productive enterprise, and it always engages in the distribution of goods and services. Economic institutions not only produce goods and services but must have an internal order which involves the control of force and the exercise of legitimate authority. These considerations have led sociologists to make a distinction between social structures conceived of in either the analytic or the concrete sense. When speaking of *concrete structures*, they refer to the institutions we are all familiar with—families, courts, factories, and the like. By *analytic structures* they mean the whole set of social ways, spread over many concrete institutions, whereby a society manages to effect the production and distribution of goods, the control of force, and its other basic functional needs. For example, when we speak of "the structure of authority" in the analytic sense, we mean the way in which authority is organized and exercised not only in political affairs but also in the neighborhood, the church, the school, the family, and even in informal groups. Analytic structures are, therefore, constructs, products of the mind, abstracted from the concrete reality of a set of specific institutions.[1]

The use of authority as an "analytic structure" and a classification of its "legitimate" forms were first introduced into sociological studies by the German sociologist, Max Weber. His concepts of charismatic, traditional, and legal-rational authority remain useful categories of analysis and will be employed in our examination of Roman institutions and society. There are, however, a number of other ways of considering the concept of authority.

[1] Alex Inkeles, *What Is Sociology?: An Introduction to the Discipline and Profession,* © 1964. Reprinted by permission of Prentice-Hall, Inc., Englewood Cliffs, New Jersey.

AUTHORITY
Carl J. Friedrich [2]

In common usage, authority is often confused with power or taken to be a synonym of power. In more learned discourse, authority has been defined as a particular kind of power, such as "formal power" or "rightful power." It has been spoken of in relation to persons, as well as to other entities, such as law or the dictionary. The problem of what makes people "accept" authority, by obeying commands or believing a message, has given rise to a variety of interpretations of authority. Authority has been juxtaposed to freedom, or to force, or to reason. It has been praised and condemned in all these contexts, and as a result, the word has been incorporated in a pejorative adjective, "authoritarian," and linked as a general characteristic to "personality" as an objectionable and eradicable trait. In most of these discussions, both on the popular and the learned level, it has been assumed that authority is a peculiar something that can be possessed, and gained or lost, as the case may be. Against such views it has been argued through the ages that there is only power based on some sort of constraint, and that authority is merely a make-belief, based upon religious faith at best.

It is illuminating to cast a glance at the Roman antecedents from which the word "authority" is derived. *Auctoritas* is . . . not readily definable in its original meaning. It has predominantly the sense related to the verb from which it is derived: *augere,*

to augment. *Auctoritas* thus supplements a mere act of the will by adding reasons to it. Such augmentation and confirmation are the results of deliberation by the "old ones." The *patrum auctoritas* is, for that reason, more than advice, yet less than a command. It is, as Mommsen comments, advice which cannot be properly disregarded, such as the expert gives to the layman, the leader in Parliament to his followers. This augmentation or implementation and confirmation had in ancient Rome, as did indeed authority elsewhere, religious overtones. While it was not intended to set limits to the free decision of the community, it was intended to prevent violations of what was sacred in the established order of things. It was believed that because such violations were a crime (*nefas*) against the divine order, they might jeopardize the divine blessing. Thus, the preservation of good auspices probably was the basic idea underlying the *patrum auctoritas,* the authority of the fathers, that is to say, of the Senate. It was a matter of adding wisdom to will, a knowledge of values shared and traditions hallowed, to whatever the people wanted to do. (Later on, the *auctoritas* became a more general notion, and something of what our modern word "author," meaning a maker or originator, suggests.)

Why bother with these ancient verbal connotations? Because they suggest the role of reasoning, they thereby help to get clearly into focus what is probably the central fact to which a great many of the situations refer in which the word "authority" is employed. When there are good reasons for doing or believing something, such action or thought acquires a quality which is otherwise lacking. This has been overlooked by that rather numerous group of writers and philosophers who thought

[2] Carl J. Friedrich, "Authority, Reason, and Discretion" in Carl J. Friedrich, ed., *Nomos,* I, *Authority* (Cambridge, Mass.: Harvard University Press, 1958), pp. 29–36. Reprinted by permission of Carl J. Friedrich and the publisher. Footnotes have been deleted.

they could build law upon power alone. The power of him who willed something was, they thought, what gave someone's decision authority. . . .

In his forthright little study on political verbiage, T. D. Weldon makes an effort at clearing away some of the thick underbrush that has grown up around the word "authority." He remarks that until recent times, no clear distinction has been drawn between power and authority, and that it is "too simple to identify 'authority' with 'force rightly or justly applied.' " He differentiates four kinds of authority, ranging from pure force to unquestioning confidence, and hence asserts that "force exercised or capable of being exercised with the general approval of those concerned is what is normally meant by 'authority.' " Thus, if the followers *want* wickedness, they will obey a wicked authority. And yet, at the start of his analysis, Weldon had pointed out that authority somehow is related to the fact that he who possesses it could produce reasons, if challenged. Such was the case of the Roman Senate, such is the case of the modern judge. To say, as Weldon does, that "the proper use of force is always authoritative" is quite inadmissible, unless this statement is made into a tautology by giving to the adjective "proper" the meaning of "reasonable," in the sense of possessing adequate reasons for him to whom the force is applied. What is more, Weldon himself seems to know this, for he tells us that when people begin to ask the question, "Why should I obey X," X is on the way to losing his authority.

This last observation deserves further exploration. For when such a question is raised, a number of answers may be given. One answer would be in terms of hierarchy and status—because he is your king or your father. Another might be in terms of religion and faith—because God has commanded you to do so. A third would be in terms of interest and advantage—because he may make you his heir and successor. A fourth would be in terms of personal emotions and loyalties—because he loves you and you are devoted to him. A fifth would be in terms of law—because article so-and-so of the civil code requires you to do it. Such a recital, though incomplete, suggests some of the values and beliefs involved in reasoning upon authority, and at the same time, it gives a first hint of the fluid, indeed the fugitive quality of power based on authority. However, these five answers do not enable us really to get at the distinctive phenomenon which the augmentation and confirmation of will by some sort of reasoning accomplishes. The escape into the psychological concomitants of this datum of political experience suggests that a crucial aspect belonging to its ontological core has not yet been laid bare.

We have, in the previous paragraph, spoken of authority in terms of obedience. This is very commonly done; indeed, in action-related situations, obedience is the predominant aspect. But there is another phase of authority which is paramount in such situations as those involving the teacher, the scholar, and the dictionary. As to the last, some very interesting special problems are presented by the authority of nonpersonal entities, such as dictionaries, laws, and the like. It might be argued that one could bracket these entities and their "authority," because their authority may be traced back to the human "authors" who created them. There is, furthermore, often a question as to who were the makers: the fathers at Philadelphia, or the long line of judges who adorned the Supreme and other courts, or yet the presidents and congressmen. From a certain standpoint, it may even be said that the Constitution as it exists today is the work of the entire American people. The problem of the "authority" of impersonal entities will, I believe, become more comprehensible, once the analysis of the rational component of authority has been further advanced.

Leaving aside, then, the authority of such impersonal entities, we return to the situation of the teacher, the scholar, the doctor, or the lawyer. Here authority seems to be related to the fact that the person wielding authority possesses superior knowledge or insight. Frequently—for instance, among scholars accepting each other's authority—the authority of X rests upon the fact that he could give extended reasons for the opinions he expounds. It is not essential for such authority, however, that these opinions are conclusively demonstrable; indeed only where they are not thus demonstrable, the phenomenon of authority in the strict sense is involved. In any case, the authority of the teacher, the scholar, the doctor, and the lawyer is infused with a rational element, and the belief in it includes the belief in superior "reasoning." It is challenged on the part of those who accept it, by asking, not, why should I obey? but, why should I agree?

Before I proceed with this analysis, it might be well to turn to a kind of primordial authority which has been particularly controversial in our time, namely parental authority. In the course of each child's development, the growth of authority may be studied and experienced. . . . In the beginning, the child is helplessly dependent and in the power of the parents. Indeed, their power is absolute force to such

a degree that the legislator has seen fit to step in and regulate by law, to control and limit, the unlimited power of the parents, at least to some extent. But this absolute power does not continue, as the child grows. A wise parent will increasingly prefer to explain what needs to be done and to be believed, to give reasons, thus replacing subjection by understanding. He will respond to the questions, "why?" and "wherefore?" and seek to develop in the child an understanding of, a participation in, the *reasons* which animate the parent in asking for obedience as well as for agreement. It is in this process that a new relationship, different from that of power and force, comes into being, and it is this relationship which I should like to designate as authority. Such authority rests upon the fact that the child increasingly gains insight into parental orders and regulations, into parental opinions and beliefs. The child learns to relate both to basic values, and thereby comes to share these values with his parents. Such insight anticipates the insight into the regulations and opinions of the larger community, the church, the school, and eventually the polity. What is important is to realize that all such discourse provides for participation of the child. By coming to understand these regulations and beliefs, the child is helped, so to speak, to shape them into proper possessions, to make them his own. Thus discipline is transformed into self-discipline. It may well happen, and often does in fact happen, that this process takes place only partially and incompletely. Power and force continue to play their role, often to the point where they create dangerous tensions and frustrations about which modern psychology and psychoanalysis have taught many revealing lessons. For, if the power of parents is wielded without such growing participation and insight on the part of the child, then either the community of the family is destroyed by the rebellion of the child, or the child's personality is destroyed by the imposition of meaningless opinions, rules, and regulations. It is this latter situation which has been the focal point of attack by many thoughtful critics who have written about the "authoritarian personality" and "authoritarian family relations," when actually what they mean is better termed "totalitarian personality," and "totalitarian family." . . . What seems to me significant about this well-known development within the family is that the phenomenon of authority is associated with "reasoning." And by reasoning I do not mean the absolute rationality alleged to be possessed by mathematics and logic, that is to say, the reasoning which calls no value judgment into play, but rather the reasoning which relates actions to opinions and beliefs, and opinions and beliefs to values, however defined.

It has, I hope, become apparent that I not only reject the use of the word "authority" for the purpose of designating any kind of power, but that when I speak of authority, I wish to say that the communications of a person possessing it exhibit a very particular kind of relationship to reason and reasoning. Such communication, whether opinions or commands, are not demonstrated through rational discourse, but they possess the *potentiality of reasoned elaboration*—they are "worthy of acceptance." Seen in this perspective, authority is a *quality* of communication, rather than of persons, and when we speak of the authority of a person, we are using a shorthand expression to indicate that he possesses the capacity to issue authoritative communications. And furthermore, when we say X possesses authority, we thereby propose to suggest that the communications which X addresses to A, B, and C are based upon reasoning that has meaning not only to X, but also to A, B, and C, in the sense of being related to knowledge which they all possess, or to opinions, beliefs, and values which they all share.

A child first learns about authority—and, indeed, about all values—in the family. Personal associations within the family are of a direct, face-to-face nature resulting in deep and enduring emotional ties. For this reason, and also because all societies are composed of family groupings, sociologists designate the family as a primary group.

The strategic significance of the family is to be found in its *mediating* function in the larger society. It links the *individual* to the larger social structure. A society will not survive unless its many needs are met, such as the production and distribution of food, protection of the young and old, the sick and pregnant, conformity to the law, the socialization of the young, and so on. Only if *individuals* are motivated to serve the needs of the society will it be able to survive. The formal agencies of social control (such as the police) are not enough to do more than force the extreme deviant to conform. Socialization makes most of us wish to conform, but throughout each day we are often tempted to deviate. Thus both the internal controls and the formal authorities are insufficient. What is needed is a set of social forces that responds to the individual whenever he does well or poorly, supporting his internal controls as well as the controls of the formal agencies. The family, by surrounding the individual through much of his social life, can furnish that set of forces.

The family then, is made up of individuals, but it is also part of the larger social network. Thus we are all under the constant supervision of our kin, who feel free to criticize, suggest, order, cajole, praise, or threaten, so that we will carry out our role obligations. . . .

Thus it is *through the family* that the society is able to elicit from the *individual* his necessary contribution. The family, in turn, can continue to exist only if it is supported by the larger society. If the society as a larger social system furnishes the family, as a smaller social system, the conditions necessary for its survival, these two types of systems must be interrelated in many important ways.[3]

The family is thus the primary socializing agent, the molder of personality, the basic mediator of cultural values. Its importance for the individual and for the functioning of the larger social system can scarcely be exaggerated. It is only recently, however, that the family has become a subject of historical investigation. R.M. MacIver, for example, though a sociologist, has provided an historical dimension to the study of kinship institutions; he regards the family as an incipient political institution which, in primitive societies, performs many functions later assumed by other social institutions.

THE FAMILY AS GOVERNMENT IN MINIATURE
R. M. MacIver[4]

. . . Regulation is a universal aspect of society. Society means a system of ordered relations. The system may be informal, folk-sustained, uncentralized, and without specific agencies, or it may be highly organized. But social regulation is always present, for no society can exist without some control over the native impulses of human beings. Political government appears when social regulation is taken over

[3] William J. Goode, *The Family* (Englewood Cliffs, N.J.: Prentice-Hall, Inc., 1964), pp. 2–3. Reprinted by permission of the publisher.

[4] Reprinted with permission of The Macmillan Company from *The Web of Government*, rev. ed., by Robert M. MacIver. © Copyright by Robert M. MacIver, 1965.

or begins to be presided over by a central social agency. At first the business of regulation is mainly a family concern, broadly protected by the custom of the inclusive group. To ascribe the beginnings of government to force or to contract or to some particular conjuncture is to ignore the fact that already in the family, the primary social unit, there are always present the curbs and controls that constitute the essence of government. Government is not something that is invented by the cunning or the strong and imposed on the rest. Government, however much exploitation of the weak by the strong it may historically exhibit, is much more fundamental than these explanations imply. It is the continuation by the more inclusive society of a process of regulation that is already highly developed within the family.

The family is bound up with all the great crises and transitions of life. It is the focus of the most intimate relationships, those in which the personality of man and of woman is most profoundly expressed and most thoroughly tested. It is the primary agent in the molding of the life-habits and the life-attitudes of human beings. It is the center of the most impressive celebrations and rituals, those associated with marriage, with death, and with the initiation of the child into the beliefs and ways of the community. It is the hearth, the home, the place where the generations are brought continuously together, where old and young must learn to make ever changing adjustments to their ever changing roles in the life-cycle.

The same necessities that create the family create also regulation. The imperative of sex has for human beings no pre-established harmony with longer-range imperatives, with the upbringing of the young and the maintenance and enhancement through the generations of the mode of life that the group, on whatever level, has acquired. The long dependence of the human young necessitates the establishment of some kind of control over sexual relations. There must be rules, and against so powerful an appetite, against the recklessness and the caprice of desire, these rules must be guarded by powerful sanctions. They must have back of them the authority of the community, bulwarked by such myths as the prevailing culture can devise against so formidable a danger.

Here is government in miniature and already government of a quite elaborate character. For sex is so closely inwrought with other concerns, and particularly with those of possession and inheritance, that its control carries with it a whole social code. The existence of the family requires the regulation of sex, the regulation of property, and the regulation of youth. If we briefly examine what is involved in these three types of regulation we shall see why the family is everywhere the matrix of government.

Let us consider the regulation of sex. It has a number of aspects. First there are mating rules, determining who may enter with whom into the kind of sexual union that contemplates the establishment of family life. Mating is hedged about by restrictions and conditions. There is generally a circle beyond which one may not mate and there is always a circle within which one may not mate. The former sustains the coherence of the community or class, the latter sustains the coherence of the family itself. There are "prohibited degrees" of kinship or family relationship within which mating is prohibited. Beyond this provision there are endless varieties of regulation exhibited by different human groups.

Then there are rules restricting sexual relations outside of mating. The main function of these rules is again to preserve the integrity of the family. Foremost among them is the practically universal incest taboo. If there is one rule that is common to all the endlessly divergent human societies that the earth knows or has known, it is this. It applies to sex relations between brother and sister, between son and mother, and between father and daughter, extending with somewhat less rigor to a kin group variably defined. The breach of this taboo arouses peculiar abhorrence, and it is so deeply embedded in human culture everywhere that it must have conveyed to the young the most profound sense of what government means. . . .

If we pursued this subject further we should find that under all conditions the family takes its particular form from the system of rules that prescribes and limits sexual relations. The family may be patriarchal or matriarchal, may be monogamous or polygamous, may conform to one or another of all the possible patterns of mating. The one universal principle is that it finds its being as well as its specific character within the shelter of a strongly sanctioned, highly authoritative code. Wherever the family exists—and it exists everywhere in human society—government already exists.

The code of the family inevitably stretches far beyond mere sexual regulation. The primary responsibilities and obligations of human beings are bred within the family. The relation of man to man is insubstantial and emotionless compared with the relation of spouse to spouse, of mother to child, of father to the household he maintains, of sibling to sibling, of children to parents, of blood-brother in the larger kin to blood-brother. These are the relations that in the context of the simple community confer on each his place and station, that animate and give meaning to his labor and his leisure, that raise a thousand questions of responsive behavior. The family is itself a way of living, and the way of living is always governed by a code.

We select from this pervasive code the regulation of property. The first form of property is land, and in all civilizations except the highly industrialized type in which we live land is overwhelmingly the most important form of property. The land belongs to the group, and the unit property-holder is the family. Each family has its plot of earth, its habitation, its home. Family and family earth are one. The mode of possession varies, and often is highly complicated. There are also generic differences characteristic respectively of hunting, fishing, pastoral, and agricultural peoples. But usually the land is divided between families rather than between individuals. The head of the family controls, rather than owns in his exclusive right.

This nexus of family and property is attested by the rules of inheritance, which generally require that on the death of the head of the family the land and other primary possessions pass to the children or next of kin. An exception is sometimes found in the case of nomad tribes devoted to hunting or cattle-raising, where there may be considerable freedom in the disposal of property to outsiders. But in the great majority of cases, where tribes are settled and engaged in the cultivation of the land, the family is closely associated with the particular soil. The land is then the family heritage; under the patriarchal system it is the patrimony, handed down from the fathers to the sons. It cannot be freely disposed of, it is virtually inalien-able. The principle mode of transferring property beyond the immediate family is as dowry, bride-price, or other conveyance attendant on the inauguration by marriage of a new family.

Furthermore, the economy of the simple community is a family economy. What is produced is shared within the family; what each provides is his or her contribution to the common stock. So much is true in degree of the family everywhere, but in the simpler community the family is a joint producer, not merely a beneficiary of the joint product. The family is, particularly in the agricultural economy, the functioning microcosm; within it there is division of labor, beyond it there is generally little. The primal division of labor, between the child-bearing female and the sustaining male, is developed and elaborated in the processes of family life. The routines of work and the customs of the economic scheme of things are learned, directed, and administered under the aegis of the family.

Thus we see that one of the major functions of government, the regulation of property, has its early locus in the circle of the family and the near-of-kin. The form of the family, whether it be matriarchal or patriarchal, monogamous or polygamous, endogamous or exogamous with respect to specific social groupings, unitary or composite, and so forth, is functionally interdependent with the code of property. This code is administered within the family and in dealings between families. It is family government and interfamily government. So in the course of things the heads of families, the *patres* become the council of the community.

In showing how the nature of the family necessitated the regulation of sex and the regulation of property and how the family itself was the primary agent in the maintenance of the customary law that determined its particular being we have not yet fathomed the significance of the family in the generation of the habits and patterns of government. Nor would that significance be adequately revealed if we went on to explain how the family was the locus of the altar as well as of the workshop, of the school as well as of the tribunal. Beyond all such associations there lies the elemental fact that man is born the most helpless and unwitting of animals, the least armed with ready instincts to fit him for survival, the slowest to develop his potentialities of autonomy; and at the same time the most receptive, the most imitative, the most educable, the most richly endowed. The family receives this amorphous being and through the long years of childhood shapes the mentality and orients it into social attitudes, imprinting on the impressionable organism the habits that become the foundation for all its later activities.

Even before the child is conscious of a self that self is being molded within the family. There are two main aspects of this process. One is the subtle unconsciously registered interaction of the nascent being with the family members, pre-eminently at first with the mother, as through the satisfaction of its animal needs it awakens gradually to a sense of social relations, of self and otherness, of dependence and demand, of love and anger. The child *makes* the first coherent society, for its coming transforms the fugitive relations of sex into the stability of the home. Of the society thus created the child is also the product. Modern social psychology and the intimations of psychoanalysis are revealing how deeply the effects of this interaction become rooted in the context of the growing personality, how they control dis-

positions seemingly developed in later situations, and how they manifest themselves in the conflicts and tensions, in the acceptances and rejections, that constitute the selective experience of the adult being.

With society, as always, goes regulation. This is the other aspect of the molding of the child. The home is the world of the child, and it is a governed world. Regulation is operative from the first, in the sequences of feeding and cleaning. Presently the child is disciplined in the exercise of his bodily functions. He is, so to speak, "house-broken." He is taught that this is right and that is wrong. As he learns the speech of the folk he learns the values that are conveyed by words. This is good and that is bad; this is honorable and that is shameful. So the long process of indoctrination and habituation begins. The child is governed in its going out and in its coming in, in its rising and in its lying down, and in its learning and in its playing, in its doing and in its thinking, in its hoping and in its fearing.

The child knows no other world, no other values. In the circle of the home affection and authority are combined, whatever the proportions may be. They are not likely to be wholly reconciled, for authority represses native inclinations. But the authority is final, as authority. There is no alternative, and there is no appeal. It may be disobeyed, but that is evasion. It may be defied, but that is rebellion. Here the authority is absolute. No other is even conceivable. Other authorities may rule outside, but to the child the outside is another world. The world of the child is a closed world of absolute authority, mitigated by affection. . . .

So far as the child is concerned the imperium of the home is always absolute at the first, and only the length of time through which it holds undisputed sway differentiates in this respect one form of culture from another. For the child the magic of the law begins as soon as it becomes aware of others and of its relation to others. What is right and what is wrong, the things it must not do and the things it must do, are delivered to it from on high, as the law was delivered to Moses. It is so ordained, it is the eternal way of things. It is incorporated in the rites and religious observances of the community. Beyond it there is no other law.

Most complex societies have developed gradually from more simple forms in which kinship institutitions were dominant. This was true of Greek and Hebrew civilizations and was equally true of Rome. The family, of course, continued to function in all these societies as the primary socializing agent even after many of its other functions had been assumed by other social institutions. Yet Rome, more than the other societies we have studied, affords an opportunity to examine the family as it relates to other social institutions in the process of social development. For in Rome the family, that is, the aristocratic family, continued to shape values and to influence the structure of politics for a longer period of time relative to the development of complex social institutions, than has been the case in most other civilizations.

Rome, which according to tradition was founded in 753 B.C. by the twins Romulus and Remus, was in fact not at first a single city but a collection of villages situated atop several hills near the Tiber River. Archeological evidence indicates that the first of these villages was established on the Palatine Hill some time in the eighth century B.C. by Latin-speaking people from the surrounding territory. The Latins were a rustic people—far less sophisticated than the Greeks who were beginning at that time to colonize southern Italy, or the Etruscans, their formidable neighbors to the north. They were primarily herdsmen and gathered in small vil-

lages at the center of a grazing area. Each Latin village was headed by a tribal chieftain who was advised by a council (senatus) of tribal elders. Sometime in the early seventh century B.C. the seven villages near the Palatine Hill formed a loose alliance called the Septimontium. They did this most probably for mutual defense, and they joined together from time to time for common religious ceremony. These seven villages seem from the very earliest times to have been divided into three tribes and thirty smaller groupings called curiae. The curiae, like the early Greek phratries, comprised all the arms-bearing men of the community—the heads of families, their sons, and free dependents. Each curia had its own religious worship and contributed a specific quota of men to the army. From time to time the thirty kinship groups were called together to form the Curiate Assembly. This early Roman political-military organization paralleled that of Greece during the Dark Ages down to the eighth century B.C., and both seem to have derived from a common Indo-European heritage.

The primary social unit among the Latins was the extended family, which included the immediate relatives by blood and marriage, a number of free dependents, and slaves. Within the household the father (paterfamilias) held absolute authority.

Those families which claimed descent from a common ancestor through the male line formed the larger unit of the gens or clan. Clan members were marked as such by their use of the clan name, the nomen, in addition to a personal name, the praenomen. At a later date, as the families comprising a gens multiplied, family names were divised to mark the particular branch of the gens to which a man belonged. For example, Julius Caesar's full name was Gaius Julius Caesar, which designated him as the individual, Gaius, of the Caesar family in the Julian clan.[5]

These kinship institutions formed the basis of Roman society well into the fifth century B.C. and left their mark on later development.

[5] Carl Roebuck, The World of Ancient Times (New York: Charles Scribner's Sons, 1966), p. 433.

Gradually in the sixth century B.C. the villages of the Septimontium came under the control of the Etruscans. Roman tradition records a succession of Etruscan kings who ruled until the Latins overthrew the monarchy in 509 B.C. The dates are not certain, but Etruscan domination for a period of about fifty years in the sixth century B.C. is verified by archeological evidence. The period was long enough for elements of the more advanced Etruscan culture to influence Roman development but not sufficiently long to obliterate the Latin tradition. Under Etruscan rule Rome ceased to be exclusively a collection of tribal villages along the Tiber and began to take on the characteristics of urban life. The Etruscans built fortications around the area of the seven villages, drained the marshland at the foot of the seven hills, and turned it into a market and meeting place—the Roman Forum. It is probable that the Romans learned the art of writing from the Etruscans, and elements of Etruscan religion—especially augury and divination—were brought into the Roman tradition.

As Rome grew in size and importance in the sixth century B.C. a class structure and specialization of economic function began to emerge. The members of the upper or patrician class were the descendants of the Latin tribal elders who, in the process of urban development, had maintained their positions as the owners of land, the leaders in war, and the heads of clans. Their dependents were known as clients. Clients were most probably in the first instance non-Romans brought into the protection of a Roman family. They worked their patron's land as tenant farmers, and, if they became citizens, supported their patron's in-

A Roman family, Sepulchral monument of Lucius Vibius, his wife and son. (Alinari)

terests in the assembly. The patron-client relationship was hereditary and an essential part of Roman kinship institutions.

The institution of slavery also enabled the patriciate to establish its social superiority. Like clientage, slavery was known in Roman society from the earliest times. Enslavement for debt occurred until the fourth century B.C. when, as in Athens during the reforms of Solon, this practice was abandoned. After that, Roman expansion in Italy made large numbers of captives available for exploitation, and slavery assumed greater economic significance. A slave, when purchased or captured, became a member of a household, and as such came under the protection as well as the absolute authority and discipline of the housefather. Only custom and possible public disapproval interfered with the father's control over his slaves. (In this respect the blood relatives were in no better position than the slaves.) As members of the household, Roman slaves were employed primarily in agriculture. Only later, in the third and second centuries B.C., were slaves regularly employed as domestic servants, or in labor gangs in the mines, or on public building projects.

Urban growth also brought into being a new class without great wealth or political privilege—the plebeians. The plebeians were traders, artisans, small landowners, and clients of the great families. The patricians erected rigid class barriers against these new elements. Marriage between patrician and plebeian was strictly forbidden. The patriciate remained a closed sect with its own religious practices and the sacred duty to defend the territory as soldiers. Social and economic leadership of Rome during the Etruscan period and for several centuries thereafter remained securely in the hands of the patrician families.

In 509 B.C., according to Roman tradition, the patriciate drove out the last of the Etruscan kings and assumed direct control of the Roman state. Recent archeological evidence suggests that this patrician "revolution" was not in fact a single event, but rather a gradual process by which the clan leaders and military commanders of Rome wrested power from the Etruscan overlords. Even though the process of change was gradual we can still regard the end of the sixth century B.C. as the point at which the Romans entered into a new stage of political and social development. During the centuries that followed (509–44 B.C.), Rome developed a set of political institutions that did not include kingship in the structure of authority, and which is usually referred to as the Republic.

[The pre-Republican] Roman constitution was founded on the institution of the monarchy. The king was the source of power, but under the direction of the patrician assembly [senatus]. It was believed that the divine forces giving the king his authority acted also in the assembly: the laws made by the assembly in collaboration with the deity had the same authority as those made by the king under divine guidance. When the monarchy disappeared, its religious functions passed to a person invested with the power to make sacrifices on behalf of the community, the "rex sacrificulus." The executive, judicial and military powers [imperium] passed to two annual magistrates called praetors. The same powers were given to two lieutenants of the praetors, known as consuls, while the praetors remained the titular holders of authority in legal matters.

When the consulate became the highest office of the Roman magistrature, the evolution of the state from the Etruscan model reached a significant point. Now the very idea of the "people" was identified with that of the "army." Military service was the single basis of any claim to citizenship, and now the military magistrates took precedence over those with religious or legal functions. Even the development of the public assemblies shows the increasing importance of military forces in their ranks as the basic element of collective life.

Gradually the consulate assumed all the attributes of royal power. The year took its name from the consuls, and either one had the right to veto the action of his colleague and subordinates. Around the city was drawn an imaginary line, the "pomerium." The territory of the state, in which the powers of the "numina," the Roman gods, were felt, and the laws inspired by them were effective, came to an end at this point, and foreign territory began. Here Rome held power by virtue of her military control of the area. But within the city no one was allowed to carry arms, the power of open violence was restricted, and the greatest care was taken to maintain good relations with the gods, for only in this way could the prosperity and happiness of the citizens be assured.[6]

Roman military strength was tested in a series of wars in Italy in the fifth and fourth centuries B.C. Rome emerged as the leading power in a league of Latin communities and eventually became the master of a confederacy which comprised the former Latin allies, the Etruscan territories, and the Greek cities of southern Italy. This Roman confederacy was the political basis of what came to be a common Italian culture.

During the Italian wars, the Romans instituted military changes which in turn altered the political and social structure of the Republic. Ranks of infantry gradually replaced the individual aristocratic warrior as the primary military unit. This new arrangement necessitated the participation of a larger number of citizens in military service. The infantry was composed of companies of one hundred soldiers (centuries). The citizenry was correspondingly divided into new territorial units called tribes, and reclassified into five groupings according to wealth, which determined each citizen's ability to equip himself for combat. The assembly of these territorial and military units, the Centuriate Assembly, gradually replaced the old Curiate Assembly and became one of the legal assemblies of the Roman people. The result, similar to Solon's and Cleisthenes' reforms in Athens, was gradually to replace the patriciate and its strict kinship basis with a new aristocracy derived from both citizen classes and based on wealth as well as ancient lineage.

These constitutional and social changes gave greater voice to the plebeian class which grew

[6] From *Political Power in the Ancient World* by Mario Attilio Levi, translated by Jane Costello, pp. 133–134. English translations copyright © 1965 by George Weidenfeld and Nicolson Ltd. Reprinted by arrangement with The New American Library, Inc., New York.

in number and strength during the two centuries following the establishment of the Republic. Early in the fifth century B.C. the plebeians formed their own assembly outside the regular framework of the constitution. This assembly in time was expanded to include all the reorganized tribes and the Tribal Assembly took its place with the Centuriate Assembly as one of the regular gatherings of the Roman people. The patriciate eventually took part in its meetings, but it nevertheless remained essentially a plebeian assembly. In it, the plebeians formulated their grievances, drew up resolutions (*plebi scita*), and elected their own officers—the tribunes of the people—who eventually gained a formal veto over all political action.

In the mid-fifth century, the plebeians successfully demanded the codification of the customs and legal practices of early Rome, the knowledge of which had previously been an exclusive possession of the patriciate. According to tradition this codification was accomplished by two commissions of ten magistrates, and the results were displayed in a public place, probably in the Forum, on twelve wooden tablets—the Twelve Tables. The eventual result, similar to the reforms of Draco and Solon in Athens, was a secularization of the law and its impartial application to a larger number of citizens. The plebeians also won the right to have members of their class elected to most of the new magistracies which were created in response to the expansion of Rome. In addition, plebeians won the right to election to one of the two consulships and to the dictatorship, an old office designed to replace the consulship temporarily in times of emergency. By 287 B.C., when plebiscites of the Tribal Assembly gained full legal validity, all legal distinctions between patricians and plebeians had been removed.

New social distinctions, however, had emerged to replace the old division between patrician and plebeian. The new aristocracy was now defined as those elected to public office and included both old patrician families and wealthy plebeians. All public office holders sat in the Senate, a much-expanded descendant of the old council of tribal elders. Membership in the Senate was hereditary, and for the most part new office holders were drawn from the ranks of the senatorial order. This new aristocracy profited directly from the policy of opening conquered Italian land for settlement and economic exploitation. They developed into a class of agricultural capitalists managing great estates *(latifundia)* worked by slave labor. Though it was forbidden by custom for an aristocrat to engage in trade, many senatorial families invested in expanding commercial corporations through clients who, in return, received legal protection and political favors from the senators. The senatorial class was thus able to support its agricultural position with commercial wealth. Throughout the Republican period the aristocracy retained its attachment to the land and its primacy in the military establishment.

Although the old hereditary patrician aristocracy gave way in the course of Roman expansion to a new aristocracy based on office-holding and wealth, and although kinship institutions no longer formed the basis of the political constitution, there was a surprising persistence within the aristocracy of the social, religious, and legal traditions of the patrician family. For this reason it is important to obtain as clear a picture as possible of the development of the Roman family. The following selection locates in the early form of the Roman family the source of much that characterized later Roman society. Through comparative linguistic analysis, C. W. Westrup has shown that the early forms of the Roman family derived from an Indo-European (what he calls Aryan) heritage shared by many peoples of the Mediterranean basin and western Asia. As a legal historian, he specifically points out the elements of Roman law which had their origin in the early family.

THE ROMAN FAMILY
C. W. Westrup[7]

Among the ancient Aryan-speaking peoples, the family was undoubtedly in the

[7] C. W. Westrup, *Introduction to Early Roman Law: The Patriarchal Joint Family* (Copenhagen: Levin and Munksgaard, Ejnar Munksgaard, 1934 and 1939), vol. II, *Joint Family and Family Property,* pp. 5–6, 13–16, 21–23; vol. III, *Patria Potestas,* pp. 143–144, 146, 168–170, 193–194, 220. Reprinted by permission.

first place a community of cult. It was founded on marriage, and the aim of marriage was to produce legitimate progeny which could perpetuate the ancestral cult and thus ensure the continued existence of the family. But the family was, in addition, an economic association necessitated by the material cultural conditions. In a remote common Aryan time, when our ancestors, passing from a nomadising hunting life to field agriculture, began to till the soil, the joint undivided [i.e., extended] family, comprising several generations, became a practical necessity.

The cultivation of the land called for joint effort. If husband and wife were to be able to procure what was necessary for the maintenance of the family, the sons, when they grew up, must remain in the home in order to till the soil in conjunction with the father. At a time when the number of slaves kept was very limited and only a single male slave—the spoil of war—or a single female slave was probably the rule, the requisite labour could only be procured in this way. By such a community of work between several generations, the transmission of the experience gained was also best ensured. Socially, too, for . . . the decrepit, the inner solidarity of the family would be further fortified by the mutual economic support afforded by this joint domestic life comprising several generations.

Even after the sons had brought home wives, they remained with their wives in their father's house. Since now undoubtedly marriages were contracted at an early age, it would no doubt often happen that three generations with their wives and children lived together in the same house, united by community of cult, community of work and community of property.

In historical Rome the family normally consisted only of the parents and the children. About the young M. Licinius Crassus, however, we have the well-known account in Plutarch that he lived with his wife and two married brothers in his father's little house and that they all every day took their meals together at the same table. About Aemilius Paulus' son-in-law, Aelius Tubero, who was himself highly esteemed for ancient Roman virtue, we are told that there lived simultaneously 16 men of his family who bore the name Aelius, that between them they had only a small house in Rome and a modest country place at Veii which they themselves were able to cultivate together, and that they all with their wives and children had their common hearth and home there.

In this domestic community of several generations we have evidently the last remnants of an earlier Roman form of joint life which can doubtless be traced back to an obsolescent common Aryan organisation, the joint undivided family, united in the house community.

The economic conditions which, in a remote past, had created the joint family and made it a practical necessity, were still in the main the same in prehistoric Rome. At a time when the Greeks were already a trading and industrial people in rapid development, the Romans were still predominantly an agricultural peasant population. And the cultivation of the infertile Roman soil—like the cultivation of the soil in the common Aryan period—demanded combination. Among the Italic, Umbro-Sabellic tribes from which the Romans must be assumed to be descended, the house community must therefore have been preserved, after the Greeks, as early as before Solon's time, had developed the individual family from the joint undivided family. . . .

This house community, the form of the family created within the joint undivided family as a result of the primitive social-economic conditions and the religious ideas of the ancients, was more than a mere form of living together. The house community was a community of work and property, a system of law in common. In the conception of the family in the legal sense, it was the domestic association uniting the family which was the actual constitutive element. The family was not a geneological concept. It was not primarily an association of blood relations. It was an association of housemates, a household. Its point of crystallisation was the house. Those who belonged to the same house formed, collectively, the family. . . .[8]

With the alteration in the social conditions resulting from the economic development [in the fifth and fourth centuries B.C.] and the new practical claims consequent thereon, there occurred a change in the form of the family. The evolution of trade and industry and the division of labour connected therewith demanded greater individual liberty. The changed social conditions created the necessary economic conditions for the emancipation of the grown-up sons. The development of slavery was probably a contributory factor. The old community of work between the several generations which gave to the joint family its form and its material foundation, became less of an economic necessity with the increased employment of slaves for the cultivation of the land. When

---

[8] [The legal relationship deriving from the joint undivided family under the Roman civil law was called "agnatic." "Agnates" were all those who were subject to the same *patria potestas* whether related by blood or not. Thus a mother was the agnatic sister of her own children and legally adopted persons. This legal relationship persisted throughout Roman history, though it gradually gave way in practice to *cognatio,* or blood relationship.]

the grown-up sons married on attaining maturity, they founded their own *households*. From the joint undivided family there arose, as is evidenced earliest among the Greeks . . . the legally independent individual family.

Among the Romans, too, probably at a comparatively late date, though presumably as far back as prehistoric times, it became the custom that the sons (and the sons' sons) upon contracting marriage founded their own households (*familiae*). Thus in Rome, also, the joint undivided family was split up into individual families comprising only the parents and their children. But legally the development was essentially different. Though forming separate households, the Roman sons' families (and sons' sons' families) did not in historic times form independent families in civil law—as the Greek individual families —but in conjunction with the father's family (and grandfather's family) they still legally constituted only one undivided family with the father (or grandfather) as the *paterfamilias*. . . .[9]

The national Roman patriarchal family organisation, where only the father's (grandfather's) family was legally independent, only the father (grandfather) was *sui iuris* [legally competent], is in reality a remnant of the ancient common Aryan joint family, preserved through a series of evolutional stages for special so-

cial and political reasons, and subsequently undergoing a further legal development.

The legal significance of the Roman family is to be found primarily in the power of the *paterfamilias* to make concrete judicial decisions based upon his knowledge of customary law. This power, like the joint undivided family itself, had its origins in prehistoric times.

In early times the formation of the so-called positive law took place exclusively by way of custom. Within the family, too, early law is throughout self-grown so-called customary law. Here, also, positive law is in the last instance created by the demands of practical life, and custom is here, too, established by concrete dooms. . . . The head of the family establishes what, in accordance with the traditions of the ancestors, is to be valid as Law and Justice in the family. Then, from this concrete judicial decision (doom), here too, the general legal maxim, the law, is abstracted and formulated.

Among the Aryan-speaking peoples the family was in early times everywhere autonomous: law is virtually formed through customs created within the family by concrete judicial interpretation of Justice. The Roman *patria potestas* itself, according to the classical jurisconsults, had its origin in custom. And the instrument of this autonomy is the head of the house. The house-father is the interpreter of the legal traditions (*mores* of the Romans) handed down from father to son. What the father had learnt as the custom of his fore-fathers he again taught his son. The *paterfamilias* does not create law. But as the person who, by virtue of the higher insight accorded him by the gods, had uncontested and incontestable knowledge of ancestral cus-

[9] [For instance, in Roman private law until the first century A.D. only the *paterfamilias* could own property. Whatever the son acquired, whether property, wife or children, he acquired for the *paterfamilias*, although the father might allow him to dispose of the property. Thus the joint undivided family survived in property law long after the individual family replaced the larger unit in practice. These distinctions did not affect the public law. Father and son alike had equal rights and obligations as citizens.]

toms, of the legal usages, he had to interpret, to "show," to say, to dictate, what was Law. . . .

Through the natural autonomy of the house, with the head of the house as the hereditary personal interpreter and upholder of the traditions, the family took shape as a legal institution. . . .

In primitive Rome the family chief was in principle *sovereign,* socially *sovereign. Tenebant non modo auctoritatem sed etiam imperium in suos* [They retained not only authority, but also command, over their families], Cicero says about the early Roman *paterfamilias.* His *potestas* was not limited by any other social authority. The rules established by custom governing the family were *leges imperfectae* [vague or undefined laws]. Only quite exceptionally, as far as we can surmise, did a precept positively ordain a punishment—or a penal effect—if a house-father arbitrarily set aside the commands of the law. Thus an ancient decree, referred by Dionysios to Romulus, seems to have punished with the forfeiture of his *patria potestas* the house-father who abused his authority as the economic ruler of the house by "selling" the son, i.e. by hiring out the son's labour, more than twice. But an instinctive respect for religious precept and ancestral custom (*mos patrius*) in connection with a practical sense of law and order had made the socially sovereign *potestas* of the *paterfamilias* a regular exercise of Justice.

The primitive Roman *paterfamilias* was a peasant and further, if required by the times, a soldier. Sober and earth-bound, he understood by experience the immediate advantage of observing the established precept, he understood the social utility of the firmness and the constancy of the rule. When Cicero, speaking of the remote times when not law but mere force prevailed, makes the individual's recognition of the *utilitas* of respecting the law a constitutive factor in the maintenance of the social order itself, it is no mere philosophical reflection he expresses, but an historical reality, bearing in mind the peculiar character of the Roman people. Like the peasantry of all ages, the Roman peasant was, besides, full of superstition; perhaps he was more superstitious than actually religious. In order to preserve the good understanding with the gods (*pax deum*), in order to please the supernatural powers, for the peace of his own soul, he submitted to what custom and usage, to what Law and Justice commanded. Further, as a soldier trained in discipline he instinctively felt the importance and necessity of submitting obediently to the dictates of the command. Among the Romans, whose whole history, as far back as it is known, is pervaded by a normative and disciplining belief in authority, obedience to the law was from the old days, more than in any other people, deeply rooted in the mind of the individual. And this spontaneous and constant adherence to established usage and "ancestral custom" was bound to create that domestic discipline and, above all, that respect and veneration for *auctoritas* which by giving strength and force to the government of the house gave the *paterfamilias* that personal authority and that intensified will to see that Law is observed and Justice done which in all primitive community is the foundation for and the condition of a regular and effective exercise of *patria potestas.*

The family was also the source of many of the characteristic features of Roman religion. The household cult had its roots in the extended or joint undivided family where religious institu-

Statuette of a Lar, protector of the Roman family. (Metropolitan Museum of Art, Rogers Fund 1919)

tions were undifferentiated from economic or political ones. Even after the extended family had given way to the individual, or nuclear, family, and other social institutions had taken over many of the functions of the primitive family, the rituals associated with the hearth and field continued to be practiced.

The early Romans believed that nature was filled with an impersonal spiritual force (*numen*) which was manifested in specific concrete events surrounding human life. These manifestations the Romans attributed to deities, some with personal names, some known only by the specific function which they performed. The Romans, even under Greek influence, did not fully personify their gods. The gods were addressed as *pater* in the way one would regard the *paterfamilias,* as one having authority and power within a specific realm, not as the Greeks might regard them, as fathers of other gods, or as the Hebrews regarded Yahweh, as the creator of man and nature. The Romans derived no geneologies for their gods, nor did they develop a mythology to express the relationship of gods and men. Their true meaning was to be found in the ordinary rather than the extraordinary events of life, in the regular functions of sowing and harvesting, birth and death, travelling and homecoming. The great gods usually associated with the functions of nature—Jupiter (sky-god),

A Roman aristocrat holding wax masks of two ancestors. These effigies were carried in funeral processions. See Polybius' description on page 52. (Alinari)

Ceres (goddess of grain), Mars (the god of war)—were called upon only when their particular function was to be performed, or on regularly appointed ceremonial days. Only the minor spirits of the household—Vesta (hearth-goddess), Janus (guardian of the doorway), the Penates (watchers of the storeroom), the Genius (spirit of the ancestral father), and the Lares (protectors of the family fields)—were attended to daily. In these ceremonies the entire family participated, for the welfare of the household depended upon the functions which these spirits represented.

Particular significance seemed to be attached to the cult of the ancestors. Long after the joint undivided family had given way in practice to the individual family, there remained a strong sense of solidarity with departed generations which had its foundation in the economic and sacred unity of the early family.

With settled life, which led to the dead being buried on the family's own land, originally in his own house, and probably near the hearth or under the threshold, the defunct of the family, the dead "fathers," became as it were part of the family. . . . A reminiscence of these old ideas is met with in the custom prevalent among the Roman nobility far down into the time of the emperors, that the images of the ancestors (*imagines majorum*) set up in the atrium were taken out of their small cupboards when a great man of the family was to be carried to his last resting-place, and borne in a pompous funeral procession in front of the dead man's bier. These *imagines* were no doubt originally the wax masks used in olden times at the customary expositions of the dead man's body to cover the face so as to hide the decomposition that quickly set in. And they were kept with the "forefathers in the atrium," at any rate originally, not to form a collection of family pictures but, as Pliny has it, in order that they might at *gentilicia funera* [clan funerals] "accompany" the dead. Always, when a member of the family was to be buried, the whole host of the deceased of the family were to be present personally. And these wax masks which had the dead man's features did not merely represent the dead. They were the dead themselves. In the image of the departed, conceived as a reality, the dead lived on.

The hearth, under which the housefather had once been buried, was the seat of the household gods and the symbol of the continued existence of the house.

In the hearth [the Roman] saw his dead ancestor's "soul." In the flame of the hearth-fire which was kindled anew each spring in honour of the first ancestor, the protector of the house, the Romans imagined, as it were, the ever-wakeful and active soul of the dead *paterfamilias*, to be living on, immortal.

It was the duty of the housewife and her daughters to kindle the hearth-fire from which the goddess Vesta watched over the welfare of the family.

When the first Latin clans joined together to form a community, the family cult became the basis of a state cult. The welfare of the community, like the welfare of the family, depended on the respect shown toward what was sacred and on the regular and correct observance of the cult. This attitude the Romans expressed by the word "*religio.*" Because Roman religion demanded the observance of precise ritual formulas, it was necessary that men with full knowledge of the technical formalities should attend to the state cult. These men formed a college of priests (*pontifices*), headed by the *Pontifex Maximus,* who drew up the calendar of festivals and advised the population of the correct formulas for legal action. The *pontifices* were assisted by minor colleges: the vestal virgins tended the hearth-fire of the state; the *fetiales* ensured that Rome always conducted diplomatic negotiations with the favor of the gods; and augurs read omens from the flight of birds or the entrails of a sacrificial animal, and were consulted by the king, or later on, by generals, before engaging in battle. It was important for later Roman development, however, that these priests did not become a special caste within society. They remained members of the patrician class and were marked only by their special knowledge of the ways of the ancestors. Under the influence of Etruscan and Greek religion the Romans singled out, as early as the sixth century B.C., a triad of great gods whose special concern was the Roman state. Jupiter, Juno and Minerva were worshipped in temples of Etruscan and Greek design. In addition, the cults of foreign gods were introduced into Rome as she extended her influence and contacts beyond Italy. Still the ancient cults remained fixed in their formal worship and continued to command the loyalty of the aristocracy and the official recognition of the state.

Roman religion as practiced in the family and state cults profoundly affected Roman aristocratic values, and these values in turn became to a considerable extent the values of the culture as a whole.

The highest Roman virtue was *pietas,* the proper observance of obligations to the gods, the state, and to the family, and the most important quality of Roman character was *gravitas,* a serious, dignified attitude to life. Material and practical as they were, the Romans learned from their religion and the regimen of their household a sense of personal duty, responsibility, and a profound respect for ancestral custom. The Romans did not embark on action lightly, but once a decision was made, they held to it with stubborn tenacity.[10]

Education, like religion, began in the family and continued to be dominated by traditional

[10] Roebuck, *The World of Ancient Times,* p. 436.

values even after educational practices began to change.

Legal historians love to emphasize the Roman family's strong constitution—the sovereign authority that was invested in the *paterfamilias,* the respect that was accorded to the mother—and nowhere is this more evident than in the matter of education. In the eyes of the Romans the obvious place in which children should grow up and be educated was the family. Even under the Empire, when it had been the custom for a long time to educate children together in schools, they still went on . . . discussing the advantages and disadvantages of the two systems; and it was not always the old one of keeping the child at home . . . that was given up.

How different from Greece! The contrast is clear from the child's earliest years. In Rome it was not a slave but the mother herself who brought up her child, and even in the greatest families she considered it an honour to stay at home so that she could do her duty and be as it were a servant to her children.

The mother's influence lasted a lifetime— hence the symbolic value of the famous tale that was handed down about Coriolanus. Coriolanus had revolted against Rome and was advancing upon the great city at the head of the Volsci. Ambassadors came out from the Roman people and pleaded with him, and they were followed by the city's priests, but despite their entreaties Coriolanus remained inflexible. Finally his mother appeared and upbraided him; and he yielded. The story may have been a myth, but it expressed a genuine feeling. We know the part played in their sons' lives in historical times, in the second and first centuries B.C., by Cornelia the mother of the Gracchi, Aurelia the mother of Caesar, and Atia the mother of Augustus, all of whom brought up their sons to become leaders of men.

A bone doll—third century B.C. (Metropolitan Museum of Art)

When the mother was unable to do her job properly, a governess was chosen to look after the children, and she was always a relative, a woman of experience whom all the family respected, and a person who knew how to maintain an atmosphere of severity and a high moral tone—even when the children were playing games.

From the age of seven onwards the child ceased, as in Greece, to be entirely in the hands of the women, but in Rome he came under his father. This is absolutely typical of the Roman system of teaching. The father was looked upon as the child's real teacher, and even later on, when there were proper teachers, they were still supposed to behave more or less like fathers.

While the girls tended to remain at home with their mothers, industriously spinning wool and doing the housework—this was still the custom when the austere Livia was bringing up Augustus's grand-daughters—the boys went off with their father, right into the "curia" even when the senate was sitting in secret, and so they saw all sides of the life ahead of them, learning from his precepts and still more from his example. The young Roman aristocrat, in his toga edged with purple—*praetextatus*—took part like the Greek *kouros* [youth] in the great feasts, singing and serving at table—but he was with his father, not his lover. . . .

When the boy was about sixteen, this home education came to an end. There was a ceremony to mark the beginning of the next stage: he took off his toga edged with purple and any other marks of childhood and put on the *toga virilis* instead. He was now a citizen. But he had not finished his education. There was his military service, and before that, usually, a year spent in "preparing for public life"—*tirocinium fori.* . . .

Theoretically the *tirocinium fori* was supposed to end after a year and the young Roman was supposed to go off to the army, but politics was far too serious a matter for it to come to an end as quickly as that. The young aristocrat went on following a successful politician around—who might be his father, but was usually someone else.

It was the same with military service. The first year was spent in the ranks: a potential leader had first to learn to obey, and in any case it would always be to the advantage of his political career if he was wounded or did something striking in battle. Young Scipio, for instance, the future Africanus, saved his father the consul when he was wounded at the battle of the Ticinus. But in actual fact the young aristocrats were not treated like ordinary conscripts, for they had tutors to look after them, and in any case they very soon left the ranks to become staff officers—*tribuni militum*—either as the result of being elected by the people or by being nominated by the general-in-chief.

Having become a staff officer, the young Roman aristocrat completed his training under some well-known man for whom he had the utmost respect and veneration.[11]

The education of a young Roman aristocrat was thus closely bound to the family, the army, and to the political life of the capital. These were the areas—family, army, and government—in which the Roman aristocrat lived out his whole life. These were the roles—father, soldier, and magistrate—which he was expected to perform. The content of his education was, therefore, practical training and above all an ethical ideal.

The Republican nobility expressed its [ethical] ideal in the concept of *virtus*. The word, like many others with which we shall have to deal, is not translatable. "Manliness" is perhaps the nearest we can get. Fundamentally it describes the peculiar nature and quality of the man, *vir*, as *senectus*, old age, describes the quality peculiar to the *senex*, old man, and *iuventus*, youth, that peculiar to the *iuvenis*, young man. But, whereas youth and

[11] From *A History of Education in Antiquity* by H. I. Marrou (trans. George Lamb), © 1956 by Sheed & Ward Inc., New York. Reprinted by permission of the publisher.

old age are defined largely by external and objective criteria, *virtus* is essentially a subjective concept. As one's notion of the particular end of man varies, so will one's definition of his proper activity and quality. Define the end of man as to achieve maximum material prosperity and *virtus* may consist in the more or less ruthless acquisition of money. Define it as the salvation of an immortal soul and *virtus* may consist in prayer, contemplation and withdrawal from the world. The Roman aristocrat was above all a political animal. Left, as we have seen, in the uninterrupted enjoyment of political power and position, he defined his ideal way of life as above all political. *Virtus,* for the Republican noble, consisted in the winning of personal preeminence and glory by the commission of great deeds in the service of the Roman state. It is with this concept, or rather complex of concepts that we shall be concerned. For from being the ideal of a narrow ruling class it became accepted as the tradition of Rome herself and through many transformations and redefinitions survived not only the class that had first given it birth but even the civilization and culture to which it first belonged.

We first meet this ideal, asserted rather than reasoned, for these are funerary inscriptions, on a series of laudatory epitaphs dating from the end of the third and the first half of the second centuries B.C. What appears to be the earliest of the series, the epitaph of L. Cornelius Scipio, begins with a splendidly confident statement of aristocratic pre-eminence: "This one man most Romans agree was the best of all good men." A. Atilius Calatinus went one better: it was not merely the Romans but "most nations" who agreed that he was "the leading man among the Roman People." Scipio's epitaph supports its opening assertion with a record of his civil offices, military successes and services to the gods. These three areas of activity, the government, the army and the state religion, comprised the whole of public life, the last no less and no differently from the other two. . . .

The Roman aristocrat was expected to show courage and wisdom, the two qualities most important for a general and a magistrate. In this context wisdom did not denote a rarified philosophic detachment or an intellectual enquiry into first causes and the nature of things. It meant practical political judgement, which was of little use unless expressed in words at meetings of the Roman People and of the Senate in such a way as to influence the course of events. It was only thus, by originating and instigating public policy, by being an *auctor publici consilii,* that the Roman politican could attain the highest form of prestige, *auctoritas.* . . .

. . . The ideal of the Roman aristocracy in its earliest expression known to us. . . . consisted in the gaining of pre-eminent *gloria* by the winning of public office and the participation in public life and by using these methods to achieve great deeds in the service of the state. It concerned not only the individual noble but the whole family, not only its living members but the dead ancestors and the unborn posterity. It imposed a proper standard of conduct. In its strict application it was a concept at once extrovert and exclusive: extrovert in its insistence on action, on deeds; exclusive in its concern for the family and in that the service of the state alone was considered a fit field for the exercise of a noble's talents. Outside the service of the Republic there existed no public office and, therefore, strictly speaking, no *gloria,* no *nobilitas,* no *auctoritas,* no *virtus.* . . .[12]

The continuing importance of the aristorcratic ideal as exemplified by a Roman *paterfamilias* is nowhere better illustrated than in the career and personality of M. Porcius Cato, or Cato the Elder (234–149 B.C.). Cato was a leading statesman and orator when Rome was establishing

[12] Reprinted from Donald Earl, *The Moral and Political Tradition of Rome.* Copyright © 1967 by Thames and Hudson. Used in the USA and Philippines by permission of Cornell University Press and in Canada by permission of Thames and Hudson. Footnotes have been omitted.

herself as the dominant power in the Mediterranean under the leadership of the great senatorial families. In spite of the changes which expansion brought, Cato doggedly held to the traditions of the agrarian patriciate. Plutarch, an important ancient biographer writing in the early second century A.D., combined recorded fact and oral legend in his life of Cato. The result is at once a vivid portrait of an important historical figure and a statement of the conservative Roman values which stem from the family. From Plutarch's biography of Cato one can also understand the importance of the Roman family as an educational institution where the young were taught by example.

CATO THE ELDER
Plutarch[13]

Marcus Cato's family is said to have originated from Tusculum, although he himself was brought up and spent his life—before he devoted himself to politics and soldiering—on a family estate in a country of the Sabines. None of his ancestors appears to have made any mark in Roman history, but Cato himself praises his father Marcus as a man of courage and a capable soldier. He also mentions that his grandfather Cato was several times decorated for valour in battle, and was awarded by the state treasury for his gallantry the price of the five horses which had been killed under him in battle.

The Romans were in the habit of describing as 'new men' all those whose ancestors had never risen to high office, but who were beginning to become prominent through their own efforts, and Cato soon acquired this title. He himself used to say that he was certainly new to honours

and positions of authority, but that as regards deeds of valour performed by his ancestors, his name was as old as any. Originally his third name was not Cato, but Priscus: he earned the name Cato later in his life on account of his remarkable abilities, for the Romans apply to a man of outstanding wisdom and experience the epithet *catus*.

In appearance he was red-haired and possessed piercing grey eyes, as we learn from the author of this rather malicious epigram,

> Red-haired, grey-eyed, snapping at all comers, even in Hades,
> Porcius, Queen Persephone will turn you away from the gate.

Ever since his early youth he had trained himself to work with his own hands, serve as a soldier, and follow a sober mode of living, and hence he possessed a tough constitution and a body which was as strong as it was healthy. He also developed his powers of speech, which he regarded almost as a second body, and, for the man who has no intention of leading an obscure or idle existence, as an indispensable instrument which serves not only the necessary but also the higher purposes of life. So he practised and perfected his oratory in the towns and villages near Rome, where he acted as an advocate for all who needed him, and he earned the reputation first of being a vigorous pleader and then an effective orator. As time went on the gravity and dignity of his character revealed themselves unmistakably to those who had dealings with him, and marked him out as a man who was clearly qualified for employment in great affairs and a position of leadership in the state. Not only did he provide his services in lawsuits without demanding a fee of any kind, but he did

[13] Plutarch, "Cato the Elder," in Ian Scott-Kilvert, trans., *Makers of Rome: Nine Lives by Plutarch* (Penguin Books, Ltd., 1965), pp. 119–121, 124, 141–144. Reprinted by permission of the publisher.

not seem to regard the prestige acquired in these contests as the principal object of his efforts. On the contrary he was far more anxious to distinguish himself in battles and campaigns against Rome's enemies, and his body was covered with honourable wounds before he had even reached manhood. He says himself that he served in his first campaign when he was seventeen years old at the time when Hannibal, at the height of his success, was laying all Italy waste with fire and sword. In battle he was a formidable fighter, who stood his ground resolutely and confronted his opponents with a ferocious expression. He would greet the enemy with a harsh and menacing war-cry, for he rightly believed and reminded others that such an appearance often frightens the enemy even more than cold steel. When he was on the march he used to carry his own armour and weapons on foot, and would be followed by a single attendant who looked after his food and utensils. It is said that he never lost his temper with this man, nor found fault with him when he served up a meal, in fact he would often join in and share the task of preparing food, so long as he was free from his military duties. On active service he drank nothing but water, except that occasionally when he was parched with thirst he would ask for vinegar, or when his strength was exhausted add a little wine.

Near his estate was a cottage which had belonged to Manius Curius, a redoubtable soldier of the past who had celebrated three triumphs. Cato often visited the place, and the small size of the farm and the house itself inspired him to meditate upon its owner, who although he had become the greatest Roman of his day, had conquered the most warlike tribes and driven Pyrrhus out of Italy, continued to till his little patch of land with his own hands and to live in this cottage, even after he had celebrated his three triumphs. It was here that the ambassadors of the Samnites had found him sitting in front of his hearth boiling turnips. They offered him large sums of gold, but he sent them away, telling them that a man who could be satisfied with such a meal did not need gold. He added that he believed it more honourable to conquer those who possessed gold than to possess it himself. Cato would return home with his mind full of these reflections; then he would look afresh at his own house and servants and review his mode of life, and would undertake still more work with his own hands and cut down any sign of extravagance. . . .

He tells us that he never wore a garment which cost more than a hundred drachmas, that even when he was praetor or consul he drank the same wine as his slaves, that he bought the fish or meat for his dinner in the public market and never paid more than thirty asses for it, and that he allowed himself this indulgence for the public good in order to strengthen his body for military service. He also mentions that when he was bequeathed an embroidered Babylonian robe, he immediately sold it, that none of his cottages had plastered walls, that he never paid more than 1,500 drachmas for a slave, since he was not looking for the exquisite or handsome type of domestic servant, but for sturdy labourers such as grooms and herdsmen, and that when they became too old to work, he felt it his duty to sell them rather than feed so many useless mouths. In general he considered that nothing is cheap if it is superfluous, that what a man does not need is dear even if it cost only a penny, and that one should buy land for tilling and grazing, not to make into gar-

First century A.D. Roman Mosaic. (Isabella Stewart Gardner Museum, Boston)

Bedroom of a villa, ca. 40–30 B.C. (Metropolitan Museum of Art)

dens, where the object is merely to sprinkle the lawns and sweep the paths. . . .

He was also a good father, a kind husband, and a most capable manager of his own household, since he was far from regarding this side of his affairs as trivial or allowing it to suffer from neglect. For this reason I think I should give some examples of his conduct in his private life. He chose his wife for her family rather than her fortune, for he believed that while people of great wealth or high position cherish their own pride and self-esteem, nevertheless women of noble birth are by nature more ashamed of any disgraceful action and so are more obedient to their husbands in everything that is honourable. He used to say that a man who beats his wife or child is laying sacrilegious hands on the most sacred thing in the world. He considered that it was more praiseworthy to be a good husband than a great senator,

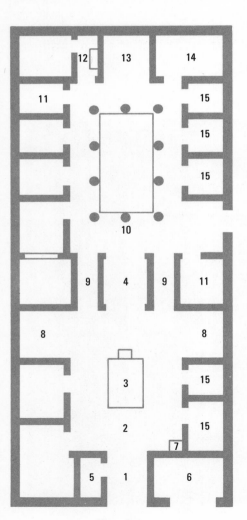

The Roman Aristocrat's House. Plan of a Roman town house, exemplifying a combination of the Italian (*atrium*) and Greek (*peristyle*) types. (From Ernest Nash, *Roman Towns*, 1944, J. J. Augustin)

1. fauces—entrance
2. atrium
3. impluvium—basin for rain water
4. tablinum—office
5. janitor—doorman
6. taberna—shop
7. lararium—altar of Lares
8. alae—wings
9. andron—corridor
10. peristyle
11. triclinium—dining room
12. culina—kitchen
13. exedra—entertaining hall
14. oecus—living room
15. cubicola—bedrooms

and was also of the opinion that there was nothing much else to admire in Socrates of old, except for the fact that he was always gentle and considerate in his dealings with his wife, who was a scold, and his children, who were half-witted. When his son was born, Cato thought that nothing but the most important business of the state should prevent him from being present when his wife gave the baby its bath and wrapped it in swaddling clothes. His wife suckled the child herself and often did the same for her slaves' children, so as to encourage brotherly feelings in them towards her own son. As soon as the boy was able to learn, his father took charge of his schooling and taught him to read, although he had in the household an educated slave called Chilo who was a schoolmaster and taught many other boys. However, Cato did not think it right, so he tells us, that his son should be scolded or have his ears pulled by a slave, if he were slow to learn, and still less that he should be indebted to his slave in such a vital matter as his education. So he took it upon himself to teach the boy, not only his letters, but also the principles of Roman law. He also trained him in athletics, and taught him how to throw the javelin,

House of the Silver Wedding, Pompeii. View of the peristyle from the atrium. (Alinari)

fight in armour, ride a horse, use his fists in boxing, endure the extremes of heat and cold, and swim across the roughest and most swiftly flowing stretches of the Tiber. He tells us that he composed his history of Rome, writing it out with his own hand and in large characters, so that his son should possess in his own home the means of acquainting himself with the ancient annals and traditions of his country. He also mentions that he was as careful not to use any indecent expression before his son as he would have been in the presence of the Vestal Virgins, and that he never bathed with him. This last seems to have been the general custom among the Romans, and even fathers-in-law avoided bathing with their sons-in-law, because they were ashamed to show themselves naked. In later times, however, the Romans adopted from the Greeks the practice of stripping in the presence of other men, and they in turn taught the Greeks to do the same even in the presence of women.

Such was Cato's approach to the noble task of forming and moulding his son for the pursuit of virtue. The boy was an exemplary pupil in his readiness to learn, and his spirit was a match for his natural goodness of disposition. But since his body was not strong enough to endure extreme hardship, Cato was obliged to relax a little the extraordinary austerity and self-discipline of his own way of life. However, his son, in spite of a delicate physique, became an excellent soldier, and fought with great distinction under Aemilius Paulus at the battle of Pydna, when the Romans defeated king Perseus. During the fighting his sword was either struck out of his hand or else slipped from his grasp when it became moist with sweat. The young man felt deeply ashamed at losing it, and so he turned to some of his companions and, rallying them to his side, charged the enemy again. The fighting was fierce, but at length he succeeded in clearing a space and there he came upon the weapon amid the heaps of arms and corpses, where the bodies of friends and enemies lay piled high upon one another. Paulus, his commander, was greatly impressed by the young Cato's courage, and a letter has came down to us written by the father to his son, in which he praises him in the highest terms for his gallantry and for the sense of honour which he showed in recovering his sword. He afterwards married Tertia, a daughter of Paulus and hence the sister of Scipio the Younger, as he afterwards became known, and the distinction of this alliance with so noble a family was quite as much due to his own achievements as to his father's. In this way Cato was justly rewarded for the care which he had devoted to his son's education.

Cato possessed a large number of slaves, whom he usually bought from among the prisoners captured in war, but it was his practice to choose those who, like puppies or colts, were young enough to be trained and taught their duties. None of them ever entered any house but his own, unless they were sent on an errand by Cato or his wife, and if they were asked what Cato was doing, the reply was always that they did not know. It was a rule of his establishment that a slave must either be doing something about the house, or else be asleep. He much preferred the slaves who slept well, because he believed that they were more even-tempered than the wakeful ones, and that those who had had enough sleep produced better results at any task than those who were short of it. And as he was convinced that slaves were led into mischief more often on account of love affairs than for any other reason, he made it a rule that the men could sleep with the women slaves of the establishment, for a fixed price, but must have nothing to do with any others.

At the beginning of his career, when he was a poor man and was frequently on active service, he never complained of anything that he ate, and he used to say that it was ignoble to find fault with a servant for the food that he prepared. But in later life, when he had become more prosperous, he used to invite his friends and colleagues to dinner, and immediately after the meal he would beat with a leather thong any of the slaves who had been careless in preparing or serving it. He constantly contrived to provoke quarrels and dissensions among his slaves, and if they ever arrived at an understanding with one another he became alarmed and suspicious. If ever any of his slaves were suspected of committing a capital offence, he gave the culprit a formal trial in the presence of the rest, and if he was found guilty he had him put to death.

When he began to devote himself more energetically to making money, he came to regard agriculture as a pastime rather than as a source of income, and he invested his capital in solid enterprises which involved the minimum of risk. He bought up ponds, hot springs, land devoted to producing fuller's earth, pitch factories, and estates which were rich in pasture-land or forest. All these undertak-

ings brought in large profits and could not, to use his own phrase, be ruined by the whims of Jupiter. He also used to lend money in what is surely the most disreputable form of speculation, that is the underwriting of ships. Those who wished to borrow money from him were obliged to form a large association, and when this reached the number of fifty, representing as many ships, he would take one share in the company. His interests were looked after by Quintio, one of his freedmen, who used to accompany Cato's clients on their voyages and transact their business. In this way he drew a handsome profit, while at the same time spreading his risk and never venturing more than a fraction of his capital.

He would also lend money to any of his slaves who wished it. They used these sums to buy young slaves, and after training them and teaching them a trade for a year at Cato's expense, they would sell them again. Often Cato would keep these boys for himself, and he would then credit to the slave the price offered by the highest bidder. He tried to encourage his son to imitate these methods, and told him to diminish one's capital was something that might be expected of a widow, but not of a man. But he certainly went too far when he ventured once to declare that the man who deserved the highest praise, indeed who should be honoured almost as a god, was the one who at the end of his life was found to have added to his property more than he had inherited.

CHAPTER 2

POLITICAL AND LEGAL INSTITUTIONS IN A COMPLEX SOCIETY:
The Expansion of Rome in the Mediterranean World

Cato used to say that our constitution was superior to those of other States on account of the fact that almost every one of these other commonwealths had been established by one man, the author of their laws and institutions. . . . On the other hand our own commonwealth was based upon the genius, not of one man, but of many; it was founded, not in one generation, but in a long period of several centuries and many ages of men. For, said he, there never has lived a man possessed of so great genius that nothing could escape him, nor could the combined powers of all the men living at one time possibly make all necessary provisions for the future without the aid of actual experience and the test of time.

Cicero, The Republic

Plato and Aristotle had appreciated the phenomenon of power, but had inserted it within a context of controlling considerations. In their view, the political association existed to serve the material and cultural needs of the members, and although power was necessary to coordinate and direct human activities in order that these needs would be best satisfied, it did not follow that power was the central mark of an association composed of contributing parts. When these considerations lost their compelling force, however, the way lay open for considering power the central political fact. The transition to the new view of power had been clearly registered in the political thought of Polybius. His *Histories* sought to account for the rapid emergence of Roman supremacy, and, as he admitted, the controlling conception in his study was the nature of power: "how it was and by virtue of what peculiar political institutions that in less than fifty-three years nearly the whole world was overcome and fell under the single domination of Rome, a thing the like of which had never happened before." From here Polybius was led to ask questions about the nature of power: what were the causes of the military successes and political expansion of Rome? why had she succeeded where other states had failed? was there a regular pattern to the waxing and waning of various types of states? And when Polybius had found his answer it turned out to be a prescription for the right organization of power by means of an institutional balance.

Sheldon Wolin, Politics and Vision

In the existence of the aristocratic families lies a solution to the puzzling fact that restraint of the individual by the customs of society had distinct limits at Rome; thence springs, the tendency of Roman law to elaborate the rights and duties of the individual, i.e., essentially of the *paterfamilias,* whose power over his off-spring, slaves, and retainers was almost unlimited.

Chester Starr, Civilization and the Caesars

In the preceding chapter we began with a consideration of the nature of authority and proceeded to a discussion of the particular structure of authority and value system which were associated with the Roman aristocratic family. In this chapter, we will direct our attention to the political institutions which the Romans developed as their city became preeminent in a league of Italian states and subsequently the capital of an empire embracing the entire Mediterranean world. The great aristocratic families dominated the process of Roman expansion, and, as a consequence, the political institutions they created were strongly influenced by the values which stemmed from the aristocratic tradition. Yet despite their respect for tradition, or perhaps because of it, the Romans were amazingly adept at confronting and controlling the new facts of power which became increasingly evident as the small city-state turned into a world-state.

But before examining the nature of the Roman state, it would be useful to define the basic characteristics of political institutions in general and to examine their role in the functioning of the social system. While political institutions here refer to formal government of the state, it should not be forgotten that political functions are performed in and by other human associations. R. M. MacIver has pointed out the degree to which regulation, the essence of government, is to be found in the primitive family. Indeed, modern anthropological studies have shown that the mere fact of living together in a common territory creates in even the most primitive societies a "political" bond as basic as the kinship bond. This view discredits an earlier view which saw political institutions as an "artificial" creation emerging only after the "na-

tural" kinship ties had begun to break down. Therefore, since political institutions are as old and as basic to society as kinship institutions, the state can be regarded as a highly developed and sophisticated form of political organization, or polity.

THE STATE
J. Roland Pennock and David G. Smith[1]

[The state] is in the first place, a political system, or polity, that includes all the people in a given territory. A state is territorially bounded, and anyone who is born within its territorial limits is automatically a member of that state, a fact that distinguishes it from all other organizations.

The characteristics of territoriality and of all-inclusiveness or inescapability point to a further and even more basic distinguishing characteristic of the state: its possession of supreme coercive authority and of some mechanism for the effective exercise of this authority. Thus government and law are marks of the state. Many organizations, including all polities, have government and rules, or laws, by which they are governed. States possess the unique element of supremacy within their territory, backed up by the authority to resort to physical violence. To this it

[1] Reprinted with permission of The Macmillan Company from *Political Science: An Introduction* by J. Roland Pennock and David G. Smith. Copyright © The Macmillan Company 1964.

should be added that the state possesses a legal monopoly of the use of violence. If others (e.g., parents) are permitted to use violence, they do so on sufferance of the state. Other organizations, when faced by dissident members, have no recourse in the final analysis other than to expel them from membership or to threaten them with divine punishment. If this threat or that of losing the privileges of membership are not sufficient to secure compliance with the rules, laws, or commands of the government of the organization, there is nothing further that the organization can do. The state on the other hand can seize the property of recalcitrants and in the final resort can seize the persons themselves and put them in jail or take their lives. The monopoly of this coercive power that the state enjoys is something that had to be fought for. In primitive societies each family or clan is likely to enforce the law—frequently by violence—for itself. Even in feudal society there are powerful and often successful rivals to the central government's claim of authority. It is precisely for this reason that we withhold the name of state from such political systems; the monopoly of the right to use violence or to say who may use it is part of what the word "state" means.

The power of the state is based upon authority, which [entails] a degree of acceptance or recognition beyond mere yielding to fear of punishment. Thus, to take an extreme example, there might be a territorial society, say on a small island, in which a few members held the others in subjection by sheer force, or threat of force, by monopolizing the firearms. They might issue orders and even establish general rules, or "laws," to which they could compel obedience. Nevertheless, unless

there was some degree of recognition among the people generally that these rules possessed authority, that the organization as a whole served some rightful purpose (however much wrong it might also be doing), we would not ordinarily call the society or the organization a state.

Finally, a state must be a legally independent unit. This condition does not mean that the state has no external ties nor that it is not subject to influence by other states. It may even be subject to legal restraints (if we recognize international law as true law) and be bound by its treaties. For our purpose, it is sufficient that the political entity in question should not be part of another political entity having the characteristics of a state and that it should not be subject to the supreme coercive authority of a state. There may be borderline cases between the situation where a state has bound itself by treaty to submit to the authority of another state in some particular case and the situation where this process has gone far enough that we would no longer recognize the independence, and so the statehood of one of the societies. In general, if one "state" permitted another to exercise power within its own territory, we should say at least that its statehood was qualified. If each state gives up some of its independence on condition that the other does likewise, statehood is not lost, unless by their joint action they have created a third organization that can qualify as a state.

The state is both a legal and sociological entity. It is sometimes viewed purely from the juristic aspect. When we speak of the continuity of the state through conquest or revolution, it is primarily legal considerations to which we refer. But it will be apparent from the preceding discussion that the state is more than a system of laws. It comprises all those elements that give it the authority and the ability to act effectively—its political culture, its government, its legal system. We may summarize by defining the state as *a political system comprising all the people in a defined territory and possessing an organization (government) with the power and authority to enforce its will upon its members, by resort, if necessary, to physical sanctions, and not subject in like manner to the power and authority of another polity.*

The development of the Roman state was conditioned from the outset by the retention of power by aristocratic families and by the fact of geographical expansion. We have seen how the plebeian class had achieved full legal equality with the patriciate during the period of the conquest of Italy. Unlike the political development of Athens in the sixth century B.C., however, the plebeian advance in Rome had not resulted in political democracy. For this extremely important historical fact several explanations can be suggested. In the first place, the process by which the plebeians achieved equality was gradual. As a result, wealthy plebeians, when they gained access to the magistracy and entered the Senate, often acquired the aristocratic outlook of their patrician colleagues. Furthermore, the number of magisterial offices remained relatively small. They were exacting and brought no pay, and nomination for office depended upon the patronage of a senator. The ranks of the magisterial oligarchy, therefore, grew only gradually. In addition, certain institutional procedures inhibited the development of democracy. The two popular assemblies, unlike the Athenian Council of the Four Hundred and Assembly, could only act on business submitted to them by the magistrates. There were no debates, and voting was usually determined by the influence which senatorial families exercised over their clients.

Perhaps more important than any of these

factors was the role played by warfare in the political development of the Roman Republic. Whereas Greece was left relatively undisturbed by foreign invasion during the evolution of democracy, Rome pursued or was forced to pursue a continuous policy of military expansion. The army thus assumed an importance in Roman society it had not had in Athens. It was composed for the most part of plebeian citizens who readily deferred to the authority of their aristocratic officers. The navy, which was more democratic in structure and which had been the chief instrument of the Athenian demos' rise to power, assumed importance in Rome only after there were vast numbers of noncitizens and slaves to man the oars. Also, because of military expansion, Rome did not long remain a polis, in the Greek sense of a small and compact citizen group. Instead she became the leader of a confederacy of Latin towns and tribal communities to which full or partial citizenship was sometimes extended. Many Roman citizens moved away from the city to occupy conquered lands opened up for sale and settlement. As a result the citizenry was scattered throughout Italy and could not be easily mobilized for political purposes. All of these factors meant that, despite constitutional forms and the vital importance of the nonaristocratic classes, effective political power remained in the hands of the senatorial oligarchy.

It is important at this point to recall that after the fourth century B.C. the Roman aristocracy was legally defined not in terms of birth or wealth but in terms of office-holding. Only ex-magistrates could sit in the Senate and thus acquire noble status.

> The [Senate] itself represented the continuity of power, while the magistrates came to office for a year, and then took their places as former holders of the highest office of state. Thus Rome had a simple, constitutional distinction between the governing class, consisting of all rightful citizens participating in the assemblies and under an obligation to do military service, and the men whose chief occupation was state administration or military command. These were the real governing

caste, whose numbers were limited to the members of a few families.[2]

The offices, or magistracies, which conferred senatorial rank upon their holders, grew in number in response to urban growth and the problems of governing conquered territory. A *praetor* was elected annually after 307 B.C. by the Centuriate Assembly to assist the two consuls. His primary responsibility was the administration of the civil law. There were four *quaestors,* who were financial officials; four *aediles,* who supervised public works and the market place; and two *censors,* who assigned each citizen to his appropriate political and military group and who exercised a general supervision of public morals. All of these offices were created during the early Republic.

By the close of the fouth century the Roman magistracy had attained the form it preserved until the end of the Republic. It consisted of a number of committees, each of which, with the exception of the quaestorship, had an independent sphere of action. They were the executive branch of the government, entrusted with enforcing the laws and carrying out the routine administration of the state in consultation with the Senate. Certain of them had military as well as civil authority. Among these committees there was a regularly established order of rank ascending as follows: quaestors, aediles, censors, praetors, consuls. Except for the censorship, which was regularly filled by ex-consuls, politicians usually advanced from one magistracy to another in this order. A distinctive feature of the committee system was the right of any magistrate to veto the action of his colleague or colleagues. This applied to the consulship as well as to the lower magistracies; but in order to avoid too frequent use of veto, the consuls alternated each month in taking charge of the

administration when both were in the city, and when both were with the army they held the chief command on alternate days. Magistrates of higher rank enjoyed greater authority (*maior potestas*) than all those who ranked below them and as a rule could forbid or annul the actions of the latter. In this way the consuls, or the dictator, were able to exercise a negative control over the activities of all other magistrates. The unity which was given to the administration by this theory of *maior potestas* was increased by the Senate, a council whose influence over the magistracy grew as the consulate lost in power and independence through the creation of new offices. All magistrates were said to have *potestas,* but only the dictator, consuls, and praetor had *imperium.* Consequently, these latter were the only ones who could exercise military command, summon the people on their own authority to assemble for elective or legislative purposes, and try civil and criminal cases of more than trivial importance. All magistrates, however, had the power to enforce their orders by the arrest of disobedient persons. The great power and the relative freedom of action enjoyed by the magistrates, who were immune to prosecution while in office, are outstanding features of the constitution. The respect for public authority which they implied is one of the characteristics of early Roman society.[3]

The next major extension of the magistracy came as a result of Roman expansion beyond the Italian peninsula. Rome first became involved with the administration of territory outside of Italy as a result of a successful war with the commercial power of Carthage over control of the island of Sicily (First Punic War, 264–241 B.C.). During this war the Romans developed a navy which enabled them in the next few years to add Sardinia and Corsica as provinces. In 225 B.C. the Romans successfully repelled an

[2] From *Political Power in the Ancient World* by Mario Attilio Levi, translated by Jane Costello, p. 135. English translation copyright © 1965 by George Weidenfeld and Nicolson Ltd. Reprinted by arrangement with The New American Library, Inc., New York.

[3] Reprinted with permission of The Macmillan Company from *A History of Rome to A.D. 565* by Arthur E. R. Boak and William G. Sinnegen. Copyright © by The Macmillan Company 1965.

invasion of Gallic peoples from the north and a few years later incorporated the territory from the Po River to the Alps as a new province— Cisalpine Gaul. This was followed by the suppression of piracy and eventual Roman administration of Illyria on the eastern Adriatic coast. A second Punic War broke out in 218 B.C. in Spain where the Carthaginian leader, Hannibal, had built up a strong military force. Hannibal marched his army of over 25,000 men and elephants across the Alps and, after winning a stunning victory at Cannae in 216 B.C., ravaged southern Italy for nearly fifteen years. The delaying tactics of the Roman dictator, Quintus Fabius Maximus, however, weakened the Carthaginian forces, and in 202 B.C. Hannibal left Italy and was defeated in battle before his capital city in northern Africa.

During the second Punic War the Macedonian king, Philip V, had allied with Carthage and continued to pose a threat to Rome's Greek allies in southern Italy and the Aegean. In a series of wars against Macedonia and the Seleucid kingdom of Antiochus III, Rome gained control of the entire eastern Mediterranean and annexed portions of Greece and Asia Minor, bringing enormous wealth into the treasury and for a time relieving Roman citizens of all direct taxation. Roman control of the Mediterranean world was completed with the final destruction of Carthage in a third Punic War. The city of Carthage was leveled to the ground and its inhabitants sold into slavery in 146 B.C. Subsequently its territories were incorporated into a new province called Africa.

These conquests of the third and second centuries B.C. comprised a wide variety of non-Latin peoples on various levels of cultural development and, thus, presented a new problem of administration for Rome. The policy of extending citizenship and establishing treaty relationships—a policy which had been pursued in Italy— was abandoned for the most part, and a system of provincial administration was developed out of the powers residing in the Roman magistracy. After 227 B.C. two praetors, armed with the military power (imperium) of consuls, were elected annually by the assembly to serve as provincial governors. Their primary responsibility was to keep order, to guard the frontier, and to see that taxes were paid. Taxes were in most cases actually collected by corporations of tax farmers (publicani) who bid for the privilege. The provincial praetors also acted as judges in disputes between Roman citizens and between various communities within the province. These local communities, city-states, and tribal kingdoms retained control over internal disputes, religious practices and local taxation. Special treaties granting full local political autonomy and immunity from taxation were granted to a few communities, especially the Hellenized city-states of the eastern Mediterranean. Two more praetorships were created in 197 B.C. in a reorganization of the Spanish provinces. The Senate stopped the creation of new offices at this point, because each new magisterial post brought with it aristocratic rank and a consequent expansion of the aristocracy. Thenceforth the Senate assigned only its own members as provincial governors for annual terms of duty.

The Senate, with about 300 active members, was never more firmly in control of the state than during the conquest of the Mediterranean. Despite the theoretical power of the popular assemblies to elect public officials, the magistracies were in fact committees of senators. The assemblies were summoned only at the will of an official and could only vote on measures or candidates submitted by the presiding magistrates. The dilution of the senatorial class by an expanding magistracy was prevented by the practice of securing the election of existing senators to serve in the provinces with the titles of propraetor and proconsul. It thus became increasingly difficult for a new man to rise into the senatorial ranks by being elected to the magistracy. The Senate was the only permanent assembly in Rome with sufficient experience and continuity to carry out a consistent foreign and military policy. The organization and administration of Rome's foreign provinces, like Rome itself, became a senatorial prerogative.

Economic change as well as these modifications in the political structure accompanied military expansion. The competition of cheap for-

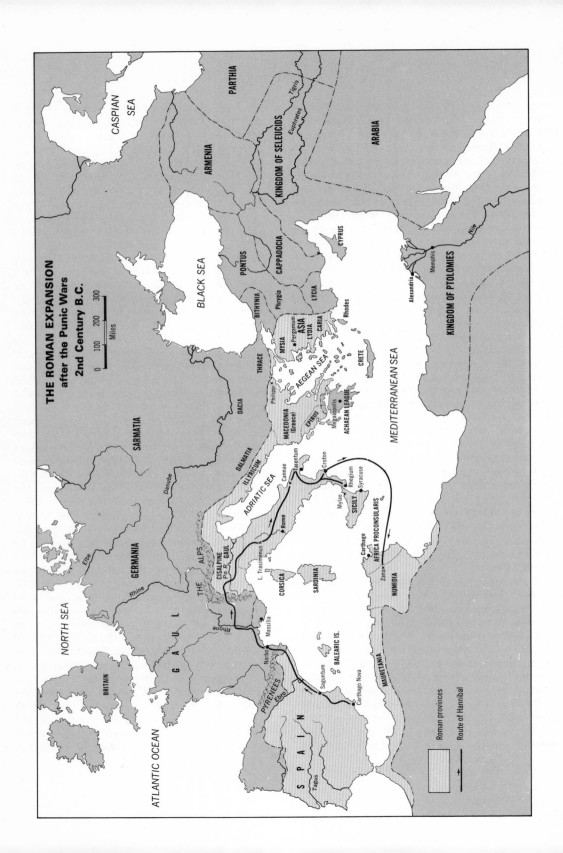

THE ROMAN EXPANSION
after the Punic Wars
2nd Century B.C.

0 100 200 300
Miles

NORTH SEA

ATLANTIC OCEAN

BRITAIN

GERMANIA

G A U L

Rhine

Elbe

SARMATIA

Danube

DACIA

CASPIAN
SEA

BLACK SEA

PARTHIA

ARMENIA

Tigris

KINGDOM OF SELEUCIDS

Euphrates

ARABIA

PONTUS

BITHYNIA

THRACE

Phrygia

CAPPADOCIA

MYSIA

ASIA

LYDIA

CARIA

LYCIA

CYPRUS

Pergamum

Rhodes

Nile

Alexandria

Memphis

KINGDOM OF PTOLOMIES

Philippi

MACEDONIA
(Greece)

EPIRUS

AEGEAN SEA

CRETE

Megalopolis

ACHAEAN LEAGUE

MEDITERRANEAN SEA

THE ALPS

PYRENEES

S P A I N

Tagus

Ebro

Saguntum

Carthago Nova

BALEARIC IS.

Narbo

Massilia

Rhone

CISALPINE
Po R. GAUL

Rome

L. Trasimenus

CORSICA

SARDINIA

DALMATIA

ILLYRICUM

ADRIATIC SEA

Cannae

Tarentum

Croton

Rhegium

Mylae

SICILY

Syracuse

Carthage

AFRICA PROCONSULARIS

Zama

NUMIDIA

MAURETANIA

Roman provinces

Route of Hannibal

Bronze figures of slaves in pillory. (British Museum)

eign grain and the difficulty of maintaining their farms while away on military service ruined many small Italian farmers. Their lands were consolidated into great estates (*latifundia*) which could specialize in commercial crops—fruit, olives, vines, sheep, and cattle—for an expanding domestic and export market. *Latifundia* also arose in the parts of Italy where Hannibal's policy of devastation had ruined small-scale farming. The development of the *latifundia* depended upon the capital supplied by the wealthy senatorial families and upon an abundant supply of slave labor furnished by the victims of Rome's foreign wars. It has been estimated that some 250,000 slaves were imported into Italy between 200 B.C. and 150 B.C., bringing the percentage to nearly three slaves for every five free men.

As Rome gradually took over the area in which Carthaginians had been the chief traders, Roman citizens began for the first time to engage in overseas trade, an activity previously left almost entirely in the hands of foreigners. In addition, contracts were let to private individuals for the construction of public works and the operation of mines. Banking and finance became important activities. Since both law and custom placed restrictions on the business activities of the senatorial order, this profitable business fell to a growing business class outside the governing oligarchy. The wealthy citizens were usually enrolled in the cavalry by the cen-

sors and were known as equestrians (*equites*). Rome became a commercial city as well as an administrative capital. In 242 B.C. a new praetor (*praetor peregrinus*) was elected to preside over the trial of disputes arising mostly from commercial exchange among foreigners, or between Roman citizens and foreigners. The city of Rome had by the first century B.C. a population of perhaps a half-million slaves, traders, foreign merchants, craftsmen, and citizens.

Prior to the second century B.C., the Romans had produced almost no literature which either eulogized or analyzed their outstanding political and military success. The poet, Ennius (239–169 B.C.), who was educated in Tarentum, a Greek city in southern Italy, wrote the first important Latin epic poem of Rome's history from its mythical founding by Aeneas to the Punic wars. It was a Greek, Polybius (201–132 B.C.), who wrote the first history of Rome's conquest of the Mediterranean lands and who first began to familiarize the Roman upper classes with Greek words and categories of political analysis.

Probably the Roman senators made their own evaluation of Polybius' analysis because they were quite familiar with the art of politics, but they found Greek theory most congenial because of the high value placed on aristocracy. The senators were pleased to discover a theoretical justification for their rule as the "best" men of the state and began to refer to themselves as *Optimates* (the best). In the political struggles of the first century B.C. convenient labels were found in the Greek political vocabulary for their opponents: tyrants for the military dictators, and demagogues for the leaders of the popular groups. The opponents of the Senate, of course, found oligarch a convenient word.[4]

Polybius had himself acquired political experience as a citizen of Megalopolis in Arcadia and as a statesman of the Achaean League, a federation of Greek city-states which maintained its independence in the balance of power between Rome and Macedonia in the early part of the second century B.C. When Roman armies subjugated the eastern Mediterranean, Polybius was brought, along with a thousand other Achaeans, to Rome as a hostage. Here he stayed for the greater part of seventeen years as the

[4] Carl Roebuck, *The World of Ancient Times* (New York: Charles Scribner's Sons, 1966), p. 496.

close friend of Scipio Aemilianus, the conqueror of Carthage. Polybius thus brought to his history a combination of Greek education, foreign objectivity, and personal knowledge of the centers of senatorial power and influence in Rome. In the sixth book of his multi-volume history of the Punic and Macedonian wars, Polybius interrupted his narrative to analyze the political and military institutions of the Roman Republic and the customs on which they were based. In your reading of this analysis consider the following questions: Do the Aristotelian categories of political analysis which Polybius employs clarify or distort the reality of Roman power? Are formal political institutions determining factors in the distribution and regulation of power? What factors explain Polybius' shift from the idealist political philosophy of Plato and Aristotle to a philosophy which is oriented around the question of power? Why do religious and military institutions play such a prominent part in Polybius' analysis? What is the ultimate source of authority in the Roman state as Polybius sees it?

Roman merchant vessel being loaded with grain. The demand for grain increased as Rome grew and imports became essential. The Romans succeeded the Phoenicians as masters of the sea. (Alinari)

Bronze head of a mule used as an ornament on a couch in the Roman Imperial Period. (Metropolitan Museum of Art)

THE ROMAN CONSTITUTION
Polybius[5]

BOOK VI

1. I am aware that some will be at a loss to account for my interrupting the course of my narrative for the sake of entering upon the following disquisition on the Roman constitution. But I think that I have already in many passages made it fully evident that this particular branch of my work was one of the necessities imposed on me by the nature of my original design; and I pointed this out with special clearness in the preface which explained the scope of my history. I there stated that the feature of my work which was at once the best in itself, and the most instructive to the students of it, was that it would enable them to know and fully realise in what manner, and under what kind of constitution, it came about that nearly the whole world fell under the power of Rome in

[5] Polybius, *The Histories*. Translated by Evelyn S. Shuckburgh, 1889.

somewhat less than fifty-three years—an event certainly without precedent. This being my settled purpose, I could see no more fitting period than the present[6] for making a pause, and examining the truth of the remarks about to be made on this constitution. . . .

What is really educational and beneficial to students of history is the clear view of the causes of events, and the consequent power of choosing the better policy in a particular case. Now in every practical undertaking by a state we must regard as the most powerful agent for success or failure the form of its constitution; for from this as from a fountain-head all conceptions and plans of action not only proceed, but attain their consummation. . . .

As for the Roman constitution, it had three elements, each of them possessing sovereign powers: and their respective

[6] [Polybius pauses at that point in his narrative when the Roman army has been destroyed by the Carthaginian general, Hannibal, at the Battle of Cannae in 216 B.C. The Punic war seems for the moment to be lost.]

share of power in the whole state had been regulated with such a scrupulous regard to equality and equilibrium, that no one could say for certain, not even a native, whether the constitution as a whole were an aristocracy or democracy or despotism. And no wonder: for if we confine our observation to the power of the Consuls we should be inclined to regard it as despotic; if on that of the Senate, as aristocratic; and if finally one looks at the power possessed by the people it would seem a clear case of a democracy. What the exact powers of these several parts were, and still, with slight modifications, are, I will now state.

12. The Consuls, before leading out the legions, remain in Rome and are supreme masters of the administration. All other magistrates, except the Tribunes, are under them and take their orders. They introduce foreign ambassadors to the Senate; bring matters requiring deliberation before it; and see to the execution of its decrees. If, again, there are any matters of state which require the authorisation of the people, it is their business to see to them, to summon the popular meetings, to bring the proposals before them, and to carry out the decrees of the majority. In the preparations for war also, and in a word the entire administration of a campaign, they have all but absolute power. It is competent to them to impose on the allies such levies as they think good, to appoint the Military Tribunes, to make up the roll for soldiers and select those that are suitable. Besides they have absolute power of inflicting punishment on all who are under their command while on active service: and they have authority to expend as much of the public money as they choose, being accompanied by a Quaestor who is entirely at their orders. A survey of these powers would in fact justify our de-

scribing the constitution as despotic—a clear case of royal government. Nor will it affect the truth of my description, if any of the institutions I have described are changed in our time, or in that of our posterity: and the same remarks apply to what follows.

13. The Senate has first of all the control of the treasury, and regulates the receipts and disbursements alike. For the Quaestors cannot issue any public money for the various departments of the state without a decree of the Senate, except for the service of the Consuls. The Senate controls also what is by far the largest and most important expenditure, that, namely, which is made by the censors every *lustrum* for the repair or construction of public buildings; this money cannot be obtained by the censors except by the grant of the Senate. Similarly all crimes committed in Italy requiring a public investigation, such as treason, conspiracy, poisoning, or wilful murder, are in the hands of the Senate. Besides, if any individual or state among the Italian allies requires a controversy to be settled, a penalty to be assessed, help or protection to be afforded—all this is the province of the Senate. Or again, outside Italy, if it is necessary to send an embassy to reconcile warring communities, or to remind them of their duty, or sometimes to impose requisitions upon them, or to receive their submission, or finally to proclaim war against them—this too is the business of the Senate. In like manner the reception to be given to foreign ambassadors in Rome, and the answers to be returned to them, are decided by the Senate. With such business the people have nothing to do. Consequently, if one were staying at Rome when the Consuls were not in town, one would imagine the constitution to be a complete aristocracy: and this

has been the idea entertained by many Greeks, and by many kings as well, from the fact that nearly all the business they had with Rome was settled by the Senate.

14. After this one would naturally be inclined to ask what part is left for the people in the constitution, when the Senate has these various functions, especially the control of the receipts and expenditure of the exchequer; and when the Consuls, again, have absolute power over the details of military preparation, and an absolute authority in the field? There is, however, a part left the people, and it is a most important one. For the people is the sole fountain of honour and of punishment; and it is by these two things and these alone that dynasties and constitutions and, in a word, human society are held together: for where the distinction between them is not sharply drawn both in theory and practice, there no undertaking can be properly administered—as indeed we might expect when good and bad are held in exactly the same honour. The people then are the only court to decide matters of life and death; and even in cases where the penalty is money, if the sum to be assessed is sufficiently serious, and especially when the accused have held the higher magistracies. And in regard to this arrangement there is one point deserving especial commendation and record. Men who are on trial for their lives at Rome, while sentence is in process of being voted —if even only one of the tribes whose votes are needed to ratify the sentence has not been voted—have the privilege at Rome of openly departing and condemning themselves to a voluntary exile. Such men are safe at Naples or Praeneste or at Tibur, and at other towns with which this arrangement has been duly ratified on oath. Again, it is the people who bestow of-

fices on the deserving, which are the most honourable rewards of virtue. It has also the absolute power of passing or repealing laws; and, most important of all, it is the people who deliberate on the question of peace or war. And when provisional terms are made for alliance, suspension of hostilities, or treaties, it is the people who ratify them or the reverse.

These considerations again would lead one to say that the chief power in the state was the people's, and that the constitution was a democracy.

15. Such, then, is the distribution of power between the several parts of the state. I must now show how each of these several parts can, when they choose, oppose or support each other.

The Consul, then, when he has started on an expedition with the powers I have described, is to all appearance absolute in the administration of the business in hand; still he has need of the support both of people and Senate, and, without them, is quite unable to bring the matter to a successful conclusion. For it is plain that he must have supplies sent to his legions from time to time; but without a decree of the Senate they can be supplied neither with corn, nor clothes, nor pay, so that all the plans of a commander must be futile, if the Senate is resolved either to shrink from danger or hamper his plans. And again, whether a Consul shall bring any undertaking to a conclusion or no depends entirely upon the Senate: for it has absolute authority at the end of a year to send another Consul to supersede him, or to continue the existing one in his command. Again, even to the successes of the generals the Senate has the power to add distinction and glory, and on the other hand to obscure their merits and lower their credit. For these high achievements are brought in tangible form before the eyes of the citizens by what are called "triumphs." But these triumphs the commanders cannot celebrate with proper pomp, or in some cases celebrate at all, unless the Senate concurs and grants the necessary money. As for the people, the Consuls are pre-eminently obliged to court their favour, however distant from home may be the field of their operations; for it is the people, as I have said before, that ratifies, or refuses to ratify, terms of peace and treaties; but most of all because when laying down their office they have to give an account of their administration before it. Therefore in no case is it safe for the Consuls to neglect either the Senate or the good-will of the people.

16. As for the Senate, which possesses the immense power I have described, in the first place it is obliged in public affairs to take the multitude into account, and respect the wishes of the people; and it cannot put into execution the penalty for offences against the republic, which are punishable with death, unless the people first ratify its decrees. Similarly even in matters which directly affect the senators— for instance, in the case of a law diminishing the Senate's traditional authority, or depriving senators of certain dignities and offices, or even actually cutting down their property—even in such cases the people have the sole power of passing or rejecting the law. But most important of all is the fact that, if the Tribunes interpose their veto, the Senate not only are unable to pass a decree, but cannot even hold a meeting at all, whether formal or informal. Now, the Tribunes are always bound to carry out the decree of the people, and above all things to have regard to their wishes: therefore, for all these reasons the Senate

stands in awe of the multitude, and cannot neglect the feelings of the people.

In like manner the people on its part is far from being independent of the Senate, and is bound to take its wishes into account both collectively and individually. For contracts, too numerous to count, are given out by the censors in all parts of Italy for the repairs or construction of public buildings; there is also the collection of revenue from many rivers, harbours, gardens, mines, and land—everything, in a word, that comes under the control of the Roman government: and in all these the people at large are engaged; so that there is scarcely a man, so to speak, who is not interested either as a contractor or as being employed in the works. For some purchase the contracts from the censors for themselves; and others go partners with them; while others again go security for these contractors, or actually pledge their property to the treasury for them. Now over all these transactions the Senate has absolute control. It can grant an extension of time; and in case of unforseen accident can relieve the contractors from a portion of their obligation, or release them from it altogether, if they are absolutely unable to fulfil it. And there are many details in which the Senate can inflict great hardships, or, on the other hand, grant great indulgences to the contractors: for in every case the appeal is to it. But the most important point of all is that the judges are taken from its members in the majority of trials, whether public or private, in which the charges are heavy. Consequently, all citizens are much at its mercy; and being alarmed at the uncertainty as to when they may need its aid, are cautious about resisting or actively opposing its will. And for a similar reason men do not rashly resist the wishes of the Consuls, because one and all may become subject to their absolute authority on a campaign.

18. The result of this power of the several estates for mutual help or harm is a union sufficiently firm for all emergencies, and a constitution than which it is impossible to find a better. For whenever any danger from without compels them to unite and work together, the strength which is developed by the State is so extraordinary, that everything required is unfailingly carried out by the eager rivalry shown by all classes to devote their whole minds to the need of the hour, and to secure that any determination come to should not fail for want of promptitude; while each individual works, privately and publicly alike, for the accomplishment of the business in hand. Accordingly, the peculiar constitution of the State makes it irresistible, and certain of obtaining whatever it determines to attempt. Nay, even when these external alarms are past, and the people are enjoying their good fortune and the fruits of their victories, and, as usually happens, growing corrupted by flattery and idleness, show a tendency to violence and arrogance—it is in these circumstances, more than ever, that the constitution is seen to possess within itself the power of correcting abuses. For when any one of the three classes becomes puffed up, and manifests an inclination to be contentious and unduly encroaching, the mutual interdependency of all the three, and the possibility of the pretensions of any one being checked and thwarted by the others, must plainly check this tendency: and so the proper equilibrium is maintained by the impulsiveness of the one part being checked by its fear of the other. . . .

19. After electing the Consuls they proceed to elect Military Tribunes—fourteen from those who had five years', and ten from those who had ten years', service. All citizens must serve ten years in the cavalry or twenty years in the infantry before the forty-sixth year of their age, except those rated below four hundred asses. The latter are employed in the navy; but if any great public necessity arises they are obliged to serve as infantry also for twenty campaigns: and no one can hold an office in the state until he has completed ten years of military service. . . .

When the Consuls are about to enrol the army they give public notice of the day on which all Roman citizens of military age must appear. This is done every year. When the day has arrived, and the citizens fit for service are come to Rome and have assembled on the Capitoline, the fourteen junior Tribunes divide themselves, in the order in which they were appointed by the people or by the Imperators, into four divisions, because the primary division of the forces thus raised is into four legions. The four Tribunes first appointed are assigned to the legion called the 1st; the next three to the 2nd; the next four to the 3rd; and the last three to the 4th. Of the ten senior Tribunes, the two first are assigned to the 1st legion; the next three to the 2nd; the two next to the 3rd; and the three last to the 4th.

20. This division and assignment of the Tribunes having been settled in such a way that all four legions have an equal number of officers, the Tribunes of the several legions take up a separate position and draw lots for the tribes one by one; and summon the tribe on whom it from time to time falls. From this tribe they select four young men as nearly like each other in age and phy-

sical strength as possible. These four are brought forward, and the Tribunes of the first legion pick out one of them, those of the second another, those of the third another, and the fourth has to take the last. When the next four are brought forward, the Tribunes of the second legion have the first choice, and those of the first the last. With the next four the Tribunes of the third legion have the first choice, those of the second the last; and so on in regular rotation: of which the result is that each legion gets men of much the same standard. . . .

21. The roll having been completed in this manner, the Tribunes belonging to the several legions muster their men; and selecting one of the whole body that they think most suitable for the purpose, they cause him to take an oath that he will obey his officers and do their orders to the best of his ability. And all the others come up and take the oath separately, merely affirming that they will do the same as the first man.

At the same time the Consuls send orders to the magistrates of the allied cities in Italy, from which they determine that allied troops are to serve: declaring the number required, and the day and place at which the men selected must appear. The cities then enrol their troops with much the same ceremonies as to selection and administration of the oath, and appoint a commander and a paymaster. . . .

26. . . . These arrangements made, the Military Tribunes take over the citizens and allies and proceed to form a camp. Now the principle on which they construct their camps, no matter when or where, is the same; I think therefore that it will be in place here to try and make my readers understand, as far as words can do so, the Roman tactics in regard to the march (agmen), the camp (castrorum metatio), and the line of battle (acies). I cannot imagine any one so indifferent to things noble and great, as to refuse to take some little extra trouble to understand things like these; for if he has once heard them, he will be acquainted with one of those things genuinely worth observation and knowledge.

Polybius describes in great detail the Roman method of laying out a camp. The camp was perfectly square and the tents of the consul,

An altar relief of the first century B.C. depicting the ceremony of the purification (*lustratio*) of the army. The warrior god, Mars, receives the sacrifice as a Roman official, clad in toga, pours a libation. This ceremony usually took place following the census. (Archives Photographiques, Paris)

tribunes and soldiers laid out in precise order. Even when camp was set for only one night a trench was dug around all four sides and a watch kept at each entrance. This required time and strict discipline but made the Roman army on the march invulnerable to surprise attack. Polybius describes the manner in which the night watch was kept and the duty, entrusted to the cavalry, of going the rounds to see that the watch was alert. If one of the watch had fallen asleep or if the patrol had been negligent of its duty, punishment was swift and severe.

Roman camp as described by Polybius. The interior checker-board pattern of tents and passageways was surrounded by an open walkway (*intervallum*) for easy communication and concentration of defense. This, in turn, was surrounded by a rampart and ditch with four gateways. (A. H. McDonald, *Republican Rome*. London: Thames and Hudson, 1966, p. 89)

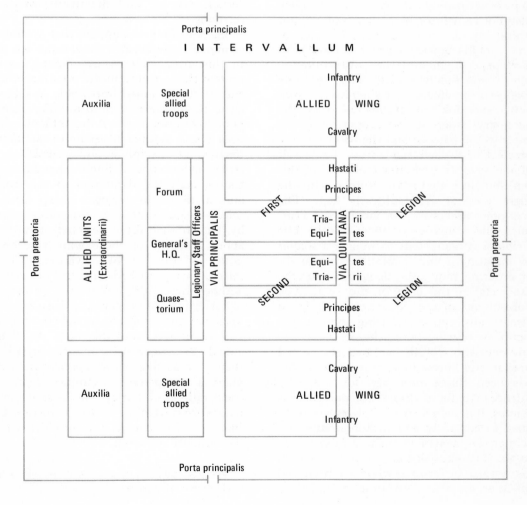

37. Then the Tribunes at once hold a court-martial, and the man who is found guilty is punished by the *fustuarium;* the nature of which is this. The Tribune takes a cudgel and merely touches the condemned man; whereupon all the soldiers fall upon him with cudgels and stones. Generally speaking men thus punished are killed on the spot; but if by any chance, after running the gauntlet, they manage to escape from the camp, they have no hope of ultimately surviving even so. They may not return to their own country, nor would any one venture to receive such an one into his house. Therefore those who have once fallen into this misfortune are utterly and finally ruined. The same fate awaits the praefect of the squadron, as well as his rear-rank man, if they fail to give the necessary order at the proper time, the latter to the patrols, and the former to the praefect of the next squadron. The result of the severity and inevitableness of this punishment is that in the Roman army the night watches are faultlessly kept. The common soldiers are amenable to the Tribunes; the Tribunes to the Consuls. The Tribune is competent to punish a soldier by inflicting a fine, distraining his goods, or ordering him to be flogged; so too the praefects in the case of the socii. The punishment of the *fustuarium* is assigned also to any one committing theft in the camp, or bearing false witness: as also to any one who in full manhood is detected in shameful immorality: or to any one who has been thrice punished for the same offence. All these things are punished as crimes. But such as the following are reckoned as cowardly and dishonourable in a soldier: for a man to make a false report to the Tribunes of his valour in order to get reward; or for men who have been told off to an ambuscade to quit the place assigned them from fear; and also for a man to throw away any of his arms from fear, on the actual field of battle. Consequently it sometimes happens that men confront death at their stations, because, from their fear of the punishment awaiting them at home, they refuse to quit their post: while others, who have lost shield or spear or any other arm on the field, throw themselves upon the foe, in hopes of recovering what they have lost, or of escaping by death from certain disgrace and the insults of their relations.

38. But if it ever happens that a number of men are involved in these same acts: if, for instance, some entire maniples have quitted their ground in the presence of the enemy, it is deemed impossible to subject all to the *fustuarium* or to military execution; but a solution of the difficulty has been found at once adequate to the maintenance of discipline and calculated to strike terror. The Tribune assembles the legion, calls the defaulters to the front, and, after administering a sharp rebuke, selects five or eight or twenty out of them by lot, so that those selected should be about a tenth[7] of those who have been guilty of the act of cowardice. These selected are punished with the *fustuarium* without mercy; the rest are put on rations of barley instead of wheat, and are ordered to take up their quarters outside the vallum and the protection of the camp. As all are equally in danger of having the lot fall on them, and as all alike who escape that, are made a conspicuous example of having their rations of barley, the best possible means are thus taken to inspire fear for the future, and to correct the mischief which has actually occurred.

---

[7] [This procedure was called *decimatio;* hence the English word "decimation."]

39. A very excellent plan also is adopted for inducing young soldiers to brave danger. When an engagement has taken place and any of them have showed conspicuous gallantry, the Consul summons an assembly of the legion, puts forward those whom he considers to have distinguished themselves in any way, and first compliments each of them individually on his gallantry, and mentions any other distinction he may have earned in the course of his life, and then presents them with gifts: to the man who has wounded an enemy, a spear; to the man who has killed one and stripped his armour, a cup, if he be in the infantry, horse-trappings if in the cavalry; though originally the only present was a spear. This does not take place in the event of their having wounded or stripped any of the enemy in a set engagement or the storming of a town; but in skirmishes or other occasions of that sort, in which, without there being any positive necessity for them to expose themselves singly to danger, they have done so voluntarily and deliberately. In the capture of a town those who are first to mount the walls are presented with a gold crown. So too those who have covered and saved any citizens or allies are distinguished by the Consul with certain presents; and those whom they have preserved present them voluntarily with a crown, or if not, they are compelled to do so by the Tribunes. The man thus preserved, too, reverences his preserver throughout his life as a father, and is bound to act towards him as a father in every respect. By such incentives those who stay at home are stirred up to a noble rivalry and emulation in confronting danger, no less than those who actually hear and see what takes place. For the recipients of such rewards not only enjoy great glory among their comrades in the army, and an immediate reputation at home, but after their return they are marked men in all solemn festivals; for they alone, who have been thus distinguished by the Consuls for bravery, are allowed to wear robes of honour on those occasions: and moreover they place the spoils they have taken in the most conspicuous places in their houses, as visible tokens and proofs of their valour. No wonder that a people whose rewards and punishments are allotted with such care and received with such feelings, should be brilliantly successful in war. . . .

43. Nearly all historians have recorded as constitutions of eminent excellence those of Lacedaemonia, Crete, Mantinea, and Carthage. Some have also mentioned those of Athens and Thebes. The former I may allow to pass; but I am convinced that little need be said of the Athenian and Theban constitutions: their growth was abnormal, the period of their zenith brief, and the changes they experienced unusually violent. Their glory was a sudden and fortuitous flash, so to speak; and while they still thought themselves prosperous, and likely to remain so, they found themselves involved in circumstances completely the reverse. The Thebans got their reputation for valour among the Greeks, by taking advantage of the senseless policy of the Lacedaemonians, and the hatred of the allies towards them, owing to the valour of one, or at most two, men who were wise enough to appreciate the situation. Since fortune quickly made it evident that it was not the peculiarity of their constitution, but the valour of their leaders, which gave the Thebans their success. For the great power of Thebes notoriously took its rise, attained its zenith, and fell to the ground with the lives of Epaminondas and Pelopidas. We must therefore conclude that it was not its constitution, but its men, that

caused the high fortune which it then enjoyed.

A somewhat similar remark applies to the Athenian constitution also. For though it perhaps had more frequent interludes of excellence, yet its highest perfection was attained during the brilliant career of Themistocles [during the Persian wars in the fifth century B.C.]; and having reached that point it quickly declined, owing to its essential instability. For the Athenian demos is always in the position of a ship without a commander. In such a ship, if fear of the enemy, or the occurrence of a storm induce the crew to be of one mind and to obey the helmsman, everything goes well; but if they recover from this fear, and begin to treat their officers with contempt, and to quarrel with each other because they are no longer all of one mind,—one party wishing to continue the voyage, and the other urging the steersman to bring the ship to anchor; some letting out the sheets, and others hauling them in, and ordering the sails to be furled,—their discord and quarrels make a sorry show to lookers on; and the position of affairs is full of risk to those on board engaged on the same voyage: and the result has often been that, after escaping the dangers of the widest seas, and the most violent storms, they wreck their ship in harbour and close to shore. And this is what has often happened to the Athenian constitution. For, after repelling, on various occasions, the greatest and most formidable dangers by the valour of its people and their leaders, there have been times when, in periods of secure tranquility, it has gratuitously and recklessly encountered disaster. Therefore I need say no more about either it, or the Theban constitution: in both of which a mob manages everything on its own unfettered impulse—a mob in the one city distinguished for headlong outbursts of

fiery temper, in the other trained in long habits of violence and ferocity. . . .

47. . . . To my mind, then, there are two things fundamental to every state, in virtue of which its powers and constitution become desirable or objectionable. These are customs and laws. Of these the desirable are those which make men's private lives holy and pure, and the public character of the state civilised and just. The objectionable are those whose effect is the reverse. As, then, when we see good customs and good laws prevailing among certain people, we confidently assume that, in consequence of them, the men and their civil constitution will be good also, so when we see private life full of covetousness, and public policy of injustice, plainly we have reason for asserting their laws, particular customs, and general constitution to be bad. Now, with few exceptions, you could find no habits prevailing in private life more steeped in treachery than those in Crete, and no public policy more inequitable. Holding, then, the Cretan constitution to be neither like the Spartan, nor worthy of choice or imitation, I reject it from the comparison which I have instituted.

Nor again would it be fair to introduce the Republic of Plato, which is also spoken of in high terms by some philosophers. For just as we refuse admission to the athletic contests to those actors or athletes who have not acquired a recognised position or trained for them, so we ought not to admit this Platonic constitution to the contest for the prize of merit unless it can first point to some genuine and practical achievement. Up to this time the notion of bringing it into comparison with the constitutions of Sparta, Rome, and Carthage would be like putting up a statue to compare with living and breathing men. Even if such a statue were faultless in point of art, the comparison of the lifeless with the living would naturally leave an impression of imperfection and incongruity upon the minds of the spectators. . . .

51. Now the Carthaginian constitution seems to me originally to have been well contrived in these most distinctively important particulars. For they had kings, and the Gerusia had the powers of an aristocracy, and the multitude were supreme in such things as affected them; and on the whole the adjustment of its several parts was very like that of Rome and Sparta. But about the period of its entering on the Hannibalian war the political state of Carthage was on the decline, that of Rome improving. For whereas there is in every body, or polity, or business a natural stage of growth, zenith, and decay; and whereas everything in them is at its best at the zenith; we may thereby judge of the difference between these two constitutions as they existed at that period. For exactly so far as the strength and prosperity of Carthage preceded that of Rome in point of time, by so much was Carthage then past its prime, while Rome was exactly at its zenith, as far as its political constitution was concerned. In Carthage therefore the influence of the people in the policy of the state had already risen to be supreme, while at Rome the Senate was at the height of its power: and so, as in the one measures were deliberated upon by the many, in the other by the best men, the policy of the Romans in all public undertakings proved the stronger; on which account, though they met with capital disasters, by force of prudent counsels they finally conquered the Carthaginians in the war.

52. If we look however at separate details, for instance at the provisions for carrying on a war, we shall find that whereas for a naval expedition the Carthaginians are the better trained and prepared —as it is only natural with a people with whom it has been hereditary for many generations to practise this craft, and to follow the seaman's trade above all nations in the world—yet in regard to military service on land, the Romans train themselves to a much higher pitch than the Carthaginians. The former bestow their whole attention upon this department: whereas the Carthaginians wholly neglect their infantry, though they do take some slight interest in the cavalry. The reason of this is that they employ foreign mercenaries, the Romans native and citizen levies. It is in this point that the latter polity is preferable to the former. They have their hopes of freedom ever resting on the courage of mercenary troops: the Romans on the valour of their own citizens and the aid of their allies. The result is that even if the Romans have suffered a defeat at first, they renew the war with undiminished forces, which the Carthaginians cannot do. For, as the Romans are fighting for country and children, it is impossible for them to relax the fury of their struggle; but they persist with obstinate resolution until they have overcome their enemies. What has happened in regard to their navy is an instance in point. In skill the Romans are much behind the Carthaginians, as I have already said; yet the upshot of the whole naval war has been a decided triumph for the Romans, owing to the valour of their men. For although nautical science contributes largely to success in sea-fights, still it is the courage of the marines that turns the scale most decisively in favour of victory. The fact is that Italians as a nation are by nature superior to Phoenicians and Libyans both in physical strength and courage; but still their habits also do much to inspire the youth with enthusiasm for such exploits. One example will be sufficient of the pains taken

by the Roman state to turn out men ready to endure anything to win a reputation in their country for valour.

53. Whenever one of their illustrious men dies, in the course of his funeral, the body with all its paraphernalia is carried into the forum to the Rostra, as a raised platform there is called, and sometimes is propped upright upon it so as to be conspicuous, or, more rarely, is laid upon it. Then with all the people standing round, his son, if he has left one of full age and he is there, or, failing him, one of his relations, mounts the Rostra and delivers a speech concerning the virtues of the deceased, and the successful exploits performed by him in his lifetime. By these means the people are reminded of what has been done, and made to see it with their own eyes—not only such as were engaged in the actual transactions but those also who were not; and their sympathies are so deeply moved, that the loss appears not to be confined to the actual mourners, but to be a public one affecting the whole people. After the burial and all the usual ceremonies have been performed, they place the likeness of the deceased in the most conspicuous spot in his house, surmounted by a wooden canopy or shrine. This likeness consists of a mask made to represent the deceased with extraordinary fidelity both in shape and colour.[8] These likenesses they display at public sacrifices adorned with much care. And when any illustrious member of the family dies, they carry these masks to the funeral, putting them on men whom they thought as like the originals as possible in height and other personal peculiarities. And these substitutes assume clothes according to the rank of the person represented: if he was a Consul or praetor, a toga with purple stripes; if a censor, whole purple, if he had also celebrated a triumph or performed any exploit of that kind, a toga embroidered with gold. These representatives also ride themselves in chariots, while the fasces and axes, and all the other customary insignia of the particular offices, lead the way, according to the dignity of the rank in the state enjoyed by the deceased in his lifetime; and on arriving at the Rostra they all take their seats on ivory chairs in their order. There could not easily be a more inspiring spectacle than this for a young man of noble ambitions and virtuous aspirations. For can we conceive any one to be unmoved at the sight of all the likenesses collected together of the men who have earned glory, all as it were living and breathing? Or what could be a more glorious spectacle?

54. Besides the speaker over the body about to be buried, after having finished the panegyric of this particular person, starts upon the others whose representatives are present, beginning with the most ancient, and recounts the successes and achievements of each. By this means the glorious memory of brave men is continually renewed; the fame of those who have performed any noble deed is never allowed to die; and the renown of those who have done good service to their country becomes a matter of common knowledge to the multitude, and part of the heritage of posterity. But the chief benefit of the ceremony is that it inspires young

---

[8] [Polybius is describing the *ius imaginum,* i.e. the "privilege of the descendants of the great families to show in their funeral processions the *imagines maiorum,* that is, the wax effigies and masks of their deceased ancestors who had held high office." This practice had its origins in age-old religious beliefs.

It is interesting to note that in Athens, legislation was passed in the seventh and sixth centuries B.C. to outlaw similar luxurious funerals. E. F. Bruck, "Political Ideology, Propaganda, and Public Law of the Romans: Ius Imaginum and Consecratio Imperatorum," *Seminar,* VII (1949), 1–25.]

men to shrink from no exertion for the general welfare, in the hope of obtaining the glory which awaits the brave. And what I say is confirmed by this fact. Many Romans have volunteered to decide a whole battle by single combat; not a few have deliberately accepted certain death, some in time of war to secure the safety of the rest, some in time of peace to preserve the safety of the commonwealth. There have also been instances of men in office putting their own sons to death, in defiance of every custom and law, because they rated the interests of their country higher than those of natural ties even with their nearest and dearest. . . .

56. Again the Roman customs and principles regarding money transactions are better than those of the Carthaginians. In the view of the latter nothing is disgraceful that makes for gain; with the former nothing is more disgraceful than to receive bribes and to make profit by improper means. For they regard wealth obtained from unlawful transactions to be as much a subject of reproach, as a fair profit from the most unquestioned source is of commendation. A proof of the fact is this. The Carthaginians obtain office by open bribery, but among the Romans the penalty for it is death. With such a radical difference, therefore, between the rewards offered to virtue among the two peoples, it is natural that the ways adopted for obtaining them should be different also.

But the most important difference for the better which the Roman commonwealth appears to me to display is in their religious beliefs. For I conceive that what in other nations is looked upon as a reproach, I mean a scrupulous fear of the gods, is the very thing which keeps the Roman commonwealth together. To such an extraordinary height is this carried among them, both in private and public

business, that nothing could exceed it. Many people might think this unaccountable; but in my opinion their object is to use it as a check upon the common people. If it were possible to form a state wholly of philosophers, such a custom would perhaps be unnecessary. But seeing that every multitude is fickle, and full of lawless desires, unreasoning anger, and violent passion, the only resource is to keep them in check by mysterious terrors and scenic effects of this sort. Wherefore, to my mind, the ancients were not acting without purpose or at random, when they brought in among the vulgar those opinions about the gods, and the belief in the punishments in Hades: much rather do I think that men nowadays are acting rashly and foolishly in rejecting them. This is the reason why, apart from anything else, Greek statesmen, if entrusted with a single talent, though protected by ten checking-clerks, as many seals, and twice as many witnesses, yet cannot be induced to keep faith: whereas among the Romans, in their magistracies and embassies, men have the handling of a great amount of money, and yet from pure respect to their oath keep their faith intact. And, again, in other nations it is a rare thing to find a man who keeps his hands out of the public purse, and is entirely pure in such matters: but among the Romans it is a rare thing to detect a man in the act of committing such a crime. . . .

57. That to all things, then, which exist there is ordained decay and change I think requires no further arguments to show: for the inexorable course of nature is sufficient to convince us of it.

But in all polities we observe two sources of decay existing from natural causes, the one external, the other internal and self-produced. The external admits of no certain or fixed definition, but the internal follows a definite order. What kind of polity, then, comes naturally first, and what second, I have already stated in such a way, that those who are capable of taking in the whole drift of my argument can henceforth draw their own conclusions as to the future of the Roman polity. For it is quite clear, in my opinion. When a commonwealth, after warding off many great dangers, has arrived at a high pitch of prosperity and undisputed power, it is evident that, by the lengthened continuance of great wealth within it, the manner of life of its citizens will become more extravagant; and that the rivalry for office, and in other spheres of activity, will become fiercer than it ought to be. And as this state of things goes on more and more, the desire of office and the shame of losing reputation, as well as the ostentation and extravagance of living, will prove the beginning of a deterioration. And of this change the people will be credited with being the authors, when they become convinced that they are being cheated by some from avarice, and are puffed up with flattery by others from love of office. For when that comes about, in their passionate resentment and acting under the dictates of anger, they will refuse to obey any longer, or to be content with having equal powers with their leaders, but will demand to have all or far the greatest themselves. And when that comes to pass the constitution will receive a new name, which sounds better than any other in the world, liberty or democracy; but, in fact, it will become that worst of all governments, mob-rule.

With this description of the formation, growth, zenith, and present state of the Roman polity, and having discussed also its difference for better and for worse, from other polities, I will now at length bring my essay on it to an end.

It is clear that Polybius recognized the importance of "customs and laws" as well as the effective balance of more formal political institutions as essential to the preservation of the Roman state. He did not note, however, what has since been regarded as the single most important institutional invention of the Romans— their legal system. Unlike the Greeks for whom law was bound to the public life of the polis and remained a branch of political philosophy or practical politics, the Romans understood the law to be a set of procedures and principles worked out by professional lawyers and legal scholars which defined the area of legitimate activity or "rights" of individual citizens. The Romans also knew an area of "public law" as differentiated from this "private law," but it was the latter for which a unique set of institutions was elaborated. These institutions were influenced in their development by the unique position of the Roman *paterfamilias* and by the special significance attached to the magisterial offices, and they reflected the changing nature of relationships between individuals and between the latter and the complex institutions of a growing empire. In much the same way as the state became clearly distinguished from society in Rome, so the legal system emerged as an institutional complex associated with the power of the state and clearly differentiated from custom. This distinction between law and custom is basic to our understanding of Roman law.

LAW
J. Roland Pennock and David G. Smith[9]

Law constitutes the rules of a political society. . . . All societies have customs that no one would think of calling law. It may be the custom to have the main meal of the day at sundown, but no one would

[9] Reprinted with permission of The Macmillan Company from *Political Science: An Introduction* by J. Roland Pennock and David G. Smith. Copyright © The Macmillan Company, 1964.

think it wrong for a family to do otherwise. Rules for worshipping the gods or performing magic may be considered religious rather than properly legal, although the line here may be vague. But rules that are socially useful, or thought to be, soon assume "rightness" in a unique sense. This peculiar quality we call "legal." Customs of this kind we speak of as "legal custom" or "customary law."

All law, customary or otherwise, has some method of enforcement, but the methods vary greatly in kind and degree. Enforcement may be left entirely to the injured individual, to members of his family, or it may be carried out by agents of the organized community. The means vary from mere expression of disapproval to the death penalty, and may include withholding of benefits, refusal to cooperate, ridicule, physical punishment, and banishment. When a society provides courts for the interpretation and application of law and organized force for its enforcement, we recognize that it has a system of law in the fullest sense of the word. Then, too, we have a state.

One of the most useful functions performed by law in any complex society is *to give definite statement to rights and duties* and to a minimally acceptable code of social behavior. Custom and informal devices may permit too much chicanery or evasion. Often in primitive society or in periods of social change, authority is shifting and obscure, and custom is surrounded by a penumbra of doubt. The certainty provided by a regime of law is sorely missed.

Both because of certainty of meaning and assurance of enforcement, law adds to the *predictability* of human behavior. Law enables men to make contracts with confidence that the other party will be com-

pelled, if necessary, to carry out his undertaking. The effective freedom of the businessman to conduct his affairs would be disastrously circumscribed if he could not rely on the law to compel payment of debts. Custom may or may not be sufficient to provide the web of structured expectations that a given situation and set of social functions requires. Pedestrians on crowded sidewalks, partly by following customary patterns and partly by on-the-spot adjustments, achieve their objectives more fully and freely than they would if subjected to a legally defined and imposed traffic pattern. Yet without traffic laws, as a result of which drivers know what to expect of each other, the movement of automobiles, buses, and trucks on city streets would be chaotic, if not impossible. The art of government lies in separating the two cases, one in which custom is sufficient or even superior to law, the other in which custom requires the corrective of explicitly enjoined and generally enforced actions.

A further service performed by law is that of substituting *peaceful settlement of disputes* for brute force. This role of law is most obvious in primitive society. Among certain Eskimo tribes, for instance, the blood feud is the normal mode of resolving disputes. These feuds smolder on, embroil more and more families, with the result that numerous tribes have been actually exterminated as a consequence of their astoundingly bloody ways of enforcing "justice." Vigilantes, lynch law, and labor violence serve as reminders that this role of law remains vital even in contemporary societies. Despite its reliance upon force as a last resort, law is the great economizer of force and violence.

Lastly, law is important as *a technique of adaptation,* particularly in adapting old forms and procedures to changed conditions, in accordance with the society's sense of justice. If, for example, a norm of behavior requires universal conformity to be effective, law and not the spontaneous activities of society is needed to enforce it. Bad business practices may drive out the good; and if, for instance, the bad practice is competition through the use of sweated labor, a few malefactors may make good practice ruinous to those who try to adhere to them. Law is clearly demanded.

The Romans were particularly successful in developing a flexible set of legal institutions which adjusted to changing customs and the new requirements of military expansion. The last two centuries of the Republic (201–27 B.C.) were the formative period of Roman law. What we know about the legal history of these centuries, however, derives largely from those periods which contemporary students of jurisprudence call classical (27 B.C.–A.D. 284) and postclassical (A.D. 284–534). It was during these two later periods that jurists developed, elaborated and systematized the law in learned digests and commentaries. The entire Roman legal tradition was codified by command of the Emperor Justinian in the sixth century A.D. following the fall of the Western Roman Empire. Justinian's famous *Corpus Juris Civilis* was the form in which Roman law was preserved in the Byzantine Empire. It was reintroduced into Western Europe in the eleventh century, and taught in medieval universities. From the *Corpus Juris Civilis* and a number of other literary sources, modern scholars have reconstructed the history of Roman law.

The most significant area of Roman legal development was private law (*jus privatum*). The Romans expanded the definition of what was private far beyond the realm of the household to include the private activities of a legal person (the *paterfamilias*) in society. Roman private law came to include methods for bringing legal action against another free person; a law of persons and family governing marriage, divorce and inheritance; a law of property (including slaveholding); and a law of obligations (contracts). This private law was distinguished from public law (*jus publicum*) which included constitutional, administrative and criminal law. At first both public and private law were aspects of the Roman civil law (*jus civile*), the law common to all citizens, and the process of distinction and elaboration was a slow one.

Classical scholars are agreed in identifying four basic sources of Roman law. Ancestral custom (*mos majorum*), embedded in the sacred traditions of the tribe, is the most difficult source to identify positively. But from the earliest times the Romans distinguished within their customary laws a sphere of secular law (*jus*) from divine or sacred law (*fas*). *Jus* meant both "right" and "law" as they applied to human relations. *Fas* was that which was permitted by sacred law (*fas est* means literally "not prohibited by taboos"), but it came to imply moral or religious precepts "enforced through priestly coercion (for instance, the duty of an heir to perform the rites of ancestor worship) or through censorial reproof (for instance, the prohibition of senseless cruelty of the chief of a family toward persons subject to his legally unrestricted paternal power)."[10] It was the area of *jus* which developed into systems of law and procedure. In the early Republic, when private law consisted primarily of the law of the family and inheritance, members of the aristocracy well acquainted with ancestral custom served as members of the college of pontiffs. Acting as state priests (*pontifices*) they would give advice (*responsum*) to individuals and magistrates concerning the precise rituals and words (*formulae*) by which cases had to be introduced before a judge. This practice of referring to the advice of knowledgeable elders was the way in which custom developed into formal Roman law.

The second source of law recognized by the Romans was statute. The enactment of any one of the three Republican assemblies had the

[10] Hans Julius Wolff, *Roman Law: An Historical Introduction* (Norman, Okla.: University of Oklahoma Press, 1951), p. 51.

force of law—*lex*. Statute, generally acknowledged today as the primary source of Western law, played a relatively minor role in the development of Roman law. The assemblies were regarded more as ratifying agencies of a magisterial program than as legislatures. Yet, paradoxically, the Twelve Tables, Rome's first written statutes, were the foundation of all Roman law, and they were preeminently *lex*. The Twelve Tables, apparently published at the demand of the plebeians in the fifth century B.C. so that the law could be generally known and less arbitrarily interpreted, were a statement of established Roman custom. They were "conditional" laws like most of the ancient codes, but in the Twelve Tables one can already see the Roman emphasis on the procedure to be followed rather than the penalties to be meted out. For instance, the opening passage runs: "If a man is summoned to court and does not go, let witnesses be called, and then let the plaintiff seize him. If he resists or runs away, let the plaintiff lay hands on him. If he is ill or aged, let the plaintiff provide an animal to carry him. If he refuses this, the plaintiff need not provide a covered carriage." [11] The Twelve Tables did not, however, prescribe the precise formulas to be used in court procedure; this area of law remained the preserve of the priests and later the magistrates.

The third and fourth sources of Roman law—the edicts of magistrates and interpretation of the law by professional jurists—deserve special attention. These two sources of legal development constitute the area of Rome's unique contribution to law and the science of jurisprudence. Both were the work of a new class of legal specialists, and both derived their authority from the powers vested in the magistracy.

The praetor, as we have seen, was a magistrate whose primary responsibility was the administration of the civil law. Specifically, he supervised day-to-day litigation between private citizens. He had no power to *make* law, but his power over "remedies," that is, the formulas by which actions could be admitted into court, was

in fact the most fruitful source of Roman law. Upon assumption of office for one year, the praetor would issue an edict, or statement of the circumstances under which he would grant new remedies. For example, a praetor's edict might run: "If it is alleged that anyone has in bad faith harboured or incited another's slave, male or female, so as to diminish his or her value, I shall give an action against him for double damages." [12] The result was a new right before the law, or in substance, a new law. The praetor could at any time—not only in his annual edict—grant a special remedy. These would be embodied in the next year's edict and so contribute to a growing body of law known as the *jus honorarium* to distinguish it from the more formal *jus civile* of the Twelve Tables and legislation. The praetorian edict was the principal means by which the highly formalistic procedure of the civil law adjusted to changes brought on by political and economic expansion. The increasing importance of the praetorian edict is attested to by the fact that by the end of the Republic there were sixteen praetors resident in Rome.

Another edict of special interest, but one about which little is known, was the edict of the *praetor peregrinus*. The edicts issued by this magistrate created a whole new body of law which consisted of remedies for cases involving foreigners to whom the rules of the Roman civil law did not apply. His edict was of special importance in the legal definition of contract because of the commercial nature of most of the litigation which came before him. It is probable that the *praetor peregrinus* adapted procedures and principles from a wide variety of legal systems when searching for formulas to accommodate cultural differences. The result was a law of a more universal character than the civil law, which came to be known as *jus gentium,* or law of nations. This new area of private law which was common to all free men, not just Roman citizens, had the effect of rejuvenating the civil law and purging it of its narrow formalism.

The last major source of Roman law was

---

[11] B. Nicholas, *An Introduction to Roman Law* (Oxford: Oxford University Press, 1962), p. 16.

[12] Nicholas, *An Introduction to Roman Law,* p. 21.

juristic interpretation. The jurists (*prudentes*) were neither practicing advocates nor magistrates, but men of respected social position who made a study of the law and who gave their opinions (*responsa*) to the magistrate, to the judge or to private individuals. They came from the same social class as those who acted as state priests, and their advice was merely a secular version of the *responsum* of the priests. The emergence of the jurists as differentiated from priests sometime in the fourth century B.C. marked the beginning of specialization within the legal profession. The *pontifices* confined their attention to sacred law; the jurists, to private law. By remaining aloof from the actual formal procedure of the court, the jurists emphasized their aristocratic station on which the authority of their advice alone stood. Only a few jurists in every generation came to be recognized as *prudens*. The importance of jurists grew with the introduction of the formulary procedure of the praetorian edict. The praetor, as an elected official, was often not well versed in the law. It was, therefore, frequently a jurist who wrote the edict, and his interpretation thus became decisive in the development of the *jus honorarium*.

The praetor, aided by the advice of eminent jurists, provided remedies before the law, but in civil cases he was not a prosecutor or a judge. As an official of the state he determined the formula by which a case might be brought to court. The praetor's formula served as a judicial contract by which the parties pledged themselves to accept the decision of a judge (*judex*) chosen by the litigants from a list of prominent citizens who undertook this function as a public duty. There were neither professional judges nor regularly established courts for private litigation in Republican Rome. The judge heard the case as presented by the parties or their advocates. He took what advice he needed from legal experts and arrived at a decision which was binding in each particular case, and from which there was no appeal. In the first and second centuries A.D., when the Empire began to take on bureaucratic forms of administration, the functions of the praetor and the *judex* in more

and more forms of action were combined in one state official, and a system of appeals through the administrative hierarchy began to take form.

The procedure just described prevailed only in civil cases, or what the Romans called *jus privatum*. In criminal cases, or in cases of treason or administrative corruption (*jus publicum*), the *imperium* of the magistrate was exercised in a direct fashion, the magistrate initiating the case, hearing the evidence and passing judgment. Appeal to the Centuriate Assembly was available in cases involving capital punishment. During the second and first centuries B.C., in a series of legislative acts, permanent courts composed of jurors chosen by lot from a list of prominent citizens were established to try criminal cases. This rudimentary jury system did not last, however, and during the Empire magistrates once again acted alone as prosecutor, jury and judge in criminal and civil cases alike. In general, the criminal system never passed through that stage of exact differentiation and definition of procedure and principle which made the civil law an important model for subsequent history.

There was no system of formal legal education during the Republic. Jurists functioned as the only teachers of law. A young man, after being formally admitted to citizenship by assumption of the toga, would be placed by his father in the charge of a leading jurist and would accompany him in daily practice, gaining a firsthand, working knowledge of the law. This practical, oral training remained the basis of legal education throughout the Republic and early Empire. But these same jurists in the course of teaching and studying the law also wrote the first law books. The oldest juristic literature seems to have consisted of lists of procedural formulas and commentaries on the Twelve Tables. As the law became more sophisticated and complex, the textbooks and commentaries of the jurists were the means by which the growing bulk of the civil law was recorded, categorized and communicated throughout the Empire.

In the written treatises of the jurists, Greek influence on Roman law for the first time became evident. Greek analytical skills, combined with the Roman respect for form and procedure, produced the system of Roman law as it was transmitted into the Western tradition. Systematization necessitated abstraction, and abstraction meant the ordering of particular legal cases into larger abstract categories. Thus the Roman jurists distinguished private law—that law marking off the area of individual freedom of acquisition and action—from public law—the law concerned with the functioning of the state (constitutional law and criminal law). And within the province of private law alone they came to recognize specific bodies of law governing slavery, marriage, guardianship (law of persons), ownership, contract, and obligation (law of things). They formally recognized, unlike the Greeks, that their law (*jus civile*) was distinct from the laws of other societies and that both were a part of a larger law common to all people (*jus gentium*). This tendency toward systematization reached its climax during the early Empire in the period of the classical jurists (27 B.C.–A.D. 284). Its beginnings, however, go back to the Republican period, more specifically to the second century B.C., when Greek philosophy and Greek methods of categorization were introduced into Rome.

The degree to which Greek philosophy influenced Roman law is much debated by scholars. Roman legal historians tend to emphasize the fact that flexible legal institutions transcending rigid primitive forms were well established before the influx of Greek philosophy, and they also point out that the jurists remained practical men of affairs whose job it was to interpret the law in day-to-day circumstances. On the other hand, the first efforts to systematize the law in the latter part of the second century B.C. coincided with the arrival in Rome of Greek scholars and teachers, among them Polybius and the Stoic philosopher, Panaetius of Rhodes (189–109 B.C.). More specifically, it seems to have been the jurist Q. Mucius Scaevola, a member of the Scipionic Circle (which included Polybius and Panaetius) who wrote the first systematic treatise on the civil law employing Greek methods of analysis. He divided the law into four general categories: the law of inherit-

ance, the law of persons, the law of things, and the law of obligations. The result was the development of an intellectual procedure which raised the study of law to the level of a science and provoked several generations of commentaries and criticisms. This legal literature became the basis for continuing reinterpretation and reevaluation of the Roman law and also became the source from which subsequent Western legal systems derived so much influence.

In the perspective of the past as well as in the world of the present, no legal system has had such prodigious consequences for the course of human relations throughout the world as that which issued from the classical Roman method of producing laws.

This is so because Roman law was developed neither by priests, whose special interest was the protection of a local creed, nor by a supreme law-giver, in whose view the purposes of the law would be identical with those of the political system effective at the time of his legislation. Instead it was developed by a class of lawyers who made it their special business to cleanse legal notions of all the particularisms adhering to them, and to abstract the concepts that would seem generally applicable. As a result of the efforts thus pursued systematically over the centuries, Roman private law was kept from being confounded with any particular religion, form of government, or generation of men. It emerged as an independent system of norms, for which validity could be claimed outside of religion, outside of government, outside of Rome, and even outside of any special epoch in time.

Such an acknowledgment of Roman originality in the field of jurisprudence does not imply that Rome did not borrow from the legal theories and practices elaborated in other cultures and earlier centuries. On the contrary, the genius of the Roman jurists lay precisely in their readiness to study law in all of its intricate manifestations, and to observe its operation in the varied civilizations of the

Mediterranean. The Roman achievement in lawmaking can be measured best, in fact, when it is compared with the law ways of the Greeks—the only nation whose cultural superiority Rome unhesitatingly accepted in all domains of thought excepting that of jurisprudence. And Rome's discerning rejection of Greek leadership in this realm, it should be noted, has stood the test of modern research in the field of ancient legal practice. For the Greeks, it has been found, were so absorbed in perfecting the state as the fulfillment of the individual's talents and aspirations that they could not conceive of any law except in association with a particular political society. Moreover, since the political society of the Greeks was synonymous by and large with the city-state, law was in their estimation just another aspect of such a political community. It was "good" or "bad" to the extent that it supported or frustrated the purposes of the state.

Now, it is certainly true that the Greeks never tired of arguing questions of "good" and "bad," "right" and "wrong"; but through all of this they associated the goal of justice with the perfectibility of the city-state rather than with that of the processes of law. As Professor McIlwain puts it, they thought of law in terms of the state, rather than of the state in terms of law. The great classical philosophers of Greece assumed, of course, that a universal norm of political life could be apprehended through human reason, and that various political societies could be judged by reference to this universal norm. Yet they never really suggested that this norm could be elaborated as a practical guide for the perfectibility of laws. Throughout their discourses on law and justice, the legal norm remained a purely intellectual standard, which could not be used as a yardstick for the testing of the legitimacy of any particular law. Such a view involved a failure to distinguish between the public law of the state (*ius publicum*) and the private rights of individuals (*ius privatum*).

But it was precisely in the recognition of this distinction that the Roman lawyers made their revolutionary contribution to political thought. In their differentiation of the *ius publicum* from the *ius privatum* the jurists of Rome made it perfectly clear that both were derived from the same essence—law, and that both were addressed to the same subject—the natural person. The Romans departed, however, from the more ancient traditions of law by establishing the proposition that private rights affect private citizens exclusively, whereas all individuals alike participate in the public law by virtue of the fact that they together constitute the state.

This legal distinction had momentous consequences for the evolution of the modern society of nations, and may be said, indeed, to represent the fundamental legal proposition of the modern Western world, for the doctrine of the state as a bond or partnership in law as set forth by Cicero became the foundation for all our Western theories of constitutionalism. The general Roman theory that law is antecedent and thus superior to the state, made it possible to think of law as a regulating force in relations between states. And the legal disengagement of the individual from the political group led in due time to the elaboration of a category of "inalienable human rights," as well as to the general realization that it is constitutionally possible to render international relations in terms of human relations.[13]

---

[13] From *Politics and Culture in International History* by A. B. Bozeman. Copyright © 1960 by Princeton University Press. Reprinted by permission of Princeton University Press.

CHAPTER 3

THE ADAPTATION OF GREEK PHILOSOPHY TO ROMAN INSTITUTIONS AND VALUES:
Cicero's Ethics, Rhetoric and Politics

Since the heyday of classical Greek philosophy the role of the philosopher, of whatever school, had come to be identified as that of a guide to life. To the Romans this meant in practice guidance to political life as well as consolation for its not unlikely results, banishment or death. In the two principal Greek influences on Roman thought, rhetoric and Stoic philosophy, practical aims were given more importance than theorizing. The subtleties of Greek rhetoric were, as Quintilian put it, made easy. Stoicism in its five centuries from Zeno to Marcus Aurelius was changing from a more or less formally articulated philosophy to a set of attitudes. . . . In this process, two Greek Stoics of the second century B.C., active in Roman circles, the philosopher Panaetius and his pupil, the historian Posidonius, were most important. The former became the counselor and friend of Scipio, the latter of Pompey. Their achievement may be summed up by saying that they identified the Stoic ideal with the Roman ideal of public virtue and service to the state, and connected with this, that they imparted to historiography its principal didactic message: moral instruction.

George H. Nadel, Studies in the Philosophy of History

Prolonged reflection on this subject leads me to the only reasonable conclusion: I believe that wisdom without eloquence is of little use to the community, but that eloquence without wisdom mostly does great harm, and never does any good.

Cicero, On Invention

. . . A Commonwealth is the property of a people [*res publica*]. But a people is not any collection of human beings brought together in any sort of way, but an assemblage of people in large numbers associated in an agreement with respect to justice and a partnership for the common good.

Cicero, The Republic

The creative period of Roman law, the Republican period, was also a period of considerable political unrest. The year 133 B.C. marks an important turning point in Roman history. The election in that year of Tiberius Sempronius Gracchus as tribune of the people marked the beginning of a century of civil strife, during which the political ascendency of the senatorial aristocracy was challenged by popular pressures and ultimately replaced by a thinly disguised form of monarchy.

The period of civil strife, the so-called Roman Revolution, posed the majority of the ruling aristocracy, the *Optimates,* or "best people," against the *Populares,* a small faction of the aristocracy which sought support among the urban and rural workers, some of the equestrian class, and Rome's Italian allies. Tiberius Gracchus was one such popular leader. As tribune he gained the passage in the Tribal Assembly of agricultural reforms aimed at stopping the growth of large estates and restoring a free peasantry. The commission appointed to supervise land redistribution was headed by Tiberius Gracchus himself but was thwarted at every move by the Senate. When, contrary to custom, Tiberius Gracchus attempted to be reelected to the tribunate, he was murdered in the Forum along with 300 of his followers. Gaius Sempronius Gracchus, elected tribune ten years later, revived his brother's program of land reform and added to it a program of state purchase and distribution of grain for sale to the Roman poor. Gaius Gracchus attracted the equestrian class to the popular cause by giving them legal right to compose juries for the trial of accused magistrates. Gaius met with only temporary success, and like his brother, died in 121 B.C. in a massacre at the center of Rome.

The civil strife associated with the Gracchi brothers was only the beginning of a century of political unrest, the history of which is dominated by powerful military leaders—Marius, Sulla, Pompey, Crassus, and Caesar. In this period military service ceased being a part of every citizen's duty and became instead a specialized profession. Marius, as consul in 105 B.C., officially dropped the property qualification for military service, thus regularizing the practice of recruiting volunteers who would serve for pay and booty. The result was to shift the loyalty of many soldiers from the state to their own legion and its commander. Constant warfare and further imperial expansion became the vested interest of a group of professional soldiers. The successful general gained a personal following and a lever of power to use in the factional politics of Rome. For the most part the great generals posed as the champions of the common people. Only Sulla gave his support to the aristocratic cause against the *Populares.*

Sulla (138–78 B.C.) rose to prominence by leading the Roman army against a revolt of the Italian allies in 90–88 B.C. and by suppressing a revolt in Asia Minor and Greece. One important result of the Italian revolt was the extension of citizenship to communities of the former allies, thus expanding the voting population by hundreds of thousands and broadening the base from which the rival political factions had to look for support. But the older assemblies of the Roman people were not adequate mechanisms for turning the desires of this expanded citizenry into constitutional decisions. This was one important reason why power was now passing into the hands of military leaders. After returning to Rome from the East in 83 B.C., Sulla secured his own appointment as dictator (an ancient office revived for a new purpose). He executed or expelled thousands of *Populares* and restored the Senate to the power it had lost under the consul, Marius, and his successor, Cinna.

The victory which Sulla secured for the *Optimates* lasted only until 70 B.C., when Sulla retired from political life and Pompey and Crassus were elected consuls. These men, along with Julius Caesar (100–44 B.C.), provided popular leadership during the intense civil conflict of the next three decades. For a time the three were allied unofficially as the First Triumvirate, but personal ambitions eventually led them in separate directions. Each man owed his success in some measure to an extraordinary military command. In 73–71 B.C. Crassus put down a slave revolt in southern Italy led by the gladiator Spartacus, finishing the job by crucify-

The interior of the Colosseum. Inaugurated in the reign of Titus, in A.D. 80, and completed by Domitian. The greatest arena in all of Rome. (Italian State Tourist Office)

Roman games and the baths. The Romans had long pursued athletics as a part of military training and the religious celebrations of the city. The first athletic entertainment was introduced into Rome in the second century B.C. along with much else from the Hellenistic East. These spectacles grew in popularity and variety to become an important part of city life for Romans of all classes. Chariot racing, realistic theatricals in which victims were murdered before the spectators' eyes, gladiatorial combat, and mass executions took place in huge amphitheatres and arenas in Rome and other cities throughout the Empire. An equally popular importation from the East was the institution of the public bath. The Romans built vast facilities where men, and sometimes women, of all social strata went in the afternoon to exercise, bathe and talk.

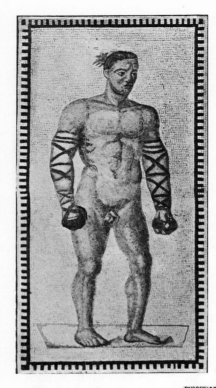 

Athletes from a mosaic in the Baths of Caracalla. (Alinari)

Interior of the Baths of Caracalla, an immense architectural complex in the center of Rome containing libraries, gymnasia, a sports stadium, and shops and offices. (Dr. Franz Stoedtner)

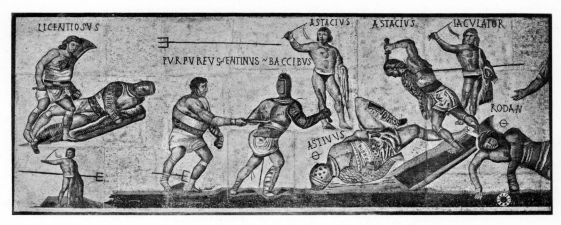

A group of gladiators from a fourth-century mosaic. (Anderson)

ing 6000 unclaimed slaves along the Appian Way. Pompey rose to power by removing the growing menace of pirates in the Mediterranean and by finally completing the conquest and reorganization of Asia Minor in 66–63 B.C. Caesar, who came from one of the oldest aristocratic families, joined the popular cause as a protégé of Crassus. He was elected quaestor in Spain in 69–68 B.C., aedile in 65, *Pontifex Maximus* in 63, praetor in 62, Spanish proconsul in 61, and consul in 59. Only in 58 B.C., when he was appointed governor of Illyricum and Cisalpine Gaul, did he gain the significant military command which had become necessary for an ambitious politician. In the course of the next nine years Caesar added the province of Gaul (modern France) to the Roman Empire.

While Caesar was occupied in Gaul, politics in the capital were reduced to gang warfare in the streets. In order to restore order, the *Optimates* won Pompey over to their side and entrusted the Republic to him as sole consul in 52 B.C. An attempt by Pompey and the Senate to remove Caesar from his command in Gaul forced him into action. Early in 49 B.C. Caesar crossed the Rubicon River which separated Italy from Cisalpine Gaul and marched on Rome. With the support of his legions and popular support from the towns of northern Italy, he forced Pompey to flee to Greece. During the next year Caesar defeated Pompey's forces and established himself as dictator until his assassination in 44 B.C.

The civil strife of the first century B.C. and the apparent triumph of Caesarism called into question the whole political and legal structure of Rome. The continued violation of accepted legal procedures by *Populares* and *Optimates* alike and the increasingly frequent use of military power threatened to destroy the respect for law and, indeed, the very dignity and authority on which the Roman public order was founded. This challenge to republican institutions and the traditional aristocratic values on which they were based was matched by the corrosive effect of foreign influences, particularly the influences arising from direct contact with Greek civilization.

There had been some knowledge of Greek culture early in Roman history largely by way of the Greek colonies in southern Italy. But now in the third and second centuries B.C., with the conquest of southern Italy and the occupation of Sicily, Greece, and part of Asia Minor, several generations of Romans saw the more sophisticated Hellenized communities at first hand. Soldiers serving in the East brought back new ideas of splendid buildings and exotic entertainments. Their officers learned something of the Greek language and the manner and style of their counterparts in diplomatic negotiations. Ambassadors came to Rome followed by teachers, physicians, merchants, and artists. Latin culture, which might, if given time, have developed sophisticated forms on its own, could not escape the overwhelming influence of the more advanced culture of the East.

The old religion of family and state cults, for instance, was subjected to foreign influences for nearly 200 years.

From the end of the third century B.C. this religion was quickened by Greek anthropomorphism and interpreted by Greek speculation, Polybius in particular helping the ruling class to realize the pragmatic value of their view of religion as an official institution. Apart from this inward transmutation, there were other consequences of Rome's advance to supremacy in the Mediterranean world. In the first place, Romans and, even more, Italians moved freely in the Hellenistic East as soldiers and merchants, and as merchants often settled there, as for instance at Delos. When so established they clung together, preserving their national individuality and reverencing the old household gods, above all the Lar and the Genius. At the same time, many of them as individuals worshipped local gods, and might on their return bring back their cults. Secondly, Romans who went to the East in positions of authority found themselves treated with the honours accorded to Hellenistic kings Flaminius received a cult and a priest at Chalcis, M'. Aquilius a priest at Pergamum. Not merely the man but his personified attributes might be worshipped: Cicero wrote to his brother Quintus "You see your virtues consecrated and set in the number of the gods." So the idea of deification was early introduced to the Roman ruling class. Finally, Rome itself attracted numerous immigrants, bringing their own cults and their own points of view. We can see manifestations of this in the statues set up in 86 B.C. to a popular praetor M. Marius in the quarters of the city and the offering to him of incense and wine, as well as the cultus of alien gods satirized in the *Eumenides* of Varro.

Thus there came to Rome both the higher and the lower elements of the Greek East.

The Hellenistic religious world contained a curious mixture of different elements, civic conservatism, individual mysticism, and scepticism. New deities, and above all Isis and Sarapis, became absorbed (as we see in their annual priesthoods of the Greek type) and obtained full civic recognition, even where there was no such motive as a desire to win Ptolemaic favour. From the cults of Cybele and Isis the Greeks formed initiations of their own type. They acquired importance, but it must not be forgotten that the cult of Isis was not primarily a religion of initiations: they were an "extra" for the devotee who could afford them. Many cult societies were formed, giving to the individual a substitute for family and local associations from which he was separated, many foundations also to secure the upkeep of his grave, which could not depend on relations and descendants. The tone of thoughtful men was marked by a certain weariness, as we see it in the end of Catullus LXIV: when our ancestors were pious, things went well; now the gods are far away and there is nothing in particular we can do about it; "I am a stranger and afraid, in a world I never made." [1]

Greek culture had a very direct influence upon Roman educational practices. Cato the Elder had tried to preserve the youth of Rome from the corrupting influence of Greek teachers by having the latter expelled from Rome in 161 B.C. and again in 154 B.C. Cato represented the last stand of the traditionalists who wanted education limited to the family and to military or political apprenticeship, although he himself was well versed in Greek rhetoric. In the second century B.C. there were still no public schools in Rome, except a few elementary "writing" schools, but it soon became regular practice for a Roman boy to attend lectures given by Greek philosophers,

[1]A. D. Nock, "Religious Developments from the Close of the Republic to the Death of Nero," *Cambridge Ancient History*, vol. X (Cambridge: Cambridge University Press, 1934), pp. 466–467. Reprinted by permission of the publisher.

rhetoricians, and physicians at a private school or in the house of one of the great families.

The best known of these households was that of Scipio Aemilianus, the conqueror of Carthage. Here Scipio's father gathered leading Greek intellectuals and books plundered from Greek libraries for the education of his son. The group thus formed was called the Scipionic Circle. It will be recalled that it was through Scipio's patronage that Polybius was able to observe Roman political institutions at first hand, and it was in part through this coterie that the various schools of Greek philosophy were introduced into Rome.

Thus the Roman aristocracy adopted Greek education for its sons. Teachers were already to hand amongst the great numbers of slaves that conquest had provided—the oldest known example being Livius Andronicus, a Greek from Tarentum who was taken to Rome as a slave after his city had been captured in 272 and later freed by his master after bringing

up his children. Roman society was very generous about emancipating its slaves—it thus did something to redeem the barbarous way it chose to obtain them.

Very soon, besides the private tuition that was given in the houses of the great, public teaching of Greek began to be given in genuine schools: Andronicus himself . . . was both tutor and schoolmaster. As well as freedmen who had set up on their own account there were slaves whose teaching abilities could be exploited by their owners: a slave who could teach was a good investment (as Cato knew) and fetched top price in the market. Not all the teachers began as slaves: Ennius was born in an allied city in Messapia. As soon as it was known that there were people in the capital anxious to learn their language, the Greeks came along to take advantage of it: in about the year 167, says Polybius, there were a large number of qualified teachers in Rome.

The Roman families, who wanted their

Boys in school—two pupils, seated on either side of the master, read the lesson from scrolls. Another boy arrives late. (The Bettmann Archive)

children to have the best education they could get, did all they could to give them a first-class training in Greek. This can be seen in the case of Aemilius Paulus, who engaged a whole staff of special Greek teachers for his sons and offered them the use of the valuable library that had belonged to King Perseus and been taken from booty seized in Macedonia.[2]

Of the Hellenistic philosophies introduced into Rome by Greek teachers, the works of the Epicureans were the first to be translated into Latin. Epicureanism[3] was also the first to find an able native Roman exponent in the person of Titus Lucretius Carus (ca. 98–55 B.C.). In his long didactic poem, *On the Nature of Things,* Lucretius outlined Epicurus' materialistic view of nature and the hedonistic ethic derived therefrom. Epicurus in the third century B.C. had developed a purely materialistic theory of the universe. All events and all things in this world and in an infinity of other worlds were to be explained in terms of atoms and their movement in the void. Epicurus assured his disciples that they need not fear death nor concern themselves with the will of the gods. "At death the atoms of the soul are dispersed and sensation ceases immediately. The gods are anthropomorphic and made out of the finest atoms. In the distances between the worlds (*intermundia*) they live a blessed and perfect life, free from any concern with this or any other world."[4] The gods and nature alike were, thus, without moral significance.

An essential feature of the Epicurean [ethic] is the cleavage it creates between the sentient being, or evaluator, and the valueless processes of the physical world. Unlike the Platonist or Stoic, the Epicurean does not find in nature any purposes or ends comparable to his own. Natural events are neither the temporal image of an eternal model, nor the constituent parts of a divinely ordered whole. There is neither harmony nor conflict between nature's ends and man's, as nature has no ends. The ever-moving atoms strive for no goals and realize no values. The ethical agent, therefore, canot identify himself with the natural world. He cannot accept and promote the cosmic order. He must stand apart, examining and testing all that comes his way, accepting little and rejecting much.

. . . Some pleasures must be rejected, as they are inseparable from greater pains, the pursuit of the good life, therefore, is not an indiscriminate attachment to pleasures, but a selection and ordering of experiences so as to ensure a stable and lasting pleasure. The ethical agent must create his own moral order from the experiences that the atoms produce in him. . . .

. . . [Moral] freedom is not merely the ability to exercise choice; it is even more the ability to avoid all that interferes with the pursuit of the good life, for one who chooses under the influence of false opinions and vain desires canot be said to be free. Moral freedom therefore requires a philosophical detachment which rejects the pursuit of wealth, fame, power, and even the more intense pleasures. It demands emancipation from hate and love and all other passions and the dissolution of desires and enthusiasms, at least so far as they are sources of unrest. It enables a person to resist forces from outside. . . . Indeed the highest freedom would seem to remove the need for making any choices at all. The Epicurean, in order to free himself from false goods, anxiety, and insecurity, enslaves himself to his system; and by identifying himself with the school he makes himself a part of the "objective" order that it establishes. Epicurus seems to have encouraged his followers thus to surrender to him their independence of judgment. He exhorted them to memorize the basic documents of the school, to train themselves in following them,

[2] From *A History of Education in Antiquity* by H. I. Marrou (trans. George Lamb). Copyright © 1956 by Sheed & Ward Inc., New York. Reprinted by permission. Footnotes have been omitted.

[3] *See Western Man,* vol. I, *The Contribution of Ancient Greece.*

[4] *The Oxford Classical Dictionary* (Oxford: Oxford University Press, 1949), p. 325.

to control all their acts by principles, to act at all times as if Epicurus were watching. Immediate responses to situations are replaced by a sober calculation of advantage and disadvantage, . . . and the chief virtue, more important even than philosophy itself, is *phronésis,* the faculty by which we determine what contributes to pleasure and what does not.[5]

Epicureanism, in proclaiming the freedom of human life from divine control, appealed to many of those Roman aristocrats for whom the traditional gods had failed to have any meaning and who were loath to turn to recently imported religions which attracted the lower strata of society. Yet it was difficult to square Epicurean egocentric ethics and elaborate materialistic metaphysics with traditional Roman beliefs. The ethical system and general view of the universe propounded by the Stoics proved to be more readily adaptable to the values of the Roman aristocracy.

Stoicism,[6] which had first developed in Hellenistic Greece, was brought to Rome in the second century by the Greek lecturers and tutors who were beginning to arrive in great numbers at that time. The first Stoic to lecture at Rome, Panaetius of Rhodes, came in 144 B.C. at the behest of Polybius and joined the group of philosophers in the household of Scipio Aemelianus. These Stoics seemed eager to please their Roman masters.

They found a place for the gods of traditional religion by a process of allegorizing, and they accepted divination. They proved by reason a number of things that the average Roman believed by instinct, such as that it was natural to love one's children and right to take part in public life, and they put for-

ward an ideal of virtuous conduct which chimed in well enough with the traditions of duty and self-sacrifice handed down from *maiores nostri.* If the virtues of *gravitas, constantia* and *magnitudo anime* were really . . . peculiarly Roman, it might even be said that the early Romans had been Stoics before they ever heard of Stoicism, for these virtues were certainly among those that made up the Stoic ideal of conduct.[7]

The original Stoic ideal of the wise man protected by his lofty indifference to material needs and emotional disturbances gave way to an emphasis on the calm and deliberate performance of duties. Living according to nature, which among some early Stoics could mean a narrow cultivation of virtue for its own sake—to the exclusion of more generally accepted benefits such as health, good looks, pleasure, wealth, and reputation—was modified to allow for the development of particular talents suited to one's station in life. This was in accord with the generally optimistic picture of the universe held by most Stoics. Nature was beneficient—guided by divine reason to provide for order and well-being —each part adapted to its special purpose. Man, through the use of his godlike faculty of reason, can understand nature and adjust himself to it.

Thus as Stoicism developed in the period of the later Roman Republic, it lost something of the narrowness of Zeno and Chrysippus. It provided a confident and optimistic view of the universe guided by divine providence with man in the centre, master of creation, gifted with reason, developing all his faculties for the organization of civilized society. It was a philosophy that flattered man's self-esteem without outraging his reason, a philosophy in which man's various instincts, social, artistic, intellectual and religious, all found recognition.[8]

---

[5] Phillip De Lacy, "Process and Value: An Epicurean Dilemma," *Transactions and Proceedings of the American Philological Association,* vol. 88 (1957), pp. 114–115, 118–119. Reprinted by permission. Footnotes have been omitted.

[6] See *Western Man,* vol. I, *The Contribution of Ancient Greece.*

[7] M. L. Clarke, *The Roman Mind: Studies in the History of Thought from Cicero to Marcus Aurelius* (Cambridge, Mass.: Harvard University Press, 1956), p. 32.

[8] Clarke, *The Roman Mind: Studies in the History of Thought from Cicero to Marcus Aurelius,* p. 41.

It was for these reasons that Stoicism held a special appeal for the Roman aristocracy. But there were those who could see in the current popularity of Stoicism and Epicureanism and in the neglect of family and civic religion signs of a weakening of the traditional Roman values. Prominent among the many Romans who became deeply concerned about this problem was Marcus Tullius Cicero (106–43 B.C.). Cicero came from a wealthy equestrian family and rose into the ranks of the magistracy and the Senate during the troubled times of Crassus, Pompey, and Caesar. He was one of the few "new men" to attain the office of consul in the first century B.C. It was during brief periods of enforced exile that he found time to write the philosophical essays which, together with his published letters and orations, have made him the most influential man of Latin letters.

Cicero's early education, like that of most wealthy Romans of the period, was in the hands of Greek tutors. As a young man he traveled to Greece and Asia Minor to study further in the rhetorical and philosophical schools of the Hellenistic East. Cicero remained a student of Greek literature throughout his life. Yet he maintained an ambivalent attitude toward Hellenic culture, recognizing Greek superiority in literature and philosophy and longing at the same time for an independent Latin culture. Cicero found in the works of Plato, for instance, models for his own literary efforts, but he refused to be bound by any particular Platonic doctrines.

It should be kept in mind in this regard that the Platonism which Cicero learned in Rome and Greece was the Platonism of the New Academy. Although the study of Plato's works had continued in the Academy at Athens after its founder's death, the principal tenets of Platonism had been lost in the welter of philosophic schools of the Hellenistic era. In the New Academy of the second century B.C., under the direction of Carneades, and later, of Posidonius, a so-called Middle Platonism was developed. It was frankly eclectic, combining elements from all the schools. Following the lead of the Skeptics, the Middle Platonists of the New Academy abandoned the belief that certain knowledge was possible. In the second century the New Academy also introduced the practice, borrowed from the rhetorical schools, of debate between teacher and student. In other words, it returned to the Socratic method. This change, however, "came at a time when scepticism had taken the place of Plato's metaphysical certitude, and its aim was to give dialectical skill rather than serious scientific knowledge."[9] It was at this Academy that Cicero studied while in Athens.

Cicero received his legal training in Rome under the first great systematizer among the jurists, Q. Mucius Scaevola. Undoubtedly he learned the law well, but Cicero did not himself become a jurist. He was ambitious for a political career and supplemented his legal training with the study of rhetoric and oratory which at that time constituted the principal education for public life. Cicero became the leading lawyer of his day, and his speeches for the defense of his clients and the prosecution of political enemies became models of Latin style. Indeed it has been said that, "Cicero moulded the Latin language into an incomparably clear and effective vehicle of thought, so that, in spite of brief reactions, his style affected centuries."[10] Cicero thus brought to bear on the problems besetting Republican Rome a thorough knowledge of law, an understanding of Greek philosophical and rhetorical schools, and practical political experience.

In all of his writings Cicero was motivated by one overriding concern—to find a philosophical basis for the restoration of order in Rome. He therefore rejected a doctrinaire adherence to the tenets of either of the currently popular Greek philosophies—Epicureanism and Stoicism —because both seemed only to contribute to factionalism. Cicero dismissed the Epicurean materialistic metaphysics as absurd. "It is astonishing," he wrote, "that, when one soothsayer meets another, he does not smile; still

---

[9] Aubrey Gwynn, *Roman Education from Cicero to Quintilian* (Oxford: Clarendon Press, 1926), p. 73.

[10] *Oxford Classical Dictionary*, p. 190.

Cicero. (Anderson)

more that, when you Epicureans come together, you can possibly refrain from laughter."[11] He objected even more strenuously to Epicurean ethics. Its insistence that the individual was free from all obligations resulted in the subversion of what he considered to be the richest and truest values of life.

But Cicero was equally critical of the more extreme Stoic position, for it made virtue the exclusive possession of the Stoic sage and rendered the everyday occurrences of life of no moral consequence. The Stoic defense of this position, he declared,

> . . . could not possibly be produced in civic life, in the law-courts, in the senate! . . . Could an advocate wind up his defence of a client by declaring that exile and confiscation of property are not evils? that they are "to be rejected," but not "to be shunned"? that it is not a judge's duty to show mercy? Or supposing him to be addressing a meeting of the people; Hannibal is at the gates and has flung a javelin over the city walls; could he say that captivity, enslavement, death, loss of country are no evils? Could the senate, decreeing a triumph to Africanus, use the formula, "whereas by reason of his valour," or "good fortune," if no one but the Wise Man can truly be said to possess either valour or good fortune? What sort of a philosophy then is this, which speaks the ordinary language in public, but in its treatises employs an idiom of its own?[12]

Cicero, obviously, favored a conception of virtue which was applicable to the realities of daily life. He was not content, however, merely to submit to present practices as a guide to proper behavior. Indeed, present practices were so distasteful to Cicero that he sought a principle of virtue which would serve as a reliable alternative and bring men to their senses. This he found in a modified form of Stoicism which stressed the Platonic elements in the Stoic ethic.

> By moral worth, then, we understand that which is of such a nature that, though devoid of all utility, it can justly be commended in kind for itself, apart from any profit or reward. . . . Good men, do a great many things from which they anticipate no advantage, solely from the motive of propriety, morality and right. For among the many points of difference between man and the lower animals, the greatest difference is that Nature has bestowed on man the gift of Reason. . . . This primary instinct leads us on to love all truth as such, that is, all that is trustworthy, simple and consistent, and to hate things insincere, false and deceptive, such as cheating, perjury, malice and injustice. Further, Reason possesses an intrinsic element of dignity and grandeur, suited rather to require obedience than to render it, esteeming all the accidents of human fortunes not merely as endurable but also as unimportant; a quality of loftiness and elevation, fearing nothing, submitting to no one, even unsubdued.[13]

The human rational faculty and the nature of Reason itself guide men to a knowledge of what is expected of them—what is good. Here Cicero is emphasizing the Stoic principle of the unity of all virtue in wisdom—the principle that recognizes that virtue is its own reward.

In his treatise, *On Duties,* written for his son Marcus in the summer of 44 B.C., Cicero was less insistent upon this standard formula and more concerned with practical rules of conduct. Nevertheless he adopted the conventional division of the subject of virtue into the four cardinal virtues of Greek tradition. Wisdom (Greek, *phronesis* or *sophia;* Latin, *sapientia*) takes first place followed by justice (Greek, *dikaiosune;*

---

[11] From Charles Norris Cochrane, *Christianity and Classical Culture* (New York: Oxford University Press, 1957), p. 40. Copyright 1944 by Oxford University Press. Reprinted by permission.

[12] *On the End of Good and Evil,* IV, 21–23, in W. T. Jones, *A History of Western Philosophy* (New York: Harcourt, Brace & World, Inc., 1952), p. 273.

[13] *On the End of Good and Evil,* II, 45–47, in Jones, *A History of Western Philosophy,* pp. 274–275.

Latin, *iustitia*), courage (Greek, *andreia;* Latin, *fortitudo*), and temperance or self-control (Greek, *sophrosune;* Latin, *prudentia*). Cicero's treatment follows closely the work of Panaetius of Rhodes. Nevertheless, by virtue of his personal stature and literary skill, Cicero's writing became the authoritative statement of the classical tradition on this subject.

CICERO'S DEFINITION OF THE FOUR CARDINAL VIRTUES
Charles Norris Cochrane[14]

Starting from [his] conspectus of human nature, Cicero undertakes to erect a scheme of ethics. Four possible ideals emerge, corresponding to the four traditional cardinal virtues. These are: (1) the life of wisdom or contemplation, (2) the life of justice and beneficence, (3) courage or loftiness and strength of mind, (4) temperance or moderation and propriety. These possibilities he considers in turn, but with a characteristically Roman bias, as when he asserts that the pursuit of individual excellence is in all cases to be subordinated to the paramount need of maintaining the security and welfare of the organized community. Thus, for Cicero no less than for Vergil, salvation is not individual, but marks the achievement of purposes which are to be realized only in the corporate life.

With this preliminary warning, Cicero proceeds to discuss wisdom or the life of contemplation. This he dismisses with a brief reference to its besetting sins—hastiness of judgement and the waste of time

[14] Charles Norris Cochrane, *Christianity and Classical Culture* (New York: Oxford University Press, 1957), pp. 48–52. Copyright 1944 by Oxford University Press. Reprinted by permission. Footnotes have been omitted.

involved in aimless and unprofitable studies which supersede activity—a kind of virtuosity by no means extinct in modern times.

Next comes justice, which, as the basis of human relationships and, in a peculiar sense, the Roman virtue, receives a much fuller treatment than the contemplative ideal. Justice is described as the bond and principle of civil society. Its content is indicated in two formulas:

> To harm no one unless provoked by injury. . . .
> To employ common goods for communal ends, private goods for one's own. . . .

Thus civil society, considered as an embodiment of justice, exists for the double purpose of redressing injuries and of enforcing rights. Of these rights the most fundamental is that of property. Tracing property to an origin in long-standing occupation, conquest, agreement, or allotment, Cicero asserts that it constitutes a right, to interfere with which is to violate the purpose which underlies human society. Justice includes also the reciprocal exchange of mutual services. . . . As such, its basis lies in good faith, i.e. fidelity to engagements. The mark of a just society will therefore be (*a*) respect for the sanctity of contract, and (*b*) a determination to see that every man receives his due. . . . From these principles it is possible to infer the character of injustice, the genesis of which may be traced to selfishness, fear, or greed. It thus becomes evident that there is a "natural" limit to the pursuit of wealth, beyond which it serves no useful purpose. To forget this limit is to open the door to unrestricted competition (*contentio*) such as had marked the economic and political imperialism of Crassus and Caesar or to "unsocial" money-making, the satisfaction of an instinct for acquisition which reflects nothing but political indifference or a miserly fear of incurring expense.

Justice involves a number of positive obligations; in describing which Cicero (notwithstandng his supposed lack of originality) attains a position radically different from that of Greek idealism in its loftiest flights. For, while affirming that this principle is the bond of men in states, Aristotle had accepted the corollary that it is without application to members of different communities, where there are "no common magistracies to enforce engagements," thereby consigning inter-state relationships to the sway of expediency or force. Cicero, however, with the long background of Roman history behind him, propounds the view that, while the use of force is characteristic of the beast, the method of settling differences appropriate to men is that of debate or discussion . . . and this rule he applies to the relations of communities no less than individuals, making it the basis for a theory of international law. From this standpoint, he denied the legitimacy of war except for the purpose of exacting redress for injuries suffered (*rebus repetitis*), and then only after a formal declaration. On the same principle, he denounced all forms of national aggrandizement which were dictated merely by the love of power and glory, thus transcending the Machiavellism of classical antiquity and proclaiming the doctrine that states as well as individuals are bound to keep faith. Latin thinking, which recognized a difference between individual and community unfamiliar to the Greeks, gave rise to other no less significant conclusions. Thus, for example, Cicero accepted the distinction between "combatants" and "non-combatants" originally proposed by the elder Cato, and maintained that the obligations of individuals

do not disappear by reason of the fact that the states of which they are members are at war. But perhaps the most remarkable implication of Cicero's theory of justice had reference not to aliens or enemies but to slaves. The Stoic Chrysippus, according to Seneca, had first enunciated the proposition that slaves are to be regarded as permanent hired employees. This Cicero accepted as a rationalization of existing Roman practice. . . .

The third virtue to be dealt with is courage or fortitude. This quality, though commonly regarded as more glorious than any of the other three, must nevertheless be associated with them if it is not to become a vice. For the spirit of fortitude is often accompanied by a love of power and by impatience of control, which give rise to acts of injustice such as those with which the society of Cicero's day was all too familiar. Emphasizing his distaste for militarism and imperialism, Cicero finds that true courage lies in the capacity for passive endurance with complete disregard for outward things, and for the active performance of great deeds attended with danger and difficulty. As such, it depends on (*a*) a correct appraisal of the good to be achieved, (*b*) freedom from all improper desires such as wealth, power, and glory. It thus presupposes a rigid subjection of the emotions to the imperatives of reason.

This is to socialize the notion of courage which, while it may dictate withdrawal from active life, on grounds, for instance, of poor health, will, in all but exceptional circumstances, call for the meticulous discharge of civic obligations. Normally, therefore, it will be exhibited in public relations and it will be apparent in the arts of peace no less than war. When it is a question of vindicating the peace, courage requires that the citizen should take up arms, but the fighting qualities are the least significant element of this virtue, and the general at any rate will need a great understanding no less than a stout heart, if he is to avoid the behaviour which so often sullies the laurels of victory. Thus for Cicero courage is a moral and intellectual rather than a physical virtue; as such, it finds its supreme embodiment in the statesman who, without thought of private advantage, makes the good of the governed his sole aim, remembering that his office is a trust. . . . Such a man will rise above partisan feeling and will speak his mind openly without hesitating to give offence; he will shun half-measures and equivocal courses; he will be lenient, affable, and courteous, strictly conscientious and exempt from passion when obliged to inflict punishment.

The fourth and last of the cardinal virtues is temperance. Temperance prescribes a rule of decorum or propriety, which is characteristically defined as behaviour compatible with the inherent dignity of human nature. It thus implies that whatever a man says or does will be appropriate to the occasion. For nature herself has imposed on each and every one a role, which he must study to fulfil. In general, therefore, the duties ordained by propriety are: to follow nature's guidance, cultivating an earnest and thoughtful disposition, and keeping the emotions within bounds. Moreover, every person has two characters to support, viz. the one which he shares with all men as rational beings and the other which is peculiar to himself as an individual. While, therefore, he must take care always to act in accordance with reason, in so doing he will adopt a course which is consistent with his own disposition and aptitudes, thus avoiding the suggestion of incongruity or awkwardness. Accordingly, while developing the com-

mon graces of humanity, he will not do so at the cost of thwarting or perverting his own development.

Thus envisaged as a question of "my station and its duties," the dictates of propriety become clear. Obligations of magistrate and subject, of citizen and alien, will depend upon and vary with their respective relations. The magistrate, for instance, will recognize that he acts in a representative capacity, "carrying the person of the state." His first obligation will therefore be to protect its dignity and prestige, and to maintain and expound its laws, remembering that these are the functions which have been entrusted to him. The private citizen, on the other hand, will seek to comport himself on a basis of equality with his fellows, avoiding any excess of abasement and self-assertion, and desiring for the commonwealth justice and tranquillity. The alien, on his part, will confine his attention to his own affairs, eschewing impertinent interference with public business which is none of his concern.

Specific injunctions of propriety include modesty and decency in behaviour and speech, together with the maintenance of a suitable establishment. This last requirement involves a discussion of the occupations appropriate to a gentleman. "Liberal" occupations are defined in general (according to a convention which is still maintained) as those which involve the exercise of more than ordinary sagacity and from which accrue results of more than ordinary utility. They therefore embrace agriculture, together with medicine, architecture, higher education, and commerce "if on a large scale."

Concluding with an effort to formulate a hierarchy of duties, Cicero reaffirms the superiority of justice to wisdom, and repeats that philosophy is without value unless it be applied to the practical purposes of life and to the advantage of mankind. Tracing the origin of civil society to social requirements rather than to necessity, he finds it to be inherently moral. This sets a limit to the claims of patriotism and disposes of any supposed obligation to defend the fatherland under all circumstances. The state, as an embodiment of the social consciousness, has no right to expect immoral conduct of its members. Accordingly, in the schematization of duties, the demands of religion come first, those of patriotism second, thirdly, domestic obligations, and, finally, the remaining obligations of civilized man. . . .

A proper knowledge of one's duties naturally required a proper education. But Cicero prescribed no elaborate program of study leading to knowledge of the good, as had Plato in the *Republic*. His aim was more modest and, he thought, more practical. In matters of philosophical belief he preferred the skepticism and eclecticism of the New Academy. For his educational ideal he turned to the rhetorical schools. What he thought was required in his day was a reuniting of wisdom and oratory, of philosophy and rhetoric.

CICERO'S EDUCATIONAL AND RHETORICAL
IDEAL
G. M. A. Grube[15]

The first book of *De Inventione* [one of Cicero's earliest works] starts with what is in effect a reworking of the old commonplace, as old as Isocrates at least, on the blessings of eloquence, of the Logos, but it is a reworking with a difference. Cicero states without equivocation that

[15] G. M. A. Grube, "Educational, Rhetorical, and Literary Theory in Cicero," *Phoenix*, 16 (1962), pp. 235–237, 239–240. Reprinted by permission.

mere rhetoric does more harm than good, a statement which his modern readers would do well to remember if they are to understand his point of view:

> Prolonged reflection on this subject leads me to the only reasonable conclusion: I believe that wisdom without eloquence is of little use to the community, but that eloquence without wisdom mostly does great harm, and never does any good.

Cicero goes on to plead for the study of moral philosophy as well as of the art of speech. Both are needed, and this is the basic principle of all his thinking and writing on education. It is interesting to find it so clearly formulated so early in his life. He then proceeds to argue that the power to persuade played a great role in leading men from savagery to civilisation "and served the highest interests of mankind." He traces "the origin of the evil," mere rhetoric, to the time when the power to persuade fell into the hands of unscrupulous men, "shrewd men" trained in the law courts, without regard for truth, who then managed to control public affairs, so that wise men retired to their study:

> And so, when rash and reckless men grasped the helm of the ship of state, violent and disastrous shipwrecks naturally followed. Eloquence then incurred such odium and disrepute that the most gifted men turned from the strife and tumult of public life as from turbulent tempests to seek harbour in some quiet and studious pursuit.

The Platonic echoes are clear and obvious, but Cicero was a Roman and a statesman; the academic ivory tower was not for him. He dedicated his whole political life to finding some *concordia ordinum,* some basis of agreement between the saner elements in the state to save the dying republic. He failed. After that failure, he repeated his plea for a system of education which would ally the pursuit of wisdom with that of eloquence. If we remember that the word *orator,* for Cicero at least, had inherited the political overtones of the Greek rhetor, the Platonic echoes continue, even though the plea this time comes from the forum outside rather than from inside the philosopher's study, and is in part directed to the philosophers themselves. This is the basic appeal of the *De Oratore* in 55 B.C.; it is found again in the *Orator* in 46, towards the end of Cicero's life.

Cicero's plea was of course very different from Plato's. He did not want his orator to be a philosopher in the Platonic sense; nor did he endorse the Stoic view that only the philosopher was the perfect speaker. But he did want his orator to have enough knowledge of philosophy, history, jurisprudence, and even science, to be able, as Isocrates had put it, to speak well on great subjects. When he says that he owes to the Academy whatever he may be as an orator, he does not mean that the study of philosophy by itself makes a great orator, for he is always careful to add that it must be supplemented by specifically rhetorical studies. These must be pursued in the rhetorical schools, but the rhetorical school alone cannot make an orator either. From this point of view his plea for a general education is a protest against the oversubtle technical training of the schools of rhetoric where nothing else was taught. . . .

It is easy to ridicule the general educa-

Cicero denouncing Cataline on the floor of the Senate—a modern fresco in the Palazzo Madama in Rome. (Anderson)

tion of the orator, even as preached by Cicero. It is always easy, for specialists in particular, to ridicule any attempt to impart general culture. In modern terms one might describe the Ciceronian curriculum as a thorough general training in philosophy (including logic, ethics, and psychology), in political science, history, and law, with a stiff Honour course in the art of speech in both Latin and Greek. Cicero is fully aware that this theory of education, and particularly his requirements in phi-

losophy and law, would startle his contemporaries, but he insists again and again that rhetoric without educational background—eloquence without wisdom as he put it in the *De Inventione*—is useless or worse. Living in a utilitarian society, Cicero, like all of us, tries to justify the time to be spent on these "academic" subjects on the grounds of their practical utility to "the orator." He does better, however, when he justifies the study of history on the simple ground that "not to know

A student orator. (Archives Photographiques—Paris)

what happened before you were born is to remain for ever a child. . . ."

. . . What Cicero is advising is very much the kind of education he had himself received, very much the education of Roman gentlemen in the late second and early first century, though more exacting. It is Roman rather than Greek, and it seems both natural and probable that it was Cicero who first gave it theoretical expression. If so, he was not restoring a Classical tradition but creating one; he has some claim to be called the father of Classical humanism, and he created it very largely by combining the Isocratean ideal of education with the Aristotelian requirements for competence in oratory. Here too he failed, and the divorce between rhetoric and philosophy continued; with the development of the practice of declamation it went in fact from bad to worse. . . .

Training in oratory, as Cicero conceived it, covered the art of self-expression in all its genres, for the orator had to use the techniques of them all. He had to learn both style and delivery, and master the ways of arousing the emotions of his audience as well. Indeed, oratory was the most difficult of all genres, and great orators were fewer than artists of any other kind. Cicero enlarges on "the incredible magnitude" of the task (*De Oratore* 1.17):

He must acquire knowledge of most things, for without it his flow of words is empty of content and ridiculous; he must shape his discourse both by selecting the right words and arranging them; he must have a thorough knowledge of the emotions with which nature has endowed man because the power and purpose of eloquence depend entirely upon his capacity to calm or to excite the minds of his listeners; and to this he must add a certain charm and wit, an erudition

worthy of a free man, swiftness and brevity both in challenge and reply combined with subtle charm and purity of language; he must, moreover, understand the past and the force of example which it provides; he cannot neglect the knowledge of law and jurisprudence. Why say more of delivery? . . . Why speak of memory which treasures all these things?

In passages like this Cicero gives a better defence than anyone else has ever done of the rhetorical education of his day. And, though he and his successors attacked certain aspects of this education, in his case its narrow technical nature, in later writers the artificial nature of school exercises, we have no record of any protest against the basic principle that the art of self-expression was the right and proper main subject of higher education.

In his writings on politics and law Cicero employed perhaps the most important of the Greek ideas to which he gave classical expression—the Stoic conception of natural law. As we have seen, the question of the relationship between human justice and the natural order had a long history in Greek thought. For the Sophists (and in Cicero's day for the Epicureans) law or *nomos* had been mere human convention, as opposed to *physis*, the law of nature. They stressed the social utility of law rather than its eternal validity. Plato, on the other hand, maintained that ". . . justice is the expression of the norm inherent in nature itself. He transfers justice from the external sphere of man's social relations to the internal world of the human soul. Justice now becomes the innate law of the soul of man and the principle of his individual and social existence."[16] Implicit in Plato's thought was the

[16] Werner Jaeger, "Praise of Law: The Origin of Legal Philosophy and the Greeks," *Scripta Minora*, II (Roma: Edizioni di historia letteratura, 1960), p. 342.

idea that a rational law, *logos* or reason made divine, governs the universe and that man partakes of that same rationality.[17] Though Plato did not explicitly express it, one implication to be drawn from this was that all men form a brotherhood; the individual human being is something more than a polis-animal, a Greek, or a barbarian—he is also a member of the community of rational human beings. Stoicism, which originated in the cosmopolitan atmosphere of the Hellenistic era, explicitly

> . . . proclaimed mankind as an all-embracing community. One god, one state, one law—this well-known formula states the doctrine of the Stoics in a clear and simple way. Man is different from other men not by his belonging to a *polis* but only by being either a wise man who recognizes the doctrine of the Stoics or a fool who does not. The true *polis* for that reason is not any existing *polis* such as Athens but in fact a community of these wise men. All of them are subject to the one God and the one law.[18]

This "one law" was defined and praised many times over by Stoics during the Hellenistic era, and in it Cicero found a rational principle on which he hoped to establish just laws and stable political institutions.

While reading the following selections from *The Laws* keep in mind the following questions: How does Cicero differ from Plato in his search for order in the political chaos of his time? What accounts for the differences? In attempting to bridge the gap between human convention (*nomos*) and the laws of nature (*physis*) did he encounter the same problems as Plato? How does he reconcile the Stoic abstract ideal of natural law with his admiration for concrete Roman republican institutions and the *jus civile*? What is the source of authority in Cicero's legal philosophy?

---

[17] See *Western Man*, vol. I, *The Contribution of Ancient Greece*.

[18] Carl J. Friedrich, *The Philosophy of Law in Historical Perspective* (Chicago: University of Chicago Press, 1958), p. 28.

THE LAWS
Cicero[19]

I. *iv.* Atticus. . . . Kindly begin without delay the statement of your opinions on the civil law.

Marcus. My opinions? Well then, I believe that there have been most eminent men in our State whose customary function it was to interpret the law to the people and answer questions in regard to it, but that these men, though they have made great claims, have spent their time on unimportant details. What subject indeed is so vast as the law of the State? But what is so trivial as the task of those who give legal advice? It is, however, necessary for the people. But, while I do not consider that those who have applied themselves to this profession have lacked a conception of universal law, yet they have carried their studies of this civil law, as it is called, only far enough to accomplish their purpose of being useful to the people. Now all this amounts to little so far as learning is concerned, though for practical purposes it is indispensable. What subject is it, then, that you are asking me to expound? To what task are you urging me? Do you want me to write a treatise on the law of eaves and house-walls? Or to compose formulas for contracts and court procedure? These subjects have been carefully treated by many writers, and are of a humbler character, I believe, than what is expected of me.

v. A. Yet if you ask what I expect of

---

[19] Reprinted by permission of the publishers and The Loeb Classical Library from (C. W. Keyes, translator), Cicero, *The Laws*. (Cambridge, Mass.: Harvard University Press, 1928), pp. 311–323, 329–335, 341–351, 379–383, 389–391.

you, I consider it a logical thing that, since you have already written a treatise on the constitution of the ideal State, you should also write one on its laws. For I note that this was done by your beloved Plato, whom you admire, revere above all others, and love above all others.

M. Is it your wish, then, that, as he discussed the institutions of States and the ideal laws with Clinias and the Spartan Megillus in Crete on a summer day amid the cypress groves and forest paths of Cnossus, sometimes walking about, sometimes resting—you recall his description—we, in like manner, strolling or taking our ease among these stately poplars on the green and shady river bank, shall discuss the same subjects along somewhat broader lines than the practice of the courts calls for?

A. I should certainly like to hear such a conversation.

M. What does Quintus say?

Quintus. No other subject would suit me better.

M. And you are wise, for you must understand that in no other kind of discussion can one bring out so clearly what Nature's gifts to man are, what a wealth of most excellent possessions the human mind enjoys, what the purpose is, to strive after and accomplish which we have been born and placed in this world, what it is that unites men, and what natural fellowship there is among them. For it is only after all these things have been made clear that the origin of Law and Justice can be discovered.

A. Then you do not think that the science of law is to be derived from the praetor's edict, as the majority do now, or from the Twelve Tables, as people used to think, but from the deepest mysteries of philosophy?

M. Quite right; for in our present conversation, Pomponius, we are not trying to learn how to protect ourselves legally, or how to answer clients' questions. Such problems may be important, and in fact they are; for in former times many eminent men made a specialty of their solution, and at present one person performs this duty with the greatest authority and skill. But in our present investigation we intend to cover the whole range of universal Justice and Law in such a way that our own civil law, as it is called, will be confined to a small and narrow corner. For we must explain the nature of Justice, and this must be sought for in the nature of man; we must also consider the laws by which States ought to be governed; then we must deal with the enactments and decrees of nations which are already formulated and put in writing; and among these the civil law, as it is called, of the Roman people will not fail to find a place.

vi. Q. You probe deep, and seek, as you should, the very fountainhead, to find what we are after, brother. And those who teach the civil law in any other way are teaching not so much the path of justice as of litigation.

M. There you are mistaken, Quintus, for it is rather ignorance of the law than knowledge of it that leads to litigation. But that will come later; now let us investigate the origins of Justice.

Well then, the most learned men have determined to begin with Law, and it would seem that they are right, if, according to their definition, Law is the highest reason, implanted in Nature, which commands what ought to be done and forbids the opposite. This reason, when firmly fixed and fully developed in the human mind, is Law. And so they believe that Law is intelligence, whose natural function it is to command right conduct and forbid wrongdoing. They think that this quality has derived its name in Greek from the idea of granting to every man his own, and in our language I believe it has been named from the idea of choosing. For as they have attributed the idea of fairness to the word law, so we have given it that of selection, though both ideas properly belong to Law. Now if this is correct, as I think it to be in general, then the origin of Justice is to be found in Law, for Law is a natural force; it is the mind and reason of the intelligent man, the standard by which Justice and Injustice are measured. But since our whole discussion has to do with the reasoning of the populace, it will sometimes be necessary to speak in the popular manner, and give the name of law to that which in written form decrees whatever it wishes, either by command or prohibition. For such is the crowd's definition of law. But in determining what Justice is, let us begin with that supreme Law which had its origin ages before any written law existed or any State had been established. . . .

Since . . . we must retain and preserve that constitution of the State which Scipio proved to be the best in the six books[20] devoted to the subject, and all our laws must be fitted to that type of State, and since we must also inculcate good morals, and not prescribe everything in writing, I shall seek the root of Justice in Nature, under whose guidance our whole discussion must be conducted.

vii. . . . That animal which we call man, endowed with foresight and quick intelligence, complex, keen, possessing memory, full of reason and prudence, has been

[20] [This is a reference to Cicero's *Republic* in which the chief speaker was Scipio Aemilianus. The best constitution was proved to be that of Rome.]

given a certain distinguished status by the supreme God who created him; for he is the only one among so many different kinds and varieties of living beings who has a share in reason and thought, while all the rest are deprived of it. But what is more divine, I will not say in man only, but in all heaven and earth, than reason? And reason, when it is full grown and perfected, is rightly called wisdom. Therefore, since there is nothing better than reason, and since it exists both in man and God, the first common possession of man and God is reason. But those who have reason in common must also have right reason in common. And since right reason is Law, we must believe that men have Law also in common with the gods. Further, those who share Law must also share Justice; and those who share these are to be regarded as members of the same commonwealth. If indeed they obey the same authorities and powers, this is true in a far greater degree; but as a matter of fact they do obey this celestial system, the divine mind, and the God of transcendent power. Hence we must now conceive of this whole universe as one commonwealth of which both gods and men are members. . . .

x. . . . Out of all the material of the philosophers' discussions, surely there comes nothing more valuable than the full realization that we are born for Justice, and that right is based, not upon men's opinions, but upon Nature. This fact will immediately be plain if you once get a clear conception of man's fellowship and union with his fellow-men. For no single thing is so like another, so exactly its counterpart, as all of us are to one another. Nay, if bad habits and false beliefs did not twist the weaker minds and turn them in whatever direction they are inclined, no one would be so like his own self as all men would be like all others. And so, however we may define man, a single definition will apply to all. This is a sufficient proof that there is no difference in kind between man and man; for if there were, one definition could not be applicable to all men; and indeed reason, which alone raises us above the level of the beasts and enables us to draw inferences, to prove and disprove, to discuss and solve problems, and to come to conclusions, is certainly common to us all, and, though varying in what it learns, at least in the capacity to learn it is invariable. For the same things are invariably perceived by the senses, and those things which stimulate the senses, stimulate them in the same way in all men; and those rudimentary beginnings of intelligence to which I have referred, which are imprinted on our minds, are imprinted on all minds alike; and speech, the mind's interpreter, though differing in the choice of words, agrees in the sentiments expressed. In fact, there is no human being of any race who, if he finds a guide, cannot attain to virtue.

xi. The similarity of the human race is clearly marked in its evil tendencies as well as in its goodness. For pleasure also attracts all men; and even though it is an enticement to vice, yet it has some likeness to what is naturally good. For it delights us by its lightness and agreeableness; and for this reason, by an error of thought, it is embraced as something wholesome. . . . Troubles, joys, desires, and fears haunt the minds of all men without distinction, and even if different men have different beliefs, that does not prove, for example, that it is not the same quality of superstition that besets those races which worship dogs and cats as gods, as that which torments other races. But what nation does not love courtesy, kindliness, gratitude,

and remembrance of favours bestowed? What people does not hate and despise the haughty, the wicked, the cruel, and the ungrateful? Inasmuch as these considerations prove to us that the whole human race is bound together in unity, it follows, finally, that knowledge of the principles of right living is what makes men better. . . .

xii. The next point, then is that we are so constituted by Nature as to share the sense of Justice with one another and to pass it on to all men. And in this whole discussion I want it understood that what I shall call Nature is [that which is implanted in us by Nature]; that, however, the corruption caused by bad habits is so great that the sparks of fire, so to speak, which Nature has kindled in us are extinguished by this corruption, and the vices which are their opposites spring up and are established. But if the judgments of men were in agreement with Nature, so that, as the poet says, they considered "nothing alien to them which concerns mankind," then Justice would be equally observed by all. For those creatures who have received the gift of reason from Nature have also received right reason, and therefore they have also received the gift of Law, which is right reason applied to command and prohibition. And if they have received Law, they have received Justice also. Now all men have received reason; therefore all men have received Justice. Consequently Socrates was right when he cursed, as he often did, the man who first separated utility from Justice; for this separation, he complained, is the source of all mischief. . . .

xiv.[21] . . . And so men pay the penalty [for crimes], not so much through decisions of the courts (for once there were no

[21] [A portion of Cicero's text is missing here.]

courts anywhere, and to-day there are none in many lands; and where they do exist, they often act unjustly after all); but guilty men are tormented and pursued by the Furies, not with blazing torches, as in the tragedies, but with the anguish of remorse and the torture of a guilty conscience.

But if it were a penalty and not Nature that ought to keep men from injustice, what anxiety would there be to trouble the wicked when the danger of punishment was removed? But in fact there has never been a villain so brazen as not to deny that he had committed a crime, or else invent some story of just anger to excuse its commission, and seek justification for his crime in some natural principle of right. Now if even the wicked dare to appeal to such principles, how jealously should they be guarded by the good! But if it is a penalty, the fear of punishment, and not the wickedness itself, that is to keep men from a life of wrongdoing and crime, then no one can be called unjust, and wicked men ought rather to be regarded as imprudent; furthermore, those of us who are not influenced by virtue itself to be good men, but by some consideration of utility and profit, are merely shrewd, not good. For to what lengths will that man go in the dark who fears nothing but a witness and a judge? What will he do if, in some desolate spot, he meets a helpless man, unattended, whom he can rob of a fortune? Our virtuous man, who is just and good by nature, will talk with such a person, help him, and guide him on his way; but the other, who does nothing for another's sake, and measures every act by the standard of his own advantage—it is clear enough, I think, what he will do! If, however, the latter does deny that he would kill the man and rob him of his money, he will not deny it because he regards it as a naturally wicked thing to do, but because he is afraid that his crime may become known—that is, that he may get into trouble. Oh, what a motive, that might well bring a blush of shame to the cheek, not merely of the philosopher, but even of the simple rustic!

xv. But the most foolish notion of all is the belief that everything is just which is found in the customs or laws of nations. Would that be true, even if these laws had been enacted by tyrants? If the well-known Thirty had desired to enact a set of laws at Athens, or if the Athenians without exception were delighted by the tyrants' laws, that would not entitle such laws to be regarded as just, would it? No more, in my opinion, should that law be considered just which a Roman interrex proposed, to the effect that a dictator might put to death with impunity any citizen he wished, even without a trial. For Justice is one; it binds all human society, and is based on one Law, which is right reason applied to command and prohibition. Whoever knows not this Law, whether it has been recorded in writing anywhere or not, is without Justice.

But if Justice is conformity to written laws and national customs, and if, as the same persons claim, everything is to be tested by the standard of utility, then anyone who thinks it will be profitable to him will, if he is able, disregard and violate the laws. It follows that Justice does not exist at all, if it does not exist in Nature, and if that form of it which is based on utility can be overthrown by that very utility itself. And if Nature is not to be considered the foundation of Justice, that will mean the destruction [of the virtues on which human society depends]. For where then will there be a place for generosity, or love of country, or loyalty, or the inclination to be of service to others or to show gratitude for favours received? For these virtues originate in our natural inclination to love our fellow-men, and this is the foundation of Justice. Otherwise not merely consideration for men but also rites and pious observances in honour of the gods are done away with; for I think that these ought to be maintained, not through fear, but on account of the close relationship which exists between man and God. *xvi.* But if the principles of Justice were founded on the decrees of peoples, the edicts of princes, or decisions of judges, then Justice would sanction robbery and adultery and forgery of wills, in case these acts were approved by the votes or decrees of the populace. But if so great a power belongs to the decisions and decrees of fools that the laws of Nature can be changed by their votes, then why do they not ordain that what is bad and baneful shall be considered good and salutary? Or, if a law can make Justice out of Injustice, can it not also make good out of bad? But in fact we can perceive the difference between good laws and bad by referring them to no other standard than Nature. . . .

II. *iv.* Once more, then, before we come to the individual laws, let us look at the character and nature of Law, for fear that, though it must be the standard to which we refer everything, we may now and then be led astray by an incorrect use of terms, and forget the rational principles on which our laws must be based.

Q. Quite so, that is the correct method of exposition.

M. Well, then, I find that it has been the opinion of the wisest men that Law is not a product of human thought, nor is it any enactment of peoples, but something eternal which rules the whole universe by its wisdom in command and prohibition.

Thus they have been accustomed to say that Law is the primal and ultimate mind of God, whose reason directs all things either by compulsion or restraint. Wherefore that Law which the gods have given to the human race has been justly praised; for it is the reason and mind of a wise lawgiver applied to command and prohibition.

Q. You have touched upon this subject several times before. But before you come to the laws of peoples, please make the character of this heavenly Law clear to us, so that the waves of habit may not carry us away and sweep us into the common mode of speech on such subjects.

M. Ever since we were children, Quintus, we have learned to call, "If one summon another to court,"[22] and other rules of the same kind, laws. But we must come to the true understanding of the matter, which is as follows: this and other commands and prohibitions of nations have the power to summon to righteousness and away from wrong-doing; but this power is not merely older than the existence of nations and States, it is coeval with that God who guards and rules heaven and earth. For the divine mind cannot exist without reason, and divine reason cannot but have this power to establish right and wrong. No written law commanded that a man should take his stand on a bridge alone, against the full force of the enemy, and order the bridge broken down behind him; yet we shall not for that reason suppose that the heroic Cocles was not obeying the law of bravery and following its decrees in doing so noble a deed. Even if there was no written law against rape at Rome in the reign of Lucius Tarquinius, we cannot say on that account that Sextus Tarquinius did not break that eternal Law by violating

[22] [The Twelve Tables]

Lucretia, the daughter of Tricipitinus! For reason did exist, derived from Nature of the universe, urging men to right conduct and diverting them from wrong-doing, and this reason did not first become Law when it was written down, but when it first came into existence; and it came into existence simultaneously with the divine mind. Wherefore the true and primal Law, applied to command and prohibition, is the right reason of supreme Jupiter. . . .

vii. So in the very beginning we must persuade our citizens that the gods are the lords and rulers of all things, and that what is done, is done by their will and authority; that they are likewise great benefactors of man, observing the character of every individual, what he does, of what wrong he is guilty, and with what intentions and with what piety he fulfills his religious duties; and that they take note of the pious and the impious. For surely minds which are imbued with such ideas will not fail to form true and useful opinions. Indeed, what is more true than that no one ought to be so foolishly proud as to think that, though reason and intellect exist in himself, they do not exist in the heavens and the universe, or that those things which can hardly be understood by the highest reasoning powers of the human intellect are guided by no reason at all? In truth, the man that is not driven to gratitude by the orderly courses of the stars, the regular alternation of day and night, the gentle progress of the seasons, and the produce of the earth brought forth for our sustenance—how can such an one be accounted a man at all? And since all things that possess reason stand above those things which are without reason, and since it would be sacrilege to say that anything stands above universal Nature, we must admit that reason is inherent in Na-

ture. Who will deny that such beliefs are useful when he remembers how often oaths are used to confirm agreements, how important to our well-being is the sanctity of treaties, how many persons are deterred from crime by the fear of divine punishment, and how sacred an association of citizens becomes when the immortal gods are made members of it, either as judges or as witnesses? . . . .

The laws thus conceived apply equally to all men. Based upon the Stoic principle of a common human rationality they are morally binding because rationally recognized. But what role, then, does the state play in determining and enforcing the law? Cicero deduces from these moral axioms the principle that

. . . a state cannot exist permanently, or at least cannot exist in any but a crippled condition, unless it depends upon, and acknowledges, and gives effect to the consciousness of mutual obligations and the mutual recognition of rights that bind its citizens together. The state is a moral community, a group of persons who in common possess the state and its law. For this reason he calls the state, in a fine phrase, the *res populi* or the *res publica,* "the affair of the people," which is practically equivalent in meaning to the older English use of the word "commonwealth." This is the ground for Cicero's argument, against the Epicureans and Skeptics, that justice is an intrinsic good. Unless the state is a community for ethical purposes and unless it is held together by moral ties, it is nothing, as Augustine said later, except "highway robbery on a large scale." A state may of course be tyrannous and rule its subjects by brute force —the moral law does not make immorality impossible—but in the measure that it does so, it loses the true character of a state.

"The commonwealth, then, is the people's affair; and the people is not every group of men, associated in any manner, but is the coming together of a considerable number of men who are united by a common agreement about law and rights and by the desire to participate in mutual advantages." (*Republic*)

The state, then, is a corporate body, membership in which is the common possession of all its citizens; it exists to supply its members with the advantages of mutual aid and just government. Three consequences follow: First, since the state and its law is the common property of the people, its authority arises from the collective power of the people. A people is a self-governing organization which has necessarily the powers required to preserve itself and continue its existence: *Salus populi suprema lex esto.* Second, political power when rightfully and lawfully exercised really is the corporate power of the people. The magistrate who exercises it does so by virtue of his office; his warrant is the law and he is the creature of the law.

"For as the laws govern the magistrate, so the magistrate governs the people, and it can truly be said that the magistrate is a speaking law, and the law a silent magistrate." (*Laws*)

Third, the state itself and its law is always subject to the law of God, or the moral or natural law—that higher rule of right which transcends human choice and human institution. Force is an incident in the nature of the state and is justified only because it is required to give effect to the principles of justice and right.

These general principles of government—that authority proceeds from the people, should be exercised only by warrant of law, and is justified only on moral grounds—achieved practically universal acceptance within comparatively a short time after Cicero wrote and remained commonplaces of political philosophy for many centuries. There was substantially no difference of opinion about them on the part of anyone in the whole course of the Middle Ages; they became a part of the common heritage of political ideas. There might, however, be considerable differences of opinion about the application of them, even among men who had not the remotest doubt about the principles themselves. Thus everyone agrees that a tyrant is despicable and his tyranny a bitter wrong against his people, but it is not obvious just what the people are entitled to do about it, or who is to act in their behalf in doing it, or how bad the abuse must be before measures are justified. In particular, the derivation of political authority from the people does not of itself imply any of the democratic consequences which in modern times have been deduced from the consent of the governed. It does not say who speaks for the people, how he becomes entitled so to speak, or exactly who "the people" are for whom he speaks—all questions of the utmost practical importance. The use of the ancient principle that political authority comes from the people to defend the modern forms of representative government was merely the adaptation of an old idea to a new situation.[23]

[23] George Holland Sabine, *A History of Political Theory,* 3rd ed. (New York: Holt, Rinehart and Winton, Inc., 1961), pp. 165–167.

CHAPTER 4

THE "PAX ROMANA":
Bureaucratization, Romanization,
and Stoic Individualism
in the Empire

If this habit of lawlessness begins to spread and changes our rule from one of justice to one of force, so that those who up to the present have obeyed us willingly are held faithful by fear alone, then, though our own generation has perhaps been vigilant enough to be safe, yet I am anxious for our descendants, and for the permanent stability of our commonwealth, which might live on for ever if the principles and customs of our ancestors were maintained.

Cicero, The Republic

At the age of nineteen, on my own initiative and at my own expense, I raised an army by means of which I liberated the Republic, which was oppressed by the tyranny of a faction. For which reason the senate, with honorific decrees, made me a member of its order in the consulship of Gaius Pansa and Aulus Hirtius, giving me at the same time consular rank in voting, and granted me the *imperium.* It ordered me as propraetor, together with the consuls, to see to it that the state suffered no harm. Moreover, in the same year, when both consuls had fallen in war, the people elected me consul and a triumvir for the settlement of the commonwealth.

Augustus Caesar, inscription placed on his own mausoleum

[The problem that imperial] politics brought to light forced the more philosophical minds to a new venture in speculation. The problems of the city state spread to the country or the region, and there seemed no end to the addition and expansion of jurisdiction. *Urbis* led to *orbis,* as in the ancient days city had led to sky. The great community was the cosmos. As civil law and the *ius gentium* dealt with the parts, so the *ius naturale* dealt with the cosmos, and Zeus, or Jupiter, was resurrected as the Great King. This has more poetry and rhetoric than it has of logic, but for a Roman it had vital reality. Both emperor and slave were helped to identify their stations and their duties in a world that rode uneasily on the surface of a chaos. The emperor was apotheosized as well as deified, and the slave, like Epictetus, could claim the dignity of cosmopolitan citizenship. Law, neither before nor since, has had such penetrative power.

Scott Buchanan, Rediscovering Natural Law

My city and country, so far as I am Antoninus, is Rome, but so far as I am a man,
it is the world.

Marcus Aurelius Antoninus, Meditations

The kind of political and social consensus which Cicero looked for in the Republic and which he thought to be the only basis of a true state was not in fact achieved. There was no union of classes, no common agreement about the limits of political ambition, no willingness to defer to ancient authority or philosophical wisdom. While traditionalism and respect for authority remained strong in the minds of a few men like Cicero, the continuation of civil war revealed both a lack of political consensus and the weakness of the institutional framework within which differences could be worked out. In short, the Republic to which Cicero's thought and sentiment were bound was no longer a viable political form. Rome had been a world empire for two centuries, and the Republican tradition no longer inspired loyalty in the vast majority of Roman citizens and subjects.

Caesar's assassination failed to restore political leadership to the Senate. Popular support and the loyalty of the armies passed to Caesar's lieutenants, Lepidus and Antony, and to Caesar's great-nephew and designated heir, Octavian. The three constituted themselves as a commission with dictatorial powers—the Second Triumvirate. Their first purpose was to crush the opposition in Rome and to punish Caesar's assassins, Cassius and Brutus, who had fled the capital and were raising armies in the provinces. Among the Triumvirs' victims in the bloody proscription which followed was Cicero, who had particularly offended Antony in a series of orations in the Senate. Antony and Octavian defeated Cassius and Brutus in Macedonia in 42 B.C. and divided political control of the Empire between them, squeezing out Lepidus. Antony received the eastern provinces, Octavian the western ones. This dual leadership lasted with periods of strained relations for nine years. Octavian, in firm control of Italy and the western

provinces, cultivated a new image of himself as the protector of Roman tradition. Antony, by contrast, seemed to be a protagonist of the Hellenistic East and to be acquiring the powers of Hellenistic kingship. In 38 B.C. he took the title of New Dionysus to signify his ambition to conquer Asia like the Dionysus of Greek legend. The following year he married Cleopatra, the queen of Egypt, to gain her support in a war against Parthia. This military enterprise was a complete failure and further strained relations between Antony and Octavian. The breach was completed when Antony publicly announced the division of the Eastern provinces into areas to be ruled by Cleopatra and by her children, the sons of Caesar and Antony. Octavian declared war against Cleopatra and her co-ruler and promised the restoration of the Republic when the Triumvirate expired. The Roman navy blockaded the Egyptian fleet at Actium in western Greece, and when Antony and Cleopatra broke out into the open sea with a few ships, Octavian pursued them back to Alexandria. There Antony's troops deserted, and the royal couple committed suicide. Octavian at the age of thirty-five was left master of the entire Empire.

Octavian returned to Rome in triumph in 29 B.C. after having settled affairs in Egypt and the eastern provinces. He at once turned his attention to the settlement of the civil war and the fulfillment of his promise to restore the Republic. His first step was to secure censorial power for himself and his fellow consul, Agrippa, and to remove from the rolls of the Senate those men recently added by Caesar and the Triumvirs, thus reducing the Senate in size from about 1000 to 600. The Senate continued to heap honors and special privileges upon Octavian as they had earlier done to Caesar. Octavian was careful, however, not to repeat his uncle's mistakes. Accordingly on January 1, 27 B.C., he formally renounced his extraordinary powers and announced the restoration of the Republic. In later years he wrote as an inscription for his tomb:

> In my sixth and seventh consulships, after I had put an end to the civil wars, having attained supreme power by universal consent, I transferred the state from my own power to the control of the Roman senate and people. For this service of mine I received the title of Augustus by decree of the senate, and the doorposts of my house were publicly decked with laurels, the civic crown was affixed over my doorway, and a golden shield was set up in the Julian senate house, which, as the inscription on this shield testifies, the Roman senate and people gave me in recognition of my valor, clemency, justice, and devotion. After that time, I excelled all in authority, but I possessed no more power than the others who were my colleagues in each magistracy.[1]

With this action Octavian, now called Augustus, went a long way toward placating the senatorial aristocracy. The familiar political machinery of the Republic was restored. The popular assemblies again elected annual magistrates, the magistrates resumed their traditional duties, and

[1] *Deeds of Augustus* in Naphtali Lewis and Meyer Reinhold, *Roman Civilization, Sourcebook II: The Empire* (New York: Harper & Row, Publishers, 1966), p. 19.

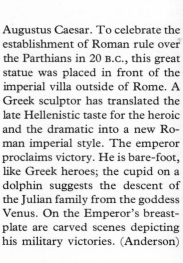

Augustus Caesar. To celebrate the establishment of Roman rule over the Parthians in 20 B.C., this great statue was placed in front of the imperial villa outside of Rome. A Greek sculptor has translated the late Hellenistic taste for the heroic and the dramatic into a new Roman imperial style. The emperor proclaims victory. He is bare-foot, like Greek heroes; the cupid on a dolphin suggests the descent of the Julian family from the goddess Venus. On the Emperor's breastplate are carved scenes depicting his military victories. (Anderson)

the Senate sent out proconsuls to govern the provinces. Gradually, however, the effective power in the Roman state shifted back into the hands of Augustus. For this reason historians usually mark Augustus' accession to power as the end of the Republican period in Roman history and the beginning of the early Imperial period, or Principate (so called because of the central importance of Augustus, the *princeps,* or first citizen).

The Senate begged Augustus not to desert the Republic following his renunciation of offices and prevailed upon him to accept proconsular responsibility for ten years for the most recently conquered and most unruly parts of the Empire —Spain, Gaul, Syria, and Egypt. It was in this vast area that military rule prevailed, and Augustus thus assumed command (*imperium*) over almost all of the armed forces of the Republic. Augustus continued to be elected annually to one of the consulships until 23 B.C., when he resigned that office in favor of the powers, although not the office, of tribune. With the tribunican power Augustus could call and preside at meetings of the Senate and assemblies, initiate legislation, and veto any unwanted actions. In addition he was given a general power (*maius imperium*) superior to that of other magistrates, although this seemed to have been more symbolic of his real power than a specific constitutional prerogative.

Despite these considerable powers, Augustus preferred whenever possible to pay respect to Republican tradition and to rely on his *auctoritas* as *princeps.* This personal prestige increased in many ways during the remaining years of Augustus' rule. In preparation for his final struggle with Antony, the young Octavian had organized the public declaration of an oath of loyalty to himself by all the inhabitants of Italy and the western provinces. As Augustus he extracted the same oath from the eastern provinces and from new territories as they were annexed. In the Hellenized sections of the eastern provinces, the new master of the Empire was deified and worshipped in public ceremonies. Augustus encouraged this cult in the provinces but forbade its practice among Roman citizens. He enhanced his popularity among the inhabitants of the capital city by personally supervising the distribution of grain and organizing an effective fire department. For the maintenance of internal security Augustus appointed a prefect of the city and put at his disposal a body of Roman troops, the urban cohorts.

These domestic reforms were accompanied by continued warfare in central Europe, and the northeastern boundaries of the Empire were extended to the Danube River. Yet at the same time Augustus was able to reduce the total number of men under arms and complete the conversion of the army into a standing professional force. The number of legions was established at twenty-five, each composed of voluntary recruits who served for sixteen years. Upon discharge, soldiers were granted land or cash bonuses paid for by an inheritance tax on Roman citizens and a tax on slaveholders.

As a part of his general constitutional settlement, Augustus attempted to initiate reforms in the religious and social life of the Roman senatorial and equestrian orders. His aim was to restore traditional social values so as to make the Italian upper classes a solid and dependable core for the administration of the Empire. Augustus was elected *Pontifex Maximus,* rebuilt temples neglected during the civil wars, and restored the public worship of the older deities of Rome and Italy, to which he added the figure of his great-uncle, Julius Caesar, and an ancestress of the Julian clan. Augustus attempted in a series of legislative acts, the *Leges Juliae,* to restore family life by placing special disabilities upon unmarried and childless persons and giving political preference to fathers as candidates for public office. In many ways Augustus' policy inaugurated a new era of respect for *Romanitas,* the moral force of Rome, which found expression in the writings of Vergil and Horace. In another respect these reforms indicated that genuinely traditional values and social institutions had lost their force, and they represented a search for alternative values and institutions. The next article examines this process in terms of the impact of imperial power (*imperium*) on an older form of authority—the *patria potestas.* In reading it the student should try to enumerate the forces working to alter kinship institutions. What were the consequences of this institutional change?

KINSHIP AND POLITICAL POWER IN FIRST CENTURY ROME
Robert A. Nisbet[2]

I propose in this paper to deal with a problem that has long been of interest to historians and sociologists of legal institutions: kinship authority (*patria potestas*) and its decline in ancient Rome. Quite apart from the intrinsic interest of the subject, we can learn much from it, I believe, of what is more generally involved in the shift of authority from one institution to another, in the rise of legal individualism, and in the dislocation of important social groups from functional significance in a social order. . . .

[2] Robert A. Nisbet, "Kinship and Political Power in First Century Rome" in Werner J. Cahnman and Alvin Boskoff, eds., *Sociology and History: Theory and Research* (New York: The Free Press, 1964), pp. 257, 261–270. Reprinted by permission of Robert A. Nisbet.

Let us summarize briefly the character of the society within which the *patria potestas* flourished. (1) It was the very opposite of an individualistic society, for the family was the irreducible unit in law, economics, religion, as well as other functional areas. (2) It was a society strong in descriptive law—tradition, convention, custom—rather than prescriptive law. (3) Pluralism, rather than monism, was the essence of the social system, although we should not underestimate the ease and effectiveness with which the early Romans could mobilize into military unity. (4) It was a society based upon legal decentralization rather than centralization, a condition emanating naturally from its pluralism. For the *patria potestas* could hardly have flourished in a society where the power of the state directly impinged upon each individual.

. . . We must turn now to the events and changes which specifically and decisively changed the character of the *patria potestas* in Rome and, with it, the foundations of order in Rome. Our subject is intimately involved in the social transfor-

A decorative fresco in the villa of Livia, wife of Augustus. (Anderson)

mation which characterized the end of the Republic and the rise of the Empire at the very end of the 1st century B.C.

We can do no better than quote some words of the Roman historian, Dio Cassius, as the means of introducing this section. "So it was," he wrote of the fateful accession of Augustus in 27 B.C., "that all the power of the people and the Senate passed over to Augustus, and from that day pure monarchy was established." Monarchy is perhaps not the word we would apply to a personal absolutism founded, not upon tradition or right of succession, but rather upon military power united with popular appeal to the masses that is best known as Caesarism. Julius Caesar had offered the vision, and, for a moment, the actuality of absolutism founded upon mass appeal; Augustus Caesar now supplied both the blueprint and the implementation of a form of totalitarian power that was to survive in one form or another for half a millennium.

The façade of the Republic was maintained in the form of the Senate, but after 27 B.C., . . . the crucial elements were "the now permanent army and its commander-in-chief, the Emperor Augustus, *Imperator Caesar divi filius Augustus*. . . . The army was the master of the State, and, in the restored Roman republic, the Emperor ruled wholly through the army and for so long as the army was willing to keep him and obey." There was, to be sure, much to recommend the new form of government. A century of bitter, destructive civil wars among the rival military commanders—based, . . . upon no social programs or objectives; merely the struggle for absolute supremacy in the state—had so thoroughly weakened the traditional foundations of the commonweal that effective rule by the Senate was impossible. It is, of course,

tribute to the majesty of the idea of the Senate that Augustus strove to make his government at all times seem to rest upon the Senate. But every Roman historian who touched upon the matter makes clear that, in fact, Augustus was the unrivalled and absolute ruler of Rome. All else was convenient fiction.

Time does not permit an examination of all the changes which were the consequence of the penetration of Augustan political power into the recesses of the social structure in Rome. Our specific concern here is the *patria potestas* and the role of the family in the new order. It is enlightening, however, to note by way of preface that changes in the *patria potestas* were themselves parts of a larger program that involved also the reconstitution of social classes in Rome, new foundations of property and wealth, the character of religion, and even the social origin of members of the Senate. . . . Legislation on the family "formed an integral part of the general policy of social and administrative reconstruction in Rome and Italy which Augustus kept steadily before him from the beginning to the end of his long reign, and it is only in connection with that policy that it can be properly studied and understood."

I will merely summarize the consequences of this broad program. There was, first, the centralization of political power. No longer would Rome be, in political terms, a decentralized and cellular society as it had been for centuries in the Republic. In the same way that the Senate had been supplanted by the Emperor as the effective source of public power, so would all other social bodies that lay intermediate to the individual and the government: social classes, gilds, and the family itself. Gradually there took form the doctrine that was, within a century, to become the basis of the texts of Roman jurists (the texts which, after their codification in the age of Justinian, were to comprise the powerful and historically significant code of Roman law). The essence of this doctrine was the axiom that law—in contrast to mere custom or tradition—flows from the sovereign alone, who must be, by definition, above the law.

Second, and functionally related to the doctrine of centralized sovereignty, was the rise of legal individualism. A century of social atomization caused by civil war and political turmoil greatly facilitated this, but the theoretical essence of legal individualism lay in the idea, closely related to the idea of sovereignty, that individuals alone are the true units of the state, not social units, and such individuals, and all the relations among them, exist under the contemplation of the legal sovereign. Everything between the state and the individual inevitably had, now, an insecure existence, for it was the state alone that could give sanction to a corporate unity. . . .

What happened to the *patria potestas* in 18 B.C. is of a piece with the other measures which were being taken to bring power firmly into the central government over association and classes throughout society. If public order was to be restored and Rome's greatness secured in the world, there must be no *imperium in imperio*, no social allegiance, not even the agnatic family, which could detract from necessary political centralization.

The professed object of the famous *Leges Juliae* in 18 B.C.—and in particular the two laws *de adulteriis* and *de maritandis ordinibus*—was moral: to clean up the moral delinquencies and to restore marriage to its once proud estate. We need not question motive. The austerity of Augustus' personal life—unchallenged by contemporaries—is perhaps sufficient proof of this. But neither can we overlook the fact that in the establishment of these laws on morality and marriage, we are dealing with the first *official* limitations in Roman history of the historic authority of the *patria potestas* over these matters. It must further be kept in mind that the new laws, far from being isolated manifestations of moral reform, constitute an integral part of that larger reconstruction of Rome which, whether dealing with water supply, fire control, education, religion or corn dole, was to lead to complete centralization. . . .

When we turn to the measures of reform adopted by Augustus it becomes clear that his efforts were by no means limited to the removal of the obstacles which impeded the growth of material prosperity or the repression of the vices which disgraced society. Great statesman as he was, he realized from the first the necessity, if either the political system which he had established was to stand or his other reforms were to have any lasting effect, of creating in a people demoralized by faction and civil war a healthy and vigorous public feeling.

For centuries, however imperfectly at times, the sole authority over adultery and other moral maters had been the power of the corporate family. Exile for personal delinquencies was not uncommon, but it was a power wielded under the authority of the *patria potestas,* not by a public magistrate nor even by the Senate unless damage to the commonweal had been done. Similarly, responsibility for marriage, for its motivation as well as for its operation, was, as we have also seen, a sacred function of the family. No public officer intruded into the decisions and ceremonies involved.

Now, at a stroke, these matters are brought within public jurisdiction. In the case of adultery, the nature of the offense was defined, the procedure fixed which was to be followed when a case arose, and the penalty laid down.

For the primitive and probably decaying jurisdiction of the *pater familias . . .* and the equally primitive right of private vengeance where the guilty parties were caught in the act, the *Lex Julia* aimed at substituting the more regular procedure of the law. So it did, but it also . . . suggests, as do Augustus' other social and moral reforms, his anxiety not merely to restore social order by assigning to each class an appropriate career, a definite status, and definite privileges, but to connect each class with himself and his rule by special ties.

So far as we know, the first object of the new law was Augustus' own daughter, a young woman who, apparently, deserved exile for the reasons given. But the genius of the punishment lay in the fact that, having just established a public law which for the first time in history arrogated such punishment to the public agency, any possible sting in its first application was taken away by the familiar spectacle of a father exiling his own daughter. Further genius was shown when, for a time, he showed considerable mercy in dealing with others guilty of adultery, turning them over to their own families. But the all important precedent had been set, and under the head of *de pudicitia* in the law, various other regulations governing public decency—behavior at public games and shows, women's attendance at athletic contests, extravagances in dress, and undue expenditures on banquets—were passed under the authority of the *Leges Juliae.*

The same kind of transfer of authority is to be seen in the sections on marriages. Here too the ostensible aim is the encouragement of marriage and the production of children, an aim on which Augustus could indeed claim the sanction of ancient custom and opinion. The aim had more than once, in earlier times, been made the subject of exhortation by various censors. But there is more in the Augustan decree. For the first time in history marriage becomes a matter of state concern and supervision. Marriage is made obligatory upon all men between the ages of twenty and sixty and upon all women between twenty and fifty. Childlessness in men over twenty-five and in women over twenty was made punishable. Widows and divorced women were also ordered to remarry within a specified time. "To enforce these regulations a system of penalties and rewards was devised. The unmarried were declared incapable of inheriting property or accepting legacies; the childless were mulcted of half the amount of such bequests."

Perhaps even more significant was the limitation placed upon the right of marriage among certain classes, specifically with persons who were not freeborn. Marriage between the freeborn and those who were not—the freedmen were a large and growing class—was forbidden to patricians. Marriages to freedmen were forbidden not only to senators but to their children, grandchildren, and great-grandchildren. Here too it might be said that the aim was moral—the reduction of the license that had grown up, often leading to the exploitation of the lower class member

as well as to dilution of ancient families. But, from our point of view the result is the same: for the first time the state intervened in a matter that had been traditionally private, reserved to the *patria potestas*.

The penalty forbidding the unmarried from inheriting property was, of course, an invasion of what we have seen to be the autonomy of the family in matters connected with its own property and income, and it is closely related to a separate act of Augustus during this period. This was the *peculium castrense*, which permitted the sons under power to retain all booty, income, and property they had acquired during military service. It will be remembered that at the basis of the *patria potestas*

was its economic solidarity, the corporate possession of property by the family alone, not its individual members. In this decree, plainly, lie the beginnings of economic individualism and, with it, of contractualism, a concept that was also to become primary in later Roman law codes. Later emperors, beginning with Hadrian, were to extend this right of individual ownership to all public employees and civil servants, eventually to all citizens. Not unrelated to Augustan decrees on property and family were those touching on membership in the Senate. Senatorial status was no longer inherited through family lines; it was to be conferred by the Emperor.

A procession of priests and members of the imperial family, from the Altar of Peace (*Ara Pacis*) dedicated in 9 B.C. in honor of the re-establishment of order by Augustus. This large altar, which was situated on the Campus Martius, reflects the attempt by Augustus to restore respect for the traditional institutions of family and state. (Alinari)

There was, finally, the religious aspect of the *patria potestas*. As we have seen, family authority was deeply rooted in the religion of the *Lares* and *Penates*. Privacy of the corporate religion of the family was one of the very pillars of the *patria potestas*. This, too, was radically modified. In 12 B.C. Augustus became Pontifex Maximus, thus uniting the political and religious life of the commonweal. But far more important from our point of view is the political penetration of the family hearth. Images of Augustus began to make their appearance within family domiciles, thus giving root to the novel and exotic efflorescence of emperor worship, a form of religion in the East that had aroused the revulsion of Romans a century or two before.

Along with the image of the *Lares* and *Penates* was placed that of Augustus. So this "genius" shared with the *Lares* the libations poured in their honor and the offerings placed for their acceptance. The worship which thus established Augustus as a household god in the homes of the people and gave him a place in one of their oldest worships was admirably fitted to serve his interests and those of the empire on a larger scale.

Thus, in three decisive ways, the *patria potestas* was challenged by the military *imperium*—in control of marriage and descent of family property; in the fragmentation of economic ownership; and, finally, in the invasion of the religious sphere. All of these momentous changes took place in the decade, 18 to 8 B.C., and they are at the heart of that simultaneous rise of individualism and political centralization in the Empire.

Relations between the state and the individual became ever more direct. The various situations in which the juridical person found himself affected him alone, and there was no more need to break or form any bond with a jealous and exclusive family group. Being no longer the foundation of the Republic, the *paterfamilias* ceased to interpose between the individual and the state. . . .

Let us turn, finally, to the question of what social forces, over a considerable period of time, had combined to form the effective bases of the Augustan decrees? Obviously these decrees did not take effect in a society totally unprepared for them. Change in an institution or concept may be the consequence of impact and intrusion from external forces, but conditions for the assimiliation of this intrusion must be present—as studies of diffusion have made clear.

Here it is tempting to take refuge in such abstractions as secularism, commercialism, and religious skepticism in Rome during the century or two leading up to Augustus. These, it is said rightly enough, formed the context that alone permitted acceptance of the radical Augustan inroads on the family and other forms of association. No one familiar with the history of Rome in this period would doubt that such generalized forces were indeed involved.

Without pretending to exclude these forces, I would like, however, to put the matter in somewhat different terms—terms that are at once more precise and more sociological. I shall illustrate this in a con-text that had been potentially present in Roman society from earliest days. This is the conflict between the *patria potestas*—the ancient authority of the family, and the *imperium militiae*—the authority over soldiers that came into being at the outbreak of any war.

The *imperium militiae* was not, strictly speaking, military power alone. "The Romans," writes Strachan-Davidson, "knew no such thing as a severance between supreme military and supreme civil authority. They merely distinguished between the space inside the walls (*domi*) and the rest of the world which was comprehended in the locative case by the word *militiae* "on service." This full imperium, then, governs all the world, less the city of Rome." So much is true, but the fact remains, and it is crucial, that it was in a military context that "the rest of the world" became of significance to the Romans, and, more important, it was in its intrinsic military role that the *imperium militiae* first conflicted with the *patria potestas*.

I stressed earlier the fact that the public power did not and could not deal with the multitude of private and social matters that came under the *patria potestas*. The opposite, however, is also true, and here I present a brilliant clarifying insight from Maine:

In every relation of life in which the corrective community might have occasion to avail itself of his wisdom and strength, for all purposes of counsel and war, the *filius familias*, the son under power *was as free as his father*. It was a maxim of Roman jurisprudence that the *patria potestas* did not extend to the *jus publicum*. Father and son voted together in the city, and fought side by side in the field; indeed, the son, as general, might command the father, or, as magistrate decide on his contracts and punish his delinquencies.

Here, I suggest, is a potential conflict of roles, a tension, that lies at the heart of our subject. So long as the public role of the *filius familias,* the son under power, was minimal, just so long was the claim of the *patria potestas* upon his allegiance an unqualified and undistracted one. There could be little conflict of authority and role. On the other hand, all that tended to maximize the son's public role—either in quality or extent—tended equally to weaken the prestige and moral authority of the *patria potestas* if only because of the greater relative sphere of matters in the son's life over which the *patria potestas* had no influence.

We are justified in assuming from the evidence that it was in times of war that the maximization of a son's public role—and, correspondingly, his sporadic releases from the *patria potestas*—was heightened. Historically, as we know, war puts a premium upon the services of the young, not the old. Ordinary civil affairs in Rome, like ordinary business affairs, could be, and were, handled by those who were *sui juris,* those who held the *patria potestas* and were not under it. The most honored title indeed of the members of the Senate was the *Patres Conscripti.* But in war, different requirements prevail, and when warfare is extended and intensified, as it became in the later Republic, these requirements can become decisive.

The conflict between kinship society and the military is one of the key conflicts of history. Kinship society is inherently cellular—composed of compact and largely autonomous groups, families, clans, and *gentes*—whereas the military, as we find it in its earliest form is, by comparison, individualistic. Between the power of the commander and the individual soldier there is no intermediate authority, for such authority would weaken both the unity and the necessary directness of command. The very directness of the military *imperium* therefore induces a kind of potential individualism in social relations if only because of its corroding effects upon intermediate groups. In the second place, military society operates primarily in terms of command—not custom, tradition, and the *mores.* In the interstices of command, accordingly, there is a degree of moral freedom unknown in kinship society, which is governed not by prescriptive law, but by the less specific and infinitely more inclusive ties of custom which, by its nature, fills in every possible crevice. In short, there is a kind of secularizing and individualizing quality in military life.

In the third place, military society, unlike kinship, is, or by its nature aspires to be, rational in its distribution of function and authority; that is, whether explicitly or implicitly, both authority and function tend to fall into hands that are most competent, irrespective of considerations of age or social prestige. It does this, that is, if it is to be successful. Kinship society, on the other hand, tends, as we have seen, to accept seniority and age as the crucial qualities of leadership, with such matters as descent and inherited prestige close in importance. We may summarize the difference between the two societies by saying that in the first—kinship—it is ascribed status that counts, whereas in the second—the military—it is achieved status that is alone significant, if victory is the prime consideration.

We know that the Romans were well aware of the differences between the two types of society and the potential consequences of military service to kinship and ordinary civil authority. An ingenious variety of checks existed to prevent possible thrusts to ascendancy of victory-intoxicated returning soldiers. For centuries there was the custom by which no militia could form within the walls and no returning militia could enter the city gates until it had disbanded outside. When the individuals reentered the city, they were thus symbolically, as well as actually, freed from the *imperium* and once again under normal civil authority, and especially the *patria potestas*. Such checks, however, whether customary or constitutional, could not forever withstand the growing number of wars, the increasing size of the forces themselves, and, perhaps most important, the constantly growing pressure for a regular standing army with continuous command.

One by one, from the end of the second century on, the old checks upon the military ceased to function. There began that fateful affinity between military service and popular following, between military triumph and political success, that, in Rome, as in many another society, was to have a transforming effect upon government and society. The key personage, undoubtedly was the brilliant but ruthless Marius at the beginning of the first century B.C. "Marius was not content to supplement his army by drawing upon the 'bravest men of Latium' and recalling to the color *evocati* or discharged veterans known to him by reputation. He employed another method of enlistment. The proletariat, . . . now legally qualified for enrollment, were signed on for a definite period of service, in all probability for twenty years." The soldier might be a citizen when he joined up, he might be uncomplainingly under civil and paternal power, but the mere length of service that he among tens of thousands of young Roman males was now to look forward to—making him in effect a mercenary, knowing little and caring less about traditional matters—

would make him restive, to say the least, when he returned on furlough or following separation.

The army, strongly detached from civil institutions, had chiefs who were absolute chiefs. Soldiers entered the service because they liked it; they hoped for loot and allotments of land. Who could give them this privilege? The general. So there grew up between the general and his men a closer association based not on the old discipline, nor even on the religion of the standard, but on mutual interest and greed.

It is therefore, I suggest, in the rising incidence of war in Roman history, especially from the second century B.C. on, that we find the setting for the tensions that were eventually to reduce the *patria potestas* to innocuousness. For it was in the circumstances of increasing warfare that more and more sons under paternal power found themselves for lengthening periods of time under the *imperium militiae,* a form of authority that differed vastly from the *patria potestas* and provided, for all its own stringency, the essential conditions of that special type of individualism that was to sap the foundations of kinship society.

The *imperium* of the Caesars continued to grow at the expense of kinship groups and the traditional Republican institutions and values closely related to them. The expansion of imperial government was, however, gradual, and the constitutional compromise (Principate) worked out by Augustus lasted for two centuries until it gave way, under social, economic, and political pressures in the early third century, to undisguised religious and military autocracy.

These two and one-half centuries are customarily divided by historians into the following periods determined by the reigning emperors and the manner of their succession.

1. The Augustan Age (27 B.C.–A.D. 14)

2. The Julio-Claudian emperors (A.D. 14–68), so called because all were related either to Augustus or his second wife, Livia.

Tiberius	A.D. 14–37
Gaius (Caligula)	A.D. 37–41
Claudius	A.D. 41–54
Nero	A.D. 54–68

3. The Flavian emperors (A.D. 68–96)

Vespasian	A.D. 69–79
Titus	A.D. 79–81
Domitian	A.D. 81–96

4. The Adoptive emperors (A.D. 96–180), or so-called "Good emperors," who reigned with the good will of the Senate. The succession was determined by the adoption and training of an heir by the ruling emperor.

Nerva	A.D. 96–98
Trajan	A.D. 98–117
Hadrian	A.D. 117–138
Antoninus Pius	A.D. 138–161
Marcus Aurelius	A.D. 161–180

5. A period of political instability and the establishment of the Severan dynasty (A.D. 180–235). The period begins with the misgovernment of Marcus Aurelius' son, Commodus (A.D. 180–193), followed by struggle for the succession and the emergence of L. Septimius Severus (A.D. 197–211) as *princeps*. During his rule and that of his sons, the Empire became an ill-disguised military despotism.

The first two centuries A.D. are frequently referred to as the era of the *Pax Romana*. During this period the entire civilized world outside of the Parthian Near East, India, and China was united under one government, and the Latin and Greek cultures achieved a kind of synthesis and spread wherever the imperial standard kept the peace. In the second century A.D., the ancient world reached the height of its material prosperity. The city of Rome was adorned with monumental public buildings, and other cities of the Empire imitated Rome on a lesser scale. Continued peace, the suppression of piracy, the extension of highways throughout the Empire, and the establishment of an imperial coinage led to an unprecedented expansion of commerce and the development of manufacturing centers in all parts of the Empire. Agriculture still remained the basic occupation of the majority of the population, and landholding constituted the bulk of wealth. Slaves supplied the labor on the great estates and in many industries. But the number of slaves began to decrease during this period due to the cessation of foreign wars and an increase in the ability of slaves to purchase their freedom. These freedmen for the most part continued to work the land as tenant farmers. Some migrated to the towns to engage in industry, trade, the civil service, or the army.

One important result of economic prosperity was thus a fluid movement of population about the Empire and a tendency for local traditions to give way to a spirit of cosmopolitanism.

Cities were built along the entire length of the far-flung frontier, where they immediately became outposts of defence as well as centers of civilization. Since each was granted extensive liberties (due provision being always made against any threat of sedition) each also functioned as a provincial school of government and citizenship. Furthermore, although the various municipal charters differed in particulars, all were replicas of the Roman constitution as far as the major organs of government were concerned. As a consequence, the city became, to a considerable extent, an internationally shared form of community life and, by virtue of this fact, an agency in the process of counteracting provincial and racial differences.[3]

[3] From *Politics and Culture in International History*, by A. B. Bozeman, p. 177. Copyright © 1960 by Princeton University Press. Reprinted by permission of Princeton University Press.

This diffusion of Roman culture, strongest in the western provinces, was matched by the extension of the legal privileges of Roman citizenship to most of the inhabitants of the Empire. In 90–89 B.C. citizenship had been extended to most Italians, and Augustus adopted a policy of granting citizenship to auxiliary soldiers upon completion of their terms of service. Claudius granted citizenship to provincials and freedmen so that they might serve in his bureaucracy, and he enrolled prominent men from the western provinces in the magistracies and Senate. The process of Romanization was completed in A.D. 212 by Caracalla, who conferred citizenship on all free residents of the Empire.

The remarkable fact that the final phase of this process of enfranchisement was the work of emperors who were firm believers in absolutist rule renders apparent the complex nature of this entire evolution, for it shows

A reconstruction of the imperial capital. From left to right: Circus Maximus, Palatine Hill, Colosseum. (The Bettmann Archive)

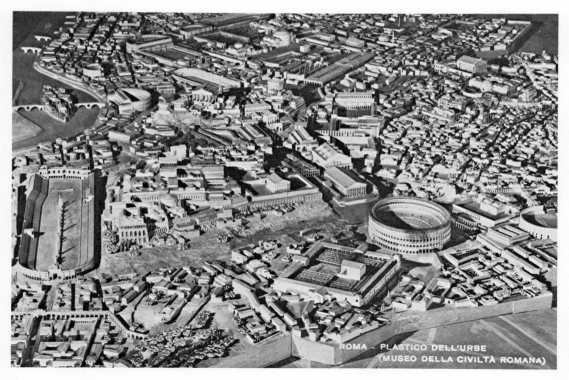

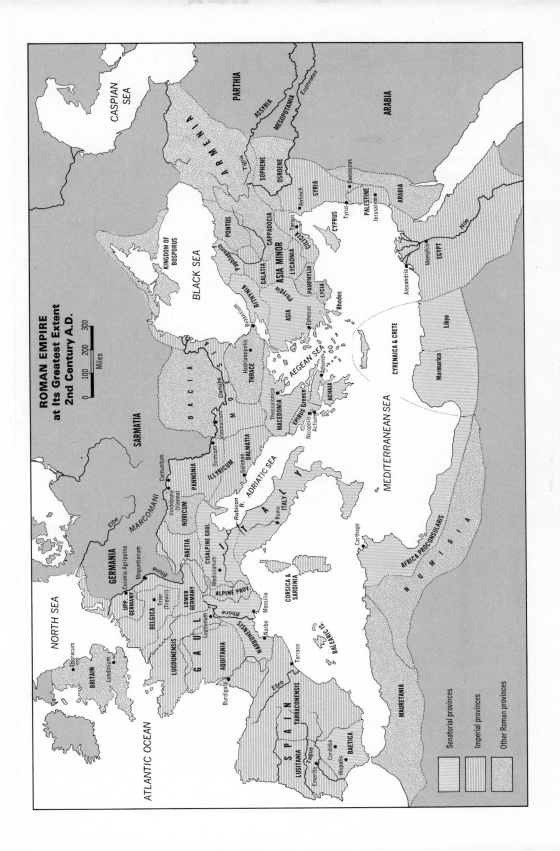

**ROMAN EMPIRE
at Its Greatest Extent
2nd Century A.D.**

0 100 200 300
Miles

CASPIAN SEA

PARTHIA

ASSYRIA

MESOPOTAMIA

Euphrates

ARABIA

ARMENIA

SOPHENE

OSROENE

Tigris

SYRIA

Damascus

Antioch

PONTUS

CAPPADOCIA

CILICIA

Tarsus

CYPRUS

Tyrus

PALESTINE

Jerusalem

ARABIA

Nile

KINGDOM OF BOSPORUS

BLACK SEA

Paphlagonia

GALATIA

LYCAONIA

PAMPHYLIA

ASIA MINOR

PHRYGIA

LYCIA

Rhodes

EGYPT

Alexandria

Memphis

BITHYNIA

ASIA

Ephesus

AEGEAN SEA

Byzantium

D A C I A

Hadrianopolis

THRACE

M O E S I A

Danube

Viminacium

Sirmium

Salonae

DALMATIA

ILLYRICUM

Thessalonica

MACEDONIA

EPIRUS

Greece

ACHAIA

Athens

Nicopolis

Actium

LIBYA

CYRENAICA & CRETE

Marmarica

MEDITERRANEAN SEA

SARMATIA

MARCOMANI

Carnuntum

Vindobona
(Vienna)

PANNONIA

NORICUM

RAETIA

CISALPINE GAUL

Rubicon R.

Mediolanum

I T A L Y

Rome

ADRIATIC SEA

Carthage

AFRICA PROCONSULARIS

N U M I D I A

GERMANIA

Elbe

Rhine

Colonia Agrippina

Moguntiacum

UPP. GERMANY

LOWER GERMANY

Trier (Trevir)

BELGICA

G A U L

Lugdunum

LUGDUNENSIS

AQUITANIA

Burdigala

NARBONENSIS

Rhone

Narbo

Massilia

ALPINE PROV.

CORSICA & SARDINIA

BALEARIC IS.

MAURETANIA

NORTH SEA

BRITAIN

Eburacum

Londinium

ATLANTIC OCEAN

S P A I N

TARRACONENSIS

Ebro

Tarraco

LUSITANIA

Emerita

BAETICA

Pacus

Corduba

Hispalis

Senatorial provinces

Imperial provinces

Other Roman provinces

Pont du Gard—a Roman aqueduct in southern France. It carried one hundred gallons of water per day for each citizen of the nearby city of Nîmes. (G. E. Kidder Smith)

that Caracalla's Edict actually capped two parallel political processes. The emperor confirmed, by his act, on the one hand a principle of equality that had had its inception in ancient republicanism, and on the other the victory of imperial authoritarianism over local rights to self-government. Moreover, the cause of internationalization had been furthered in the Roman commonwealth of many races not only by deliberate efforts to perfect administrative devices, but also—as in earlier empires—by less coordinated policies directed toward the propagation of a basic fund of education and the allowance of the widest possible competition between the sciences, arts, and crafts that had previously been developing separately in the several provinces. The Romans seem to have been more successful than their predecessors in this field of broad human relations, perhaps because they were always ready to recognize their own deficiencies and to appropriate serviceable ideas from friend and foe alike. Their increasingly close contacts with the East, furthermore, had convinced them that Hellenistic learning could not be matched anywhere; and they therefore permitted and even fostered its free development alongside their own Latin culture. Roman intellectuals were expected to know Greek, and a certain Roman governor of Asia delivered his judicial decisions according to the requirements of the case—to the consternation of native Greeks—sometimes in ordinary Greek, and sometimes in one or another of the four dialects that had become provincial written languages. The same respect for knowledge explains also why Plutarch's thesis that the Greeks could boast of men and warriors easily comparable to the heroes of Roman history met with general approval and helped to convince his contemporaries that there was a heritage outside of the narrow bounds of Roman experience in which all men could share.[4]

Education expanded and was modernized to meet the new conditions. The number of institutions of primary, secondary, and higher education grew substantially in the Imperial period, although education was available only to the children of the wealthy who could afford to pay the teachers' fees. The prestige of scholars—that is, the masters of the liberal arts, grammar, and rhetoric—increased so that many were granted imperial subsidies and special privileges under the Roman law. In the higher schools, the Ciceronian ideal of wisdom combined with eloquence gave way for the most part to pure rhetoric or the teaching of eloquence for strictly aesthetic purposes. "The chief aim of Roman education was to realize through literature and art an ideal of humanism that was unconcerned with, unconstrained by, any sordid technical or utilitarian considerations."[5] Even young lawyers studied this literary rhetoric, leaving the technical details of the law to specialists. There did grow up, however, a few special schools in which

the increasingly systematized and theoretical law was taught to aspiring jurists. And the study of the Greek language and philosophy continued to flourish in the cities of the East, especially in Athens.

This vast empire of diverse people and cultural traditions was governed by a centralized and bureaucratized government which had developed from a complex combination of institutional devices inherited from the Republic and created by the *princeps*. The Senate continued for a long time to enjoy great prestige, although its function became primarily ceremonial. The popular assemblies fell into disuse. Senatorial proconsuls, equestrian army officers, scribes from the class of freedmen, and local notables acting as municipal magistrates were all engaged in the business of government.

During the first two centuries after Christ the governmental machinery that formally bound together the far-flung Empire was continuously expanded and centralized. In this process the demands and needs of the subjects had far greater influence than any conscious will of a ruler, and the day-to-day conduct of the administration was as largely determined by the permanent bureaucracy as by its titular masters. Historians of the age rarely noted these developments, which have been ferreted out by patient modern study of inscriptions which give public careers and state edicts.

Under Augustus the central administration had been a relatively small group of aides, freedmen, and slaves; and at this time provincial government was largely an improvisation from republican experience. Governors of major provinces were senators representing either the Senate or the emperor; minor provinces as well as Egypt were assigned to equestrians; most taxes were collected locally under the supervision of senatorial quaestors, or equestrian and freedman procurators. Justice, too, lay largely in local hands, though appeals could be made to governors and their judicial deputies or even to the emperor's court.

---

[4] Bozeman, *Politics and Culture in International History,* pp. 179–180. Reprinted by permission.

[5] From *A History of Education in Antiquity* by H. I. Marrou (trans. George Lamb), p. 288. © 1956 by Sheed & Ward Inc., New York. Reprinted by permission of the publisher.

As far as the central administration was concerned, much continued to be directly in the hands of the rulers. Military control, in particular, remained too vital to the emperors to be assigned to a special department, even if the Praetorian Prefects occasionally served as advisers on military matters as well as on the conduct of the civil administration. For general advice the emperors also had an informal council or *consilium* of "friends." Claudius, the first great systematizer of the imperial bureaucracy, grouped major offices in several great departments, which eventually came to be *ab epistulis* (imperial correspondence), *a libellis* (petitions), *a cognitionibus* (judicial matters), *a rationibus* (supervision of financial matters), and *a studiis* (records and reference).

More and more these posts and other major fiscal offices came into the hands of equestrians, rather than of freedmen. Under Hadrian, the military and civil careers of equestrians were largely separated so that men specialized in one or the other field, beginning on the civil side with the position of tax attorney (*advocatus fisci*); and the higher equestrian offices were carefully graded by salary and by titles such as *vir*

egregius, vir perfectissimus, and *vir eminentissimus* (a senator was *vir clarissimus*). Special administrations for inheritance taxes, customs (levied at several major customs lines within the Empire as well as on the frontiers), and other taxes grew in size and complexity. Provincial dues now passed through the local *fisci* to the central treasury or *fiscus,* which supervised the emperor's great holdings.

By the second century the imperial administration, both central and provincial, had become the most extensive and detailed structure that the Mediterranean world as a whole had known. Its operations were governed by a professional code of efficiency, reasonable honesty, and support of Greco-Roman culture, proper education in which was a prime prerequisite for public office. The letters between Trajan and Pliny the Younger, as governor of Bithynia, throw our clearest light on the sincere efforts of ruler and agents alike to secure the welfare of the governed.

Two aspects of this generally beneficial development were less desirable. One was the tendency of the central government to invade the sphere of action of the local communities, both because it was more efficient

Hadrian's Wall—the northernmost frontier of the Empire, on the Scottish border—built in A.D. 122. (British Tourist Authority)

A Roman road in Yorkshire, northern Britain. (British Tourist Authority)

and because the cities, as we shall see later, were running into financial difficulties. Theoretically it would have been possible for the cities to gain a new function and a sense of importance by having a voice in the centralized government; but this did not occur. Some of the wealthiest men became, as individuals, members of the Senate or imperial bureaucracy; but on an organized level their only vehicle of expression was in the provincial or district assemblies of the imperial cult, which occasionally sent ambassadors and petitions to the ruler. Influence, rather, streamed in the other direction as the imperial government laid down rules for local operations, as the court of the governor became a more important arena for cases, and as municipal posts became assigned responsibilities for wealthy men whether they wished to hold them or not. Since the cities were the essential framework of ancient culture, this loss of local autonomy and local purpose was a dangerous sign for the future.

The second problem was the unceasing expansion of the bureaucracy. More and more officials had to be paid; the imperial court grew more elaborate and expensive; and the functions of the government ever increased.

In the latter aspect one interesting development was that of social welfare. Humanitarian views on slaves and women, who became more emancipated than ever before, cost nothing in themselves even when translated into official decrees for the protection of slaves, women, and children promulgated by Hadrian. But provisions for feeding poor children in Italy (the *alimenta,* begun by Nerva and Trajan) did involve expenses, as did occasional public attention to education, libraries, and other social services. So long as the Empire was prosperous, the costs of government were bearable, and the subjects continued to elevate their "father" ever higher in gratitude for earthly blessings. Would they continue to do so if prosperity ceased?[6]

Under the Caesars there was a continuous tendency to rationalize this vast administrative system and to bring it under central direction. In time the Empire came to approximate the model of bureaucratic or legal-rational authority which Max Weber designated as his third type of "domination" or authority.

[6] From *A History of the Ancient World* by Chester G. Starr, pp. 582–584. Copyright © 1965 by Oxford University Press, Inc. Reprinted by permission.

The Pantheon, built by Hadrian on the site of a former temple to the Roman gods. It was both a temple, housing statues of the gods, and a secular symbol, its overarching dome signifying both the cosmos and Roman rule. (Alinari)

MAX WEBER'S CONCEPT OF
RATIONAL AUTHORITY
Robert A. Nisbet[7]

Rational authority . . . is characterized by bureaucracy, by rationalization of the personal relationships which are the substance of traditional society. Legal dom-

[7] From *The Sociological Tradition* by Robert A. Nisbet (New York: Basic Books, Inc., Publishers, 1966), pp. 143, 145–146. Reprinted by permission of the publisher.

ination exists in a society when "a system of rules that is applied judicially and administratively in accordance with ascertainable principles is valid for all members of the corporate group." Although this mode of authority is not equalitarian—it has its own strata of function and responsibility—it cannot help but place an emphasis on equality that is lacking in the traditional order. All are equal under the rules governing them specifically. The emphasis is on the rules rather than on persons or on mores. The organization is supreme and, by its nature, strives toward increasing rationalization of itself through reduction of the influence played by kinship, friendship, or the various other factors, including money, that so strongly influence the traditional system. Function, authority, hierarchy, and obedience all exist here, as they do in the traditional order, but they are conceived to flow strictly from the application of organizational reason. . . .

Of all conceptual elements in Weber's theory of authority, the one for which he is most famous is bureaucracy. Bureaucracy falls, as we have seen, within Weber's category of rational domination; it is the mode of hierarchy that supplants patri-

monial, charismatic, and/or traditional authority when economy or government (or religion, education, the military, or any other institution in society) becomes structured in the following specific ways:

Foremost is "the principle of fixed and official jurisdictional areas, which are generally ordered by rules, that is, by laws or administrative regulations." Ordinary activities become distributed as official duties, and the authority to give commands is distributed in a stable and foreseeable way, thus replacing the random and sporadic character of kinship or patrimonial authority. Provision is made "for the regular and continuous fulfillment of these duties and for the execution of the

Interior of the Pantheon by the eighteenth-century painter, Panini. (National Gallery of Art, Washington, D.C., Samuel H. Kress Collection)

corresponding rights." In public government such a system is always identified as bureaucracy, but the same basic system exists in modern business and is known as management.

From the basic principle of fixed and official jurisdiction flow such vital practices and criteria as the regularization of channels of communication, authority, and appeal; the functional priority of the office to the person occupying it; the emphasis upon written and recorded orders, in place of random, merely personal, commands or wishes; the sharp separation of official from personal identity in the management of affairs and the superintending of finances; the identification of, and provision for the training of "expertness" in a given office or function; the rigorous priority of official to merely personal business in the governing of an enterprise; and, finally, the conversion of as many activities and functions as possible to clear and specifiable rules; rules that, by their nature, have both preceptive and authoritarian significance.

Such is the essence of Weber's definition of bureaucracy. But to leave the matter here would be to leave it in the realm of the merely descriptive and taxonomic. What gives distinction to Weber's theory of bureaucracy is the manner in which he relates it to the main currents of European political, economic, and social history. *Bureaucratization* becomes for Weber a powerful manifestation of the historical principle of rationalization. The growth of bureaucracy in government, business, religion, and education is an aspect of the rationalization of culture that has also transformed, in Weber's view, the nature of art, drama, music, and philosophy. Bureaucracy is, in short, a historical process through which we may account for much of what distinguishes the modern from the medieval world (and also, of course, for analogous differentiations in the ancient and Asiatic worlds; bureaucracy in Weber is a means of illuminating Chinese, Indian, and ancient Roman society as well as European).

Intellectual life did not remain unaffected by this transformation of the sociopolitical order. The change which Stoicism underwent provides one of the best illustrations of the new intellectual climate. Early Stoicism, as we have seen, influenced the individualization and rationalization of the law, administration, and education. Later Stoicism, by contrast, increasingly appealed to individuals cast adrift from the security of family and small community. Its formulas for the maintenance of individual tranquillity and *autarky* seemed to meet a personal need for anchorage. It seems safe to assume that it was for this reason that the religious element in Stoicism assumed greater and greater prominence.

For a time after the Augustan settlement senators and literary men used arguments from Stoic natural law—much in the manner of Cicero—to oppose the "tyranny" of the *princeps*, particularly when emperors attempted to bypass senatorial election and establish the principle of hereditary succession. Yet the Senate, itself divided by factions, was unable to resist the growing power of the emperor. Emperor-worship became more and more prevalent throughout the Empire, and the republican virtues of piety, gravity, and manliness were replaced as official attributes of the emperor by justice, clemency, foresight, and liberality, virtues which could be exercised only by a superior toward an inferior. Later Stoics, confronted by the overwhelming fact of arbitrary and almost absolute imperial power and majesty, were, therefore, not as sure as Cicero had been of the correspondence between existing institutions and the principles of nature. The Stoic continued to advocate "action in accord with nature, as revealed to man through reason. [But] this meant that instead of subordinating himself to an ordered system of social relationships, the individual must liberate himself from the constraint of both institutions and the ideology supporting them."[8] This new turn in Stoic philosophy was clearly reflected in the writings of Lucius Annaeus Seneca (4 B.C.–A.D. 65). Seneca was born in Cordoba, Spain, became tutor to the future emperor, Nero, amassed a huge fortune while holding public office, and became Nero's chief adviser in the first years of the young emperor's reign. Upon the accession of Nero to the imperial throne, Seneca wrote a discourse in which he showed full recognition of the powers of the *princeps*—powers which could be tempered only with mercy (*clementia*).

ON MERCY
Seneca[9]

I have undertaken, Nero Caesar, to write on the subject of mercy, in order to serve in a way the purpose of a mirror, and thus reveal you to yourself as one destined to attain to the greatest of all pleasures. For, though the true profit of virtuous deeds lies in the doing, and there is no fitting reward for the virtues apart from the virtues themselves, still it is a pleasure to subject a good conscience to a round of inspection, then to cast one's eyes upon this vast throng—discordant, factious, and unruly, ready to run riot alike for the destruction of itself and others if it should

[8] David Brion Davis, *The Problem of Slavery in Western Culture* (Ithaca, N.Y.: Cornell University Press, 1966), p. 73.

[9] Reprinted by permission of the publishers and The Loeb Classical Library from John W. Basore, translator, Seneca, *Moral Essays*, Vol. I (Cambridge, Mass.: Harvard University Press, 1928), pp. 357–359, 371–373.

break its yoke—and finally to commune with oneself thus: "Have I of all mortals found favour with Heaven and been chosen to serve on earth as vicar of the gods? I am the arbiter of life and death for the nations; it rests in my power what each man's lot and state shall be; by my lips Fortune proclaims what gift she would bestow on each human being; from my utterance peoples and cities gather reasons for rejoicing; without my favour and grace no part of the wide world can prosper; all those many thousands of swords which my peace restrains will be drawn at my nod; what nations shall be utterly destroyed, which banished, which shall receive the gift of liberty, which have it taken from them, what kings shall become slaves and whose heads shall be crowned with royal honour, what cities shall fall and which shall rise—this it is mine to decree. With all things thus at my disposal, I have been moved neither by anger nor youthful impulse to unjust punishment, nor by the foolhardiness and obstinacy of men which have often wrung patience from even the serenest souls, nor yet by that vainglory which employs terror for the display of might—a dread but all too common use of great and lordly power. With me the sword is hidden, nay, is sheathed; I am sparing to the utmost of even the meanest blood; no man fails to find favour at my hands though he lack all else but the name of man. Sternness I keep hidden, but mercy ever ready at hand. I so hold guard over myself as though I were about to render an account to those laws which I have summoned from decay and darkness into the light of day. I have been moved to pity by the fresh youth of one, by the extreme old age of another; one I have pardoned for his high position, another for his humble state; whenever I found no excuse for pity, for my own sake I have spared. To-day, if the immortal gods should require a reckoning from me, I am ready to give full tale of the human race."

This pronouncement, Caesar, you may boldly make, that whatever has passed into your trust and guardianship is still kept safe, that through you the state suffers no loss, either from violence or from fraud. . . .

. . . For if—and this is what thus far it is establishing—you are the soul of the state and the state your body, you see, I think, how requisite is mercy; for you are merciful to yourself when you are seemingly merciful to another. And so even reprobate citizens should have mercy as being the weak members of the body, and if there should ever be need to let blood, the hand must be held under control to keep it from cutting deeper than may be necessary. The quality of mercy, then, as I was saying, is indeed for all men in accordance with nature, but in rulers it has an especial comeliness inasmuch as with them it finds more to save, and exhibits itself amid ampler opportunities. For how small the harm the cruelty of a private citizen can do! But when princes rage there is war. . . . Let a prince, therefore, appropriating to himself the spirit of the gods, look with pleasure upon one class of his citizens because they are useful and good; others let him leave to make up the count; let him be glad that some of them live, some let him merely endure.

Seneca's protestations failed to influence Nero to moderation and mercy. Through intrigues and murder, including the murder of his own mother, Nero assumed full control of the state, intimidated the Senate, and forced Seneca into exile. In a series of letters to a friend, Seneca turned from politics to philosophical contemplation and self-scrutiny.

ON LEISURE
Seneca[10]

You will say to me: "What are you doing, Seneca? Are you deserting your party? Surely you Stoics say: 'We shall engage in affairs to the very end of life, we shall never cease to work for the common good, to help each and all, to give aid even to our enemies when our hand is feeble with age. We are those who grant no exemption from service by reason of years, and, as that most gifted poet puts it,

Upon our hoary heads we thrust the helm.

We are those who hold so strongly that there should be no leisure before death that, if circumstance permits, we take no leisure for death itself.' Why in the very headquarters of Zeno do you preach the doctrines of Epicurus? Why, if you are tired of your party, do you not with all speed desert it rather than betray it?" For the present I shall have only this reply to make to you: "What more do you expect of me than that I should imitate my leaders? And what then? I shall not go whither they despatch me, but whither they lead me."

Right now I shall prove to you that I am not in revolt against the teachings of the Stoics; for they themselves have not revolted against their own teachings either. And yet I might plead a very good excuse

[10] Reprinted by permission of the publishers and The Loeb Classical Library from John W. Basore, translator, Seneca, *Moral Essays*, Vol. II (Cambridge, Mass.: Harvard University Press, 1928), pp. 183–189.

even if I did follow their examples and not their teachings. What I have to say I shall develop under two heads, showing, first, that it is possible for a man to surrender himself wholly to the contemplation of truth, to search out the art of living, and to practise it in retirement, even from his earliest years; secondly, that, when a man has now earned release from public service and his life is almost over, it is possible that he may with perfect justice do the same thing and turn his mind to quite different activities, after the manner of the Vestal virgins, whose years are allotted to varied duties while they are learning to perform the sacred rites, and, when they have learned, they begin to teach. . . .

Let us grasp the idea that there are two commonwealths—the one, a vast and truly common state, which embraces alike gods and men, in which we look neither to this corner of earth nor to that, but measure the bounds of our citizenship by the path of the sun; the other, the one to which we have been assigned by the accident of birth. This will be the commonwealth of the Athenians or of the Carthaginians, or of any other city that belongs, not to all,

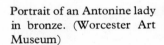

Portrait of an Antonine lady in bronze. (Worcester Art Museum)

but to some particular race of men. Some yield service to both commonwealths at the same time—to the greater and to the lesser—some only to the lesser, some only to the greater. This greater commonwealth we are able to serve even in leisure—nay, I am inclined to think even better in leisure—so that we may inquire what virtue is, and whether it is one or many; whether it is nature or art that makes men good; whether this world, which embraces seas and lands and the things that are contained in the sea and land, is a solitary creation or whether God has strewn about many systems of the same sort; whether all the matter from which everything is formed is continuous and compact, or whether it is disjunctive and a void is intermingled with the solid; what God is—whether he idly gazes upon his handiwork, or directs it; whether he encompasses it without, or pervades the whole of it; whether the world is eternal, or is to be counted among the things that perish and are born only for a time. And what service does he who ponders these things render unto God? He keeps the mighty works of God from being without a witness!

A Flavian matron. (Alinari)

ON WISDOM AND RETIREMENT;
ON THE NATURAL FEAR OF DEATH
Seneca[11]

I now return to the advice which I set out to give you—that you keep your retirement in the background. . . . To advertise one's retirement is to collect a crowd. When you withdraw from the world, your business is to talk with yourself, not to have men talk about you. But what shall you talk about? Do just what people are fond of doing when they talk about their neighbours,—speak ill of yourself when by yourself; then you will become accustomed both to speak and to hear the truth. Above all, however, ponder that which you come to feel is your greatest weakness. Each man knows best the defects of his own body. And so one relieves his stomach by vomiting, another props it up by frequent eating, another drains and purges his body by periodic fasting. Those whose feet are visited by pain abstain either from wine or from the bath. In general, men who are careless in other respects go out of their way to relieve the disease which frequently afflicts them. So it is with our souls; there are in them certain parts which are, so to speak, on the sick-list, and to these parts the cure must be applied.

What, then, am I myself doing with my leisure? I am trying to cure my own sores. If I were to show you a swollen foot, or an inflamed hand, or some shrivelled sinews in a withered leg, you would permit me to lie quiet in one place and to apply lotions to the diseased member. But my trouble is greater than any of these, and I cannot show it to you. The abscess, or ulcer, is deep within my breast. . . .

Leisure without study is death; it is a tomb for the living man. What then is the advantage of retirement? As if the real causes of our anxieties did not follow us across the seas! What hiding-place is there, where the fear of death does not enter? What peaceful haunts are there, so fortified and so far withdrawn that pain does not fill them with fear? Wherever you hide yourself, human ills will make an uproar all around. There are many external things which compass us about, to deceive us or to weigh upon us; there are many things within which, even amid solitude, fret and ferment.

Therefore, gird yourself about with philosophy, an impregnable wall. Though it be assaulted by many engines, Fortune can find no passage into it. The soul stands on unassailable ground, if it has abandoned external things; it is independent in its own fortress; and every weapon that is hurled falls short of the mark. Fortune has not the long reach with which we credit her; she can seize none except him that clings to her. Let us then recoil from her as far as we are able. This will be possible for us only through knowledge of self and of the world of Nature. The soul should know whither it is going and whence it came, what is good for it and what is evil, what it seeks and what it avoids, and what is that Reason which distinguishes between the desirable and the undesirable, and thereby tames the madness of our desires and calms the violence of our fears. . . .

. . . I classify as "indifferent,"—that is, neither good nor evil,—sickness, pain, poverty, exile, death. None of these things is

[11] Reprinted by permission of the publishers and The Loeb Classical Library from R. M. Gummere, translator, Seneca, *Epistulae Morales*, Vol. II (Cambridge, Mass.: Harvard University Press, 1917), pp. 45-49, 243-245, 247-251.

intrinsically glorious; but nothing can be glorious apart from them. For it is not poverty that we praise, it is the man whom poverty cannot humble or bend. Nor is it exile that we praise, it is the man who withdraws into exile in the spirit in which he would have sent another into exile. It is not pain that we praise, it is the man whom pain has not coerced. One praises not death, but the man whose soul death takes away before it can confound it. All these things are in themselves neither honourable nor glorious; but any one of them that virtue has visited and touched is made honourable and glorious by virtue; they merely lie in between, and the decisive question is only whether wickedness or virtue has laid hold upon them. . . .

. . . There are vast distinctions among these qualities which we call "average." For example, death is not so indifferent as the question whether your hair should be worn evenly or unevenly. Death belongs among those things which are not indeed evils, but still have in them a semblance of evil; for there are implanted in us love of self, a desire for existence and self-preservation, and also an abhorrence of dissolution, because death seems to rob us of many goods and to withdraw us from the abundance to which we have become accustomed. And there is another element which estranges us from death: we are already familiar with the present, but are ignorant of the future into which we shall transfer ourselves, and we shrink from the unknown. Moreover, it is natural to fear the world of shades, whither death is supposed to lead. Therefore, although death is something indifferent, it is nevertheless not a thing which we can easily ignore. The soul must be hardened by long practice, so that it may learn to endure the sight and the approach of death.

Seneca's attitude toward death served him well. When Nero purged the Senate of conspirators against his life, Seneca was among those ordered to commit suicide.

Epictetus (ca. A.D. 55–ca. 135), a slave from Phrygia in Asia Minor, even more clearly than Seneca, reflects the religious turn of later Stoicism. Little is known of Epictetus' life, other than the fact that he was a slave in Rome during the reign of Nero, was driven out of the city in A.D. 98 along with other philosophers by the Emperor Domitian, and settled in Nicopolis in Epirus, where he lived in poverty and lectured to a devoted circle of disciples. The starting point of Epictetus' moral teaching was that one God is the father of men and gods and that a divine providence governs the universe.

> If what philosophers say of the kinship between God and men be true, what has any one to do; but, like Socrates, when he is asked what countryman he is, never to say that he is a citizen of Athens, or of Corinth, but of the universe? . . . He . . . who understands the administration of the universe, and has learned that the principal and greatest and most comprehensive of all things is this vast system, extending from men to God; and that from Him the seeds of being are descended, not only to one's father or grandfather, but to all things that are produced and born on earth; and especially to rational natures, as they alone are qualified to partake of a communication with the Deity, being connected with him by reason; why may not such a one call himself a citizen of the universe? Why not a son of God? And why shall he fear anything that happens among men? Shall kinship to Caesar, or any other of the great at Rome, enable a man to live secure, above contempt, and void of all fear whatever; and shall not the having God for our maker, and father, and guardian, free us from griefs and alarms? [12]

[12] Epictetus, *Discourses*, I, 3. Thomas Wentworth Higginson translation.

Above all else, Epictetus sought freedom from his own anxiety and from dependence upon circumstances and the will of others.

ON FREEDOM
Epictetus[13]

Since, . . . neither they who are called kings nor the friends of kings live as they like, who, then, after all, is free? Seek, and you will find; for you are furnished by nature with means for discovering the truth. But if you are not able by these alone to find the consequence, hear them who have sought it. What do they say? Do you think freedom a good? "The greatest." Can any one, then, who attains the greatest good, be unhappy or unsuccessful in his affairs? "No." As many, therefore, as you see unhappy, lamenting, unprosperous,—confidently pronounce them not free. "I do." Henceforth, then, we have done with buying and selling, and such like stated conditions of becoming slaves. For if these concessions hold, then, whether the unhappy man be a great or a little king,—of consular or bi-consular dignity,—he is not free. "Agreed."

. . . Well; do you think freedom to be something independent and self-determined? "How can it be otherwise?" Him, then, whom it is in the power of another to restrain or to compel, affirm confidently to be by no means free. And do not heed his grandfathers or great-grandfathers; or inquire whether he has been bought or sold; but if you hear him say from his heart and with emotion, "my master," though twelve Lictors should march before him, call him a slave. And if you should hear

[13] Epictetus, *Discourses*, IV, 1. Thomas Wentworth Higginson translation.

him say, "Wretch, that I am! what do I suffer!" call him a slave. In short, if you see him wailing, complaining, unprosperous, call him a slave, even in purple. . . .

"Have we so many masters, then?" We have. For, prior to all such, we have the *things* themselves for our masters. Now they are many; and it is through these that the men who control the things inevitably become our masters too. For no one fears Caesar himself; but death, banishment, confiscation, prison, disgrace. Nor does any one love Caesar unless he be a person of great worth; but we love riches, the tribunate, the praetorship, the consulship. When we love or hate or fear such things, they who have the disposal of them must necessarily be our masters. Hence we even worship them as gods. For we consider that whoever has the disposal of the greatest advantages is a deity; and then further reason falsely, "but such a one has the control of the greatest advantages; therefore he is a deity." For if we reason falsely, the final inference must be also false.

"What is it, then, that makes a man free and independent? For neither riches, nor consulship, nor the command of provinces, nor of kingdoms, can make him so; but something else must be found." . . .

. . . I have placed my pursuits under the direction of God. Is it His will that I should have a fever? It is my will too. Is it His will that I should pursue anything? It is my will too. Is it His will that I should desire? It is my will too. Is it His will that I should obtain anything? It is mine too. Is it not His will? It is not mine. Is it His will that I should be tortured? Then it is my will to be tortured. Is it His will that I should die? Then it is my will to die. Who can any longer restrain or compel me, contrary to my own opinion? No more than Zeus. . . . A person who reasons thus, understands and considers that, if he joins himself to God, he shall go safely through his journey.

"How do you mean, join himself?" That what ever is the will of God may be *his* will too: that whatever is not the will of God may not be his. "How, then, can this be done?" Why, how otherwise than by considering the workings of God's power and his administration? What has he given me to be my own, and independent? What has he reserved to himself? He has given me whatever depends on will. The things within my power he has made incapable of hindrance or restraint. . . .

"Are you free yourself, then?" you may ask. By Heaven, I wish and pray for it. But I own I cannot yet face my masters. I still pay a regard to my body, and set a great value on keeping it whole; though, for that matter, it is not whole. But I can show you one who was free, that you may no longer seek an example. Diogenes was free. "How so?" Not because he was of free parents, for he was not; but because he was so in himself; because he had cast away all which gives a handle to slavery; nor was there any way of getting at him, nor anywhere to lay hold on him, to enslave him. Everything sat loose upon him, everything only just hung on. If you took hold on his possessions, he would rather let them go than follow you for them; if on his leg, he let go his leg; if his body, he let go his body; acquaintance, friends, country, just the same. For he knew whence he had them, and from whom, and upon what conditions he received them. But he would never have forsaken his true parents, the gods, and his real country [the universe]; nor have suffered any one to be more dutiful and obedient to them than he; nor would any one have died more readily for his country than he. For he never had to

inquire whether he should act for the good of the whole universe; for he remembered that everything that exists belongs to that administration, and is commanded by its ruler. . . .

Study these points, these principles, these discourses; contemplate these examples if you would be free, if you desire the thing in proportion to its value. And where is the wonder that you should purchase so good a thing at the price of others, so many, and so great? Some hang themselves, others break their necks, and sometimes even whole cities have been destroyed for that which is reputed freedom; and will not you for the sake of the true and secure and inviolable freedom, repay God what he hath given when he demands it? Will you not study not only, as Plato says, how to die, but how to be tortured and banished and scourged; and, in short, how to give up all that belongs to others. If not, you will be a slave among slaves, though you were ten thousand times a consul; and even though you should rise to the palace you will never be the less so. And you will feel that, though philosophers (as Cleanthes says) do, perhaps, talk contrary to common opinion, yet it is not contrary to reason. For you will find it true, in fact, that the things that are eagerly followed and admired are of no use to those who have gained them; while they who have not yet gained them imagine that, if they are acquired, every good will come along with them; and, then, when they are acquired, there is the same feverishness, the same agitation, the same nausea, and the same desire for what is absent. (For freedom is not procured by a full enjoyment of what is desired, but by controlling the desire.) And in order to know that this is true, take the same pains about these which you have taken about other things. Hold vigils to acquire a set of principles that will make you free. Instead of a rich old man pay your court to a philosopher. Be seen about his doors. You will not get any disgrace by being seen there. You will not return empty or unprofited if you go as you ought. However, try at least. The trial is not dishonorable.

Stoicism was a philosophy (or religion) for the individual whatever his station in life. Seneca was a wealthy provincial aristocrat; Epictetus was a slave and teacher. The third and last great exponent of later Roman Stoicism was the emperor himself—Marcus Aurelius Antoninus—who guided the destinies of Rome from A.D. 161–180. Marcus Aurelius did not enjoy the leisure of either forced or voluntary exile in which to contemplate and write. He thus expressed his philosophy in quick notes to himself often jotted down while on active military duty. He spent almost all of his time as emperor either on the frontier fighting back barbarian incursions which were beginning to be a serious threat to imperial security, or in distant parts of the Empire putting down revolts within the army. He was able to maintain order during his lifetime, but his reign is usually regarded by historians as the last before a long period of imperial decline.

MEDITATIONS
Marcus Aurelius[14]

II.

Begin the morning by saying to thyself, I shall meet with the busybody, the ungrateful, arrogant, deceitful, envious, unsocial. All these things happen to them by reason of their ignorance of what is good and evil. But I who have seen the nature

[14] Marcus Aurelius, *The Thoughts,* translated by George Long, 1873.

of the good that it is beautiful, and of the bad that it is ugly, and the nature of him who does wrong, that it is akin to me, not [only] of the same blood or seed, but that it participates in [the same] intelligence and [the same] portion of the divinity, I can neither be injured by any of them, for no one can fix on me what is ugly, nor can I be angry with my kinsman, nor hate him. For we are made for co-operation, like feet, like hands, like eyelids, like the rows of the upper and lower teeth. To act against one another, then, is contrary to nature; and it is acting against one another to be vexed and to turn away.

2. Whatever this is that I am, it is a little flesh and breath, and the ruling part. Throw away thy books; no longer distract thyself: it is not allowed; but as if thou wast now dying, despise the flesh; it is blood and bones and a network, a contexture of nerves, veins, and arteries. See the breath also, what kind of a thing it is; air, and not always the same, but every moment sent out and again sucked in. The third, then, is the ruling part; consider thus: Thou art an old man; no longer let this be a slave, no longer be pulled by the strings like a puppet to unsocial movements, no longer be either dissatisfied with thy present lot, or shrink from the future. . . .

11. Since it is possible that thou mayest depart from life this very moment, regulate every act and thought accordingly. But to go away from among men, if there are gods, is not a thing to be afraid of, for the gods will not involve thee in evil; but if indeed they do not exist, or if they have no concern about human affairs, what is it to me to live in a universe devoid of gods or devoid of providence? But in truth they do exist, and they do care for human things, and they have put all the means in

man's power to enable him not to fall into real evils. And as to the rest, if there was anything evil, they would have provided for this also, that it should be altogether in a man's power not to fall into it. Now that which does not make a man worse, how can it make a man's life worse? But neither through ignorance, nor having the knowledge but not the power to guard against or correct these things, is it possible that the nature of the universe has overlooked them; nor is it possible that it has made so great a mistake, either through want of power or want of skill, that good and evil should happen indiscriminately to the good and the bad. But death certainly, and life, honor and dishonor, pain and pleasure,—all these things equally happen to good men and bad, being things which make us neither better nor worse. Therefore they are neither good nor evil.

17. Of human life the time is a point, and the substance is in a flux, and the perception dull, and the composition of the whole body subject to putrefaction, and the soul a whirl, and fortune hard to divine, and fame a thing devoid of judgment. And, to say all in a word, everything which belongs to the body is a stream, and what belongs to the soul is a dream and vapor, and life is a warfare and a stranger's sojourn, and after-fame is oblivion. What then is that which is able to conduct a man? One thing, and only one, philosophy. But this consists in keeping the daemon within a man free from violence and unharmed, superior to pains and pleasures, doing nothing without a purpose, nor yet falsely and with hypocrisy, not feeling the need of another man's doing or not doing anything; and besides, accepting all that happens, and all that is allotted, as coming from thence, wherever it is, from whence he himself came; and,

finally, waiting for death with a cheerful mind, as being nothing else than a dissolution of the elements of which every living being is compounded. But if there is no harm to the elements themselves in each continually changing into another, why should a man have any apprehension about the change and dissolution of all the elements? For it is according to nature, and nothing is evil which is according to nature.

This in Carnuntum.[15]

IV.

3. . . . Remember to retire into this little territory of thy own, and above all do not distract or strain thyself, but be free, and look at things as a man, as a human being, as a citizen, as a mortal. But among the things readiest to thy hand to which thou shalt turn, let there be these, which are two. One is that things do not touch the soul, for they are external and remain immovable; but our perturbations come only from the opinion which is within. The other is that all these things, which thou seest, change immediately and will no longer be; and constantly bear in mind how many of these changes thou hast already witnessed. The universe is transformation: life is opinion.

24. Occupy thyself with few things, says the philosopher, if thou wouldst be tranquil.—But consider if it would not be better to say, Do what is necessary, and whatever the reason of the animal which is naturally social requires, and as it requires. For this brings not only the tranquillity which comes from doing well, but also that

[15] Carnuntum was a town of Pannonia, on the south side of the Danube, about thirty miles east of Vindobona (Vienna). Orosius (vii. 15) and Eutropius (viii. 13) say that [Marcus Aurelius] remained three years at Carnuntum during his war with the Marcomanni.

which comes from doing few things. For the greatest part of what we say and do being unnecessary, if a man takes this away, he will have more leisure and less uneasiness. Accordingly, on every occasion a man should ask himself, Is this one of the unnecessary things? Now a man should take away not only unnecessary acts, but also unnecessary thoughts, for thus superfluous acts will not follow after.

27. Either it is a well-arranged universe or a chaos huddled together, but still a universe. But can a certain order subsist in thee, and disorder in the All? And this too when all things are so separated and diffused and sympathetic.

43. Time is like a river made up of the events which happen, and a violent stream; for as soon as a thing has been seen, it is carried away, and another comes in its place, and this will be carried away too.

VI.

44. If the gods have determined about me and about the things which must happen to me, they have determined well, for it is not easy even to imagine a deity without forethought; and as to doing me harm, why should they have any desire towards that? For what advantage would result to them from this or to the whole, which is the special object of their providence? But if they have not determined about me individually, they have certainly determined

Marcus Aurelius—the philosopher as bearer of the *imperium*. (Anderson)

The brutality of conquest. Dramatic reliefs from the Column of Marcus Aurelius showing the rounding up and execution of German prisoners. The full emotion of horror breaks through the classical style of the sculpture. (Anderson)

about the whole at least, and the things which happen by way of sequence in this general arrangement I ought to accept with pleasure and to be content with them. But if they determine about nothing,—which it is wicked to believe, or if we do believe it, let us neither sacrifice nor pray nor swear by them, nor do anything else which we do as if the gods were present and lived with us,—but if however the gods determine about none of the things which concern us, I am able to determine about myself, and I can inquire about that which is useful; and that is useful to every man which is conformable to his own constitution and nature. But my nature is rational and social; and my city and country, so far as I am Antoninus, is Rome, but so far as I am a man, it is the world. The things then which are useful to these cities are alone useful to me.

VIII.

49. Say nothing more to thyself than what the first appearances report. Suppose that it has been reported to thee that a certain person speaks ill of thee. This has been reported; but that thou hast been injured, that has not been reported. I see that my child is sick. I do see; but that he is in danger, I do not see. Thus then always abide by the first appearances, and add nothing thyself from within, and then nothing happens to thee. Or rather add something like a man who knows everything that happens in the world.

XII.

25. Cast away opinion: thou art saved. Who then hinders thee from casting it away?

26. When thou art troubled about anything, thou hast forgotten this, that all things happen according to the universal nature; and forgotten this, that a man's wrongful act is nothing to thee; and further thou hast forgotten this, that everything which happens, always happened so and will happen so, and now happens so everywhere; forgotten this too, how close is the kinship between a man and the whole human race, for it is a community, not of a little blood or seed, but of intelligence. And thou hast forgotten this too, that every man's intelligence is a god and is an efflux of the Deity; and forgotten this, that nothing is a man's own, but that his child and his body and his very soul came from the Deity; forgotten this, that everything is opinion; and lastly thou hast forgotten that every man lives the present time only, and loses only this.

As a review of your reading of Seneca, Epictetus, and Marcus Aurelius, it would be helpful to consider the following questions: What understanding do these philosophers have of the individual and his role in political and social relationships? What is the motive for ethical behavior in Stoicism? What is its sanction? Do traditional Roman values still retain validity for these writers in a greatly changed society? Is there a basis in their writings for a universal morality transcending traditional values?

CHAPTER 5

THE CRISIS OF THE THIRD CENTURY:
The Empire and the Church

At the time of the Roman empire, during the first centuries of our era, religion replaced politics as the problem that was becoming more and more of the first importance to the greatest number of educated people. When political freedom was lost, and all that was wanted by the majority was peace and order, the individual found an expression of his inner life and personal liberty in religion, and he was willing even to lay down his life for his religious convictions—a phenomenon for which it would be hard to find a parallel in the classical age of Greece, though in that age many paid with their lives for their political faith.

Werner Jaeger, Early Christianity and Greek Paideia

Great as was the early Church's spiritual message of hope, evocative as were its doctrines of salvation in the City of God, the remarkable success of Christianity among the atomized masses of the Roman Empire cannot be separated from the earthly security which the tightly organized, communally oriented, Christian groups offered. The new religion of Christianity gave to its members a profound sense of social status and collective involvement as well as a burning message of deferred salvation.

Robert A. Nisbet, The Quest for Community

Formally, the Christian faith was given legal recognition on a par with other cults; in fact, Constantine became a Christian, favoured the Church and took the first steps towards the suppression of pagan cults and the establishment of Christianity, a policy brought to fulfillment under Theodosius at the end of the century. The Church was faced with new opportunities and new dangers. Its morale, kept at a high level by the sternly selective process of persecution (though the early Church must not be idealized), might drop as the faith became fashionable. Other-worldliness might not survive fuller contact with this world, with fuller social responsibility, not to mention ease and wealth. On the other hand, here was the chance to preach and teach on an altogether new scale, to baptize the whole life of the empire whether by the indirect influence of the individual Christians or directly by pressure upon the central organs of the State.

S. L. Greenslade, The Church and the Social Order

Commodus, son of Marcus Aurelius, depicted as Hercules. (Alinari)

The third century was a turning point in the social, political, religious, and intellectual life of Rome. The institutional arrangements of the Principate and the rational perspective from which they were viewed did not survive a century of economic distress and political disintegration. Roman unity was only maintained at a price which changed the basic character of the Empire. It will be our purpose in this chapter to examine the nature of this transformation, to see what effect it had upon men's minds and upon their political institutions and behavior, and to evaluate the role played by the Christian Church in the reorganization of the Empire. Finally we will examine the effect of these changes upon the Church itself.

There were signs of weakness in the imperial structure during the last decades of the era of the "good emperors." Marcus Aurelius had had

to spend most of his time as emperor leading the army on the northern and eastern frontiers against the movement of German tribes which had begun to be a menace in the second century. Whether due to overpopulation and a shortage of food supplies, pressures from other tribes in the interior, the attraction of riches in the Empire, or a combination of all these factors, incursions by German tribes mounted at an increasing rate in the third century and required constant military action by Rome. The cost of the maintenance of legions on the frontier was added to the growing cost of the administrative bureaucracy and constituted a continuous drain on the imperial treasury. These costs were met by more exacting taxation. All of these problems might have been overcome but for a disastrous combination of economic crises and political anarchy in the third century. The sharp cleavage between rich and poor which had characterized all ancient civilizations had not been overcome even in the prosperity of second-century Rome. The wealthy upper classes of the provincial cities provided much of the financial support for the Empire, but they remained few in number. They tended to invest their wealth in land but continued to live in the cities. The countryside of Italy and the provinces thus remained poor and largely untouched by urban civilization. The Italian pattern of large estates extended to the provinces, but absentee ownership, a decline in available slave labor, sporadic military requisitions, and the devastation of war resulted in a steady decline in agricultural production. The drain of precious metal to the East to pay for luxury imports and the debasement of the imperial coinage resulted in inflation.

The accession of Marcus Aurelius' son, Commodus, in A.D. 180 marked the beginning of political disintegration. Commodus was vain and politically incompetent. For twelve years he paid more attention to gladiatorial combat, in which he personally participated, than to the problems of government, and when he was strangled at the connivance of one of his mistresses in 192 the ensuing contest for imperial power resulted in civil war. The army again became the key to imperial politics. Septimius Severus, an able soldier and educated provincial, was able to gain control of the state for himself and his family with the active support of the army. The Severan

Caracalla. (Staatliche Museum of Berlin)

dynasty, which included Septimius (A.D. 193–211), Caracalla (A.D. 211–217), and Severus Alexander (A.D. 222–235), temporarily restored order by rewarding the military with political privileges and successive raises in pay. The imperial administration and equestrian ranks were opened to veterans, many of whom were only recently Romanized Germans. The army, itself, was enlarged to about 400,000, and came to be composed more and more of mercenary soldiers whose loyalty depended upon the government's ability to pay. Despite Severus Alexander's attempt to restore some power to the Senate, the net effect of Severan rule was to deprive the Senate of all functions except the registration of imperial decrees. Privileges won under the Severans made the army an ever more vocal and powerful influence in determining policy and the imperial succession. The two loci of power

in the state were now clearly the army and the bureaucracy.

In 235, German tribes broke through the Rhine defenses. Severus Alexander failed to turn them back and was killed by mutinous troops. For fifty years, factions within the army made and unmade emperors. Civil anarchy in Rome tempted the Goths and other German tribes to raid and plunder all along the European frontier and even into Italy and the western provinces. The eastern provinces were threatened by a revived Persian power, and in 270, were taken over by the rulers of Palmyra, a prosperous city on the caravan routes of Syria and successor to Persian military power in the East. Rivals to the imperial throne appeared in Spain and Gaul. At the same time a plague spread from Egypt to the other provinces, killing perhaps a third of the population in some areas.

An example of the realistic portrait sculpture of the middle of the third century. This life-like rendering of the individuality of its subject caught in a moment of time gave way by the end of the century to stylized, mask-like portraits whose subjects have lost their distinctively human qualities and their place in time. Compare this portrait, and the ones of Cicero (page 71) and Caracalla (page 126), with the one of Constantine (page 161). (Worcester Art Museum)

The complete disintegration of the Empire was prevented by the accession, toward the end of the third century, of strong military emperors. Aurelian (A.D. 270–275), the so-called "Restorer of the World," regained the eastern provinces from Palmyra and defeated the rivals to the throne in Gaul. It was Aurelian who began to build defensive walls around the imperial city. The stability he had gained by force of arms was reinforced by the introduction of the worship of the unconquered sun, *Sol Invictus,* as a formal state cult. An effective reorganization of both the administration and the army was carried out by Diocletian (A.D. 284–305) and his successors. Diocletian was a lower-class general from Illyria (modern Yugoslavia), who was proclaimed emperor by his troops after the death of Aurelian and a rapid succession of rulers. Diocletian began by sharing his military responsibilities with other generals. Within a few years a wholly new system of command had evolved. Diocletian shared the supreme rank of Augustus with another general, Maximian, who supervised the western provinces from Milan in northern Italy. Diocletian retained control of the imperial bureaucracy and exercised military command of the East from Nicomedia in Asia Minor. In 293, Diocletian extended this system to a four-fold division of military command by choosing two Caesars to assist the existing Augusti. The Tetrarchy, as the new system was called, proved a military success against foreign invaders as long as it lasted. Each military commander operated from a fortified base near the frontier, coming to the aid of the others in time of emergency. Nicomedia, Sirmium, Milan, and Trier became, in effect, the capital cities of the Empire.

Diocletian remained the senior partner of the Tetrarchy, calling himself *dominus* or lord, from which derives the name, Dominate, used by historians to refer to the later Empire. Diocletian ruled the administrative machinery of the Empire by fiat and decree, taking advice only from an appointed group of court retainers, the consistory. Full ceremony and rigid etiquette borrowed from oriental kingship surrounded the court. Subjects admitted to an audience with the emperor had to prostrate themselves and kiss the border of the emperor's purple robe. Diocletian called himself the earthly representative of Jupiter, and Maximian, the deputy of Hercules. He was not worshipped as divine, but flatterers often referred to him as a god.

Supporting the emperor was a vast bureaucracy divided into military and civil sections. The praetorian prefect supervised the civil government which was divided into four prefectures, twelve dioceses under vicars, and newly defined and more uniform provinces, which initially numbered ninety-six. The last vestiges of municipal independence were removed when city government became a function of the state bureaucracy. Municipal affairs, especially the collection of taxes, which formerly had been handled either by tax farmers or by bureaucratic officials, became obligatory services laid upon the members (*curiales*) of the town council or curia. Military reorganization followed the same pattern of clearly delimited functions. A frontier force, operating out of fortified villages surrounded by land which the soldiers (mostly Romanized barbarians) farmed themselves, was distinguished from a central professional reserve force—located in cities behind the frontier—ready to march swiftly to any place they might be needed. This basic reorganization of the state formed the institutional basis of the Dominate and lasted in its essential form even beyond the division of the Empire between East and West at the end of the fourth century.

The reforms of Diocletian reflected the changes in the social structure which had resulted from a century of political anarchy, disease, and invasion. The economic weaknesses of the early part of the century were compounded in the later part by inflation which Diocletian tried to curb by fixing prices and reforming the coinage. The urban middle class, and with it, the civic basis of classical culture, was slowly being destroyed by taxation and state regulation. The lower classes in the cities were organized into guilds by the government and were required to render specific services and, when necessary, to pay taxes in kind. The trend away from small-

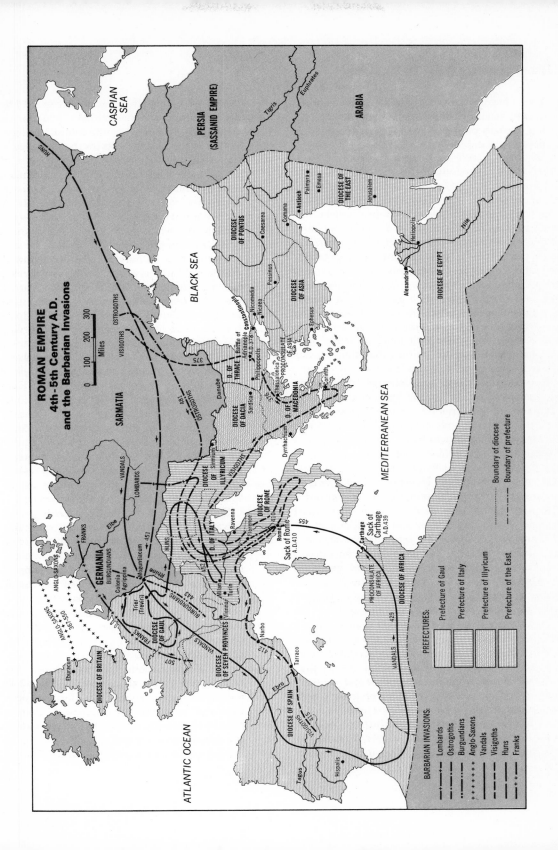

ROMAN EMPIRE
4th-5th Century A.D.
and the Barbarian Invasions

Miles
0   100   200   300

CASPIAN SEA

PERSIA
(SASSANID EMPIRE)

ARABIA

Tigris

Euphrates

DIOCESE OF PONTUS

Caesarea

Comana

Pessinus

Palmyra

Antioch

Emesa

Heliopolis

Jerusalem

Alexandria

DIOCESE OF THE EAST

DIOCESE OF EGYPT

Nile

DIOCESE OF ASIA

Nicomedia

Nicaea

Constantinople

A.D. 378
Battle of
Adrianople

Philippopolis

Ephesus

PROCONSULATE
OF ASIA

Corinth

D. OF THRACE

Danube

DIOCESE OF DACIA

Sardica

D. OF MACEDONIA

Thessalonica

MACEDONIA

Dyrrhachium

BLACK SEA

MEDITERRANEAN SEA

SARMATIA

OSTROGOTHS

VISIGOTHS

375

481

DIOCESE OF ILLYRICUM

Sirmium

VISIGOTHS

Ravenna

Florence

Rome

Sack of Rome
A.D. 410

410

D. OF ITALY

DIOCESE OF ROME

455

Carthage

Sack of Carthage
A.D.439

PROCONSULATE
OF AFRICA

DIOCESE OF AFRICA

429

VANDALS

GERMANIA

LOMBARDS

VANDALS

FRANKS

Elbe

Colonia
Agrippina

Moguntiacum

Rhine

Trier
(Treviri)

BURGUNDIANS

BURGUNDIANS

Milan

Turin

Viennae

451

HUNS

452

443

DIOCESE OF GAUL

FRANKS

DIOCESE OF SEVEN PROVINCES

Narbo

412

507

VANDALS

Tarraco

416

VISIGOTHS

DIOCESE OF SPAIN

Ebro

Tagus

Hispalis

ATLANTIC OCEAN

ANGLO-SAXONS

ANGLO-SAXONS
361-550

Eburacum

DIOCESE OF BRITAIN

HUNS

HUNS

BARBARIAN INVASIONS:
Lombards
Ostrogoths
Burgundians
Anglo-Saxons
Vandals
Visigoths
Huns
Franks

PREFECTURES:
Prefecture of Gaul
Prefecture of Italy
Prefecture of Illyricum
Prefecture of the East

Boundary of diocese
Boundary of prefecture

scale farming was accelerated as peasants sought security on large estates, becoming tenant farmers or serfs working under compulsory burdens of production.

The end result of this development was an unchangeable, firmly crystallized order. All classes, or at least all except the privileged class, were bound to their professions, "the peasant farmer to his land and forced labor, the state-employed worker to his workshop, the trader . . . to his business or his corporation, the small property owner to his duties in connection with the *munera* [obligatory services to the state, such as furnishing animals for the public post], the large property owner to the curia, the soldier to his military service, and so on." The individual no longer lived independently but within the state. He was no longer seen in his natural environment within life's organic groupings, in lively harmony with his surroundings, but as a firmly incorporated immovable part in the cadre of the state. As with the individual, so also with the communities. The municipalities no longer lived within themselves, but in the state; we no longer see them in vigorous self-growth, but firmly incorporated into the great symmetrical order of the state. In contrast to the organic expansion based on the concrete and individual life, so to speak, along an elementary growth line reaching upward from below, we now find an orientation directed downward from above, a higher order descends and is implanted into the elements— "an orientation is imposed from above upon the whole social and economic order." The characteristic feature of this higher order is the uniform simplification, the coordination of equal elements and the crystalline consolidation of the whole. Everywhere the finer social differentiations disappear and the sharp edges and the broad planes of the blocklike mass of the state break through. The rich articulation which distinguished the life of the Principate had been lost forever. The individuals and the natural civic organisms in which

they were grouped, more and more seemed to disappear into the massive and monotonous formations envisioned by the central administration as supporting walls for the Dominate's state structure.

The increasing standardization and equalization of life, the blocklike fusion of the civic organisms, was revealed characteristically in the increasing militarization of society—indeed in the whole way of life. The soldier-emperors' simplification of the government according to a military pattern was followed by a general militarization of the civil service and an assimilation of the civil into martial law. The whole administration of the state was increasingly organized and conceived according to military categories. Civil service was regarded as military service. Every civil servant, from the highest to the lowest, counted as an officer or a soldier. In all *officia* (public office), there are, according to Lactantius, *milites* (soldiers), and their service is a *militia* (war service). The wages for civil officials are *stipendia* (soldier's pay). Subordinate civil servants are *cohortales*, i.e., belonging to a *cohors* (a military detachment). As the civil service was commonly called *militia*, a new name—*militia armata*—had to be invented to distinguish military service.

Such a martial conception regarding civil servants demonstrates that the state demanded the same discipline and obedience of its civil administration as that which was required of the army. Before the highest authority, the *dominus*, every form of protest is silenced. His bidding is a command to be obeyed blindly. The people subordinate themselves, each and every one without exception, *en bloc* to this command. It is this unconditional, mass obedience which suggests the associations with the soldier, the military unit, and thereby with the whole militaristic terminology. Even Christian obedience of the period expresses itself, characteristically enough, in this style; God's servants are *milites Christi*.

This military way of life, which also be-

Reconstruction of Diocletian's Palace at Split on the Dalmatian coast. The palace is a fortress laid out in the form of a Roman army camp. It reflects both the military necessities of the age and the block-like regularity of the social and political order of the Dominate. (Alinari)

comes apparent in the imperial art and architecture of the period, is in the strictest accord with the peculiar pattern of the Dominate. The military aspect of man, that is, exactly the aspect which binds him to rank and file, letting him disappear as a person into a number within a unit, into a solid block, into a sum of uniform elements. Militarization, therefore, marks the basic characteristic in the form structure of the Dominate, in sharp contrast to the earlier Empire. The contrast between the military and the civil orders is just the contrast between mechanical coordination and organic grouping, between the natural formations in free life and a massive alignment in rank and square, between individual, natural motions and movements *en bloc*. Both in community life and in art the large block formations and mass movements now appeared ever more clearly behind the

continually thinning veil of traditional antique forms.[1]

During the Severan period, the anarchy, and the restoration which followed, there were indications of major changes in popular culture. The educated classes still retained much of their admiration for the Greco-Roman heritage, but there had been signs even earlier that philosophy and art were moving away from their rational base to introspection and emotionalism. These changes were most notable in religious life where innumerable pagan cults were joined by the new Christian religion from Palestine and Asia Minor. Consider the following questions

[1] H. P. L'Orange, *Art Forms and Civic Life in the Late Roman Empire* (Princeton, N.J.: Princeton University Press, 1965), pp. 5–8. Reprinted by permission of Princeton University Press. Copyright © 1965 by Princeton University Press.

when reading the next selection: What was the relationship between the social changes of the third century and the proliferation of cultic and mystery religions? What is the function of religion in the maintenance of political consensus and stability? What was the basis for the Roman policy of religious toleration? Why were the Christians persecuted?

PAGANISM AND CHRISTIANITY
A. H. M. Jones[2]

It is impossible to give a coherent account of the paganism of the later Roman empire, for it was not a coherent system. It was a strange amalgam of beliefs and cults from many lands and every stage of culture, ranging from a lofty if rather vague pantheism to the crudest animal worship. It was bound together only by mutual toleration, and indeed respect, and by a strong tendency to syncretism, whereby gods of different lands were identified one with another, and their myths woven together within the general framework of Greek mythology.

The official heads of the pantheon were the state gods of Rome, with whom had long been identified the Greek Olympians. But it may be doubted whether, outside Italy and Greece, their original homes, these gods gave much spiritual solace to their worshippers. The educated classes, it is true, the senatorial and official nobility, and the older and wealthier families of city councillors who formed the provincial aristocracy, had a deep-rooted sentimental attachment to them. They had been brought up on the Greek or Latin classics from childhood, and associated with the

ancient gods their splendid heritage of art and literature and the glorious history of Greece and Rome. But apart from its literary and historical associations, the official pantheon meant little to the later pagan world. The official worship of the emperors, dead and living, had even less religious content. No one really believed that the emperors were gods—no one, for instance, ever prayed to them in sickness or danger for health and safety. Their cult was merely the traditional mode of paying respect to the head of the state, usually a mere form, sometimes a vehicle for a genuine emotion of loyalty to the empire. Most members of the educated aristocracy, while punctiliously performing the old-world ceremonies, and finding in them an aesthetic and nostalgic pleasure, found spiritual consolation, either in philosophy or in one of the more emotional oriental cults.

Philosophy had by this time travelled far from its Greek starting point. It was no longer inspired by intellectual curiosity, but had become fundamentally religious: in the philosophical textbooks of the day it was common to set forth the doctrine as a revelation by a divine sage, such as Hermes the Thrice Greatest, the Egyptian Thoth. The dominant schools of the age, Neo-Platonism and Neo-Pythagoreanism, were dualist systems of belief, which held that matter was evil, the body was a tomb, and that salvation lay in subduing the flesh and contemplating in the purity of the spirit the Godhead, the mysterious One of which the human intellect could predicate nothing. This philosophy was not incompatible with popular religion. The Supreme Godhead was generally conceived as manifesting himself in a series of emanations, and to the vulgar he revealed himself in allegories.

[2] A. H. M. Jones, *Constantine and the Conversion of Europe* (London: Hodder & Stoughton, Ltd. 1948), pp. 29–44. Reprinted by permission of The English Universities Press Limited.

The attitude of the educated to the faith of the masses was thus one of rather condescending reverence. Even the most childish myths and the most beastly rites, not only of Greece and Rome, but of the lower cultures, were regarded as divinely inspired. To the wise, who could penetrate their inner meaning, they were allegorical representations of sublime truths; for the vulgar, who believed in them literally, they were the highest form of the divine truth to which their souls, blinded by the fog of the material world, could attain. Nor was philosophy incompatible with a belief in astrology and magic. The universe moved in one great harmony, and the courses of the sun and the moon and the stars were all part of the same vast movement as the lives of men. The wise man, who had broken free of the trammels of this material universe, could, by his spiritual powers, overcome mere material obstacles: most of the famous philosophers of the day were reputed to be wonder-workers.

At the bottom end of the scale a welter of local cults received the devotion of the peasantry and of the bulk of the urban proletariat, particularly in the smaller cities, whose character was predominantly rural. The Egyptians worshipped their beast-headed gods, and the sacred animals were venerated during their life and on their death solemnly embalmed. In the huge temples multitudes of shaven priests in white linen robes officiated in age-old rituals in an ancient language which they dimly understood. In Syria and in Punic North Africa the villagers and towns-people worshipped a multitude of local Baals and Ashtoreths with fertility rites which shocked Christian ideas of sexual morality. The ritual prostitution at Heliopolis, and more particularly at Apheca,

whose river ran red each year with the blood of the slaughtered Adonis, was later to justify Constantine in closing these two great temples. Farther north lay Emesa, where men worshipped the stone that the Sun God had sent down from heaven, and Doliche, the centre of another meteoric cult, which the legions had carried westwards to the Balkans. In Asia Minor the dominant figures, under a bewildering variety of names, Cybele of Pessinus, Ma of Comana, Artemis of Ephesus, were the Great Mother and her youthful son and consort, in whose honour their frenzied worshippers castrated themselves. Among the Thracians, mounted warrior gods were worshipped, and farther west in Illyricum, the Unconquered Sun was the chief object of devotion. In Celtic lands nature-worship prevailed, and reverence was paid to gods and goddesses of the springs and rivers and forests, and above all to the sun.

By the mass of the peasants and townsmen their gods were conceived as local potentates, the protectors of their village or town. The nomes of Egypt each had their own patron deities, with their appropriate sacred animals, and savage brawls were common, when the inhabitants of a nome which venerated Souchos and regarded crocodiles as sacred killed a hippopotamus, the totem of a neighbouring nome. Even a god or goddess who was worshipped over a wide area was often qualified by a local adjective, and possessed a separate local personality. Many-breasted Artemis of the Ephesians, though she was equated with Artemis of Greek mythology, was the peculiar patroness of Ephesus, and Ephesians abroad would pay their reverence to her, rather than to the local Artemis. But among the more cultured classes local gods were freely identified, often on the slenderest grounds, with figures of the Greek and Roman pantheon, and on inscriptions the local deity is more often than not disguised as Zeus or Jupiter, Aphrodite, Venus or Hercules. In this way the multitudinous and diverse cults of the empire were bound up into some loose semblance of unity. In some more cultivated circles this process of syncretism was carried to its logical conclusion, and all gods and goddesses were regarded as local manifestations, either of the particular god or divine group which they favoured, or, if they were philosophically inclined, of the Ineffable One.

Between the philosophic pantheism of the aristocracy and the local cults of the masses stood the mystery religions. Their appeal lay particularly to the cosmopolitan population of the larger towns, slaves and freedmen who had been cut off from their native cults, traders and merchants and seamen who spent their lives travelling from place to place; and also in the cosmopolitan atmosphere of the army and the civil service, where men from diverse countries mingled. Their main clientele was thus the urban middle and lower classes. They penetrated hardly at all to the rural areas, the villages and small towns, whose inhabitans were for the most part satisfied with their traditional local gods. On the other hand, they made a considerable appeal to the aristocracy, who were no longer emotionally satisfied with the official pantheon, and did not all find an adequate solace in philosophy.

One of the distinctive features of these cults was, as the name given to them implies, that they were secret. Their rites and their theology were only revealed to initiates, often gradually by successive stages of initiation. Another was their interest in a future life: they all, with more or less vagueness, assured to their initiates bliss in some world beyond the grave. All again attempted in some degree to allay the sense of sin. They offered purification, primarily by tabus and ritual acts, although most included some moral teaching. All again were of oriental origin, and owed much of their success to their exotic flavour and to the glamour of ancient learning popularly attributed to the immemorial East.

The oldest-established of these cults in the West was the worship of the Great Mother of Pessinus and her consort Attis. The black stone which was her fetish, accompanied by her Phrygian eunuch priests, had been solemnly conveyed from Pessinus to Rome on the order of the Sibylline books in the dark days of the second Punic war, when the official Roman cults had failed to allay popular alarm and despondency. The senate had, however, been somewhat dismayed by the barbaric and orgiastic character of her ritual, and strictly secluded her worship to her temple on the Palatine; the devotion of the Roman people was given in the western form of annual chariot races. In the reign of Claudius, however, this seclusion was broken, and the worship of the Great Mother began to spread among the populace both of Rome and of the Italian and provincial towns, where it enjoyed a certain prestige above other oriental cults in virtue of its official approbation by the Roman state.

We can reconstruct with some accuracy the ritual of its great spring festival. It opened on 15th March with a procession of the Reed Bearers, which probably commemorated the discovery of the goddess of Attis, who had, like Moses, been exposed on the reedy banks of a river, the Phrygian Sangarius. This day was marked by the sacrifice of a bull. There followed a week

The worship of Isis. A priest clothed in linen emerges from the·temple carrying an urn containing the sacred water of the goddess. The congregation of men and women observe as other priests and priestesses prepare the sacrificial altar. The palm trees and ibises indicate the Egyptian origin of the cult. (Alinari)

of fasting. Then the pine tree which symbolised Attis was cut and decked and a day of mourning followed. The next day, the 24th March, was the Day of Blood, when the devotees of the goddess, working themselves up into a religious frenzy by music and dance, slashed themselves with knives and finally castrated themselves with a flint. A night of watching followed, and on the 25th the resurrection of Attis was celebrated with joyous festivities. Finally, after a day of rest, the statue of the goddess was carried in solemn procession to be bathed in the sea. So much the vulgar crowd saw. For those who wished to penetrate deeper into the inner meaning of the rites, there was a sacramental meal, where the worshippers "ate from the drum, and drank from the cymbal, and became initiate of Attis."

A later arrival in the Latin west, at first banned by the Roman Government, but given official recognition by Caligula, was Isis, with her consort Serapis and their son Horus. The cult was a conflation of Greek and Egyptian elements. The art form of the representations of the Triad in purely human guise, the bearded father, and the mother and child, was Greek. On the other hand, the temples of Isis were built in a more or less Egyptian style, and the priests were vested in the Egyptian manner and made music with the sistrum. The liturgy seems to have been conducted in Greek, but reproduced the daily ritual routine of the Egyptian temples—the opening of the shrine at dawn, the washing and vesting of the god, and so on to the closing of the shrine at sunset. The principal festival of the year occurred in the autumn, and symbolised in dramatic form the myth of the death and dismemberment of Serapis by Typhos, the search by Isis for the fragments of the body and the resurrection of Serapis. The inner meaning of these rites and myths was revealed only by stages to worshippers, who had to pass through three degrees of initiation.

The third and most recent cult was that of the Persian Mithras, which, for long domiciled in eastern Asia Minor, seems first to have migrated westwards late in the first century A.D. Mithras was a god of heavenly light, often identified with the sun, the champion of justice and truth against the dark powers of evil. The chief incident of his career, which is the subject of the majority of Mithraic sculptures, was the slaughter of the bull, from whose body arose all vegetable and animal life useful to man. The faithful passed through seven grades of initiation, becoming in turn Ravens, Bridesmen, Soldiers, Lions, Persians, Runners of the Sun and Fathers. The rites, which were celebrated in caves or crypts, included a sacramental meal of bread and wine and the taurobolium, wherein the worshipper, crouching in a cavity in the floor, was literally washed in the blood of a bull, slaughtered on a grating above, thus acquiring the vital force of the bull whom Mithras had slain for the benefit of mankind. This rite became very popular and was also associated with the cult of the Great Mother.

Some general characteristics of the age require underlining. It was in the first place an intensely religious period. Except among a small coterie of Epicureans, rationalism or scepticism was non-existent. Everyone, from the most highly educated intellectual to the most ignorant peasant and worker, believed intensely in the power of supernatural forces and their interest in human affairs. Men believed that good or ill-fortune depended on the unseen, and sought, according to their temperament and belief, to divine the inevitable future, to constrain the supernatural by magic, to placate the anger of the gods or win their favour, or enter into a communion with the divine which would place them beyond the reach of earthly troubles.

In the second place, the religion of the age was to a great degree other-worldly and escapist. Despairing of true happiness for themselves in this life or of the triumph of peace, justice and prosperity on earth, men turned their thoughts to a future life beyond the grave or to a spiritual life detached from the material world. In the mystery religions, as has been pointed out above, the dominant motif was to seek assurance for a life after death. As Attis was slain and rose again, so those who gained mystic communion with him and learned his secrets would live in blessedness after their earthly death. As Osiris was torn in pieces and brought to life, so those who were instructed in the ancient lore of Egypt would know the password to the world beyond. Souls purified by his mysteries Mithras would escort through the seven planetary spheres to the highest heaven, where they would live forever in eternal light. In philosophical circles there was a strong tendency to regard the material world as inherently evil, and the body "a cloak of darkness, a web of ignorance, a prop of evil, a bond of corruption, a living death, a conscious corpse, a portable tomb." Its adepts sought release from the evils of this world in contemplation of and communion with the Ineffable One.

This is not to say that either religion or philosophy gave no practical moral teaching. The philosophers taught that the soul must be purged of carnal appetites and passions by the practice of virtue in order to attain the purity requisite for contemplating the divine. The doctrine of Mithraism was that the universe was a battleground of the forces of Light and Darkness, Evil and Good, and that worshippers of Mithras must join his fight to attain union with him. In the cult of Isis, too, moral purity was demanded from her worshippers, if they were to hope to be acquitted in the judgment beyond the grave and achieve eternal bliss. Morality was, however, save perhaps in the Mithraic system, regarded as the concern of the individual, a means of purifying his soul and gaining for it full illumination or future blessedness. Neither philosophy nor religion took any interest in social justice, or had any hope or even desire of remedying the evils of the world.

Paganism was scarcely at all organised, and to a very large extent lacked a professional priesthood. Cults were maintained by the Roman state, by villages and by private societies. The Roman state conducted through its magistrates and official priests the worship of the Roman gods. It also exercised a police jurisdiction over all cults, regulating or banning those which it considered inimical to the material, moral or spiritual interests of the empire. But beyond this negative, and very lax, control, the central government did not interfere. The majority of local cults were maintained by the cities of the empire, who appointed their priests and financed them either from the municipal revenues or from special sacred funds and endowments. Villages similarly often had their own temples and priests. The mystery cults were congregational in character. A body of worshippers formed a club, choosing their own priest, and paying for the expenses of worship by subscription.

A full-time professional priesthood existed in Egypt. It was an hereditary body, and its recruitment was regulated by an official of the Roman government, who scrutinised the pedigree and physical fitness of entrants, and examined them in their knowledge of hieroglyphics. He also inspected the temples to ensure that the cult was properly conducted and that the priests devoted the whole of their time to their sacred duties and observed the rules of their order as to shaving their heads and wearing linen garments. It is probable that in the empire-wide cult of Isis, the priesthood was full-time and professional, since the elaborate daily ritual could not otherwise have been maintained, but there is nothing to show that the priests belonged to the Egyptian sacred caste. It is possible that other oriental temples were served by professional priests, and that oriental cults which spread to the West, such as Mithraism, required the full-time services of a regular clergy. But even in widespread cults like those of Isis and of Mithras there was no central authority which laid down doctrine, regulated ritual or authorised the appointment of priests. In the great majority of local cults the priesthoods were filled by local worthies, who combined or alternated their sacred duties with other public offices. Most priests were elected by the local council, either, like most offices, for a year, or, as a special honour, for life: some priesthoods, which carried with them the enjoyment of considerable revenues, were sold by auction; a few were hereditary in the family of the founder of the cult.

Inchoate and unorganised though it was, paganism was very pervasive. Religion was intimately interwoven with public and social life. Sessions of the senate at Rome began with the burning of incense on the altar of Victory, and it is probable that the meetings of city councils opened with some religious service. Magistrates were expected in the course of their duties to make sacrifices to the gods on behalf of their city and to take part in religious processions and celebrations. Practically all public entertainments were festivals in honour of the gods, and theatrical shows, athletic competitions and chariot races were opened with prayers and sacrifices.

All education was based on the study of the ancient poets, and the very themes for composition were drawn from pagan mythology.

Christianity in many ways resembled the mystery religions. The Christians had their Saviour God, Who had died and risen again. They had their degrees of initiation into His mysteries, and they had their secret sacramental meal, in which the inner circle of initiates entered into communion with Him: like the other cults, they organised themselves in congregations, maintaining their priests by subscription. The religion, moreover, appealed to the same social strata as the other mystery cults, to the urban middle and lower classes: it, too, hardly touched the rural masses. With the upper classes it had made less headway than the other mystery cults.

But it had one great difference from the other cults. Its adherents refused to worship the other gods, and even abhorred them as demons. Hence they tended to be exclusive and clannish. They would not attend public festivals or athletic sports or theatrical shows. They even made difficulties about dining out, since most of the meat in the shops had been sacrificed to idols. They avoided joining the army, either because they might, in the course of their military duties, have to attend pagan worship, or because as soldiers of the Lord they could not give their allegiance to a power which they sometimes equated with the Prince of Darkness. For similar reasons their richer members refused to hold office in the cities or sit on the council and subscribe to the needs of the town.

Driven in upon themselves, the Christian communities developed a very strong corporate spirit and a closely knit though flexible organisation. The congregation of each city and its priests and deacons were ruled with absolute authority by a bishop, chosen for life by a rather complicated procedure, which combined approval by the clergy and laity of the town with the assent of neighbouring bishops, one of whom at least had to confer upon the candidate his charismatic grace. The congregations of the various cities had always kept in close touch by correspondence, and it gradually became customary to settle differences of doctrine and discipline by conferences of bishops.

From the beginning the Christians were, like the Jews whom they so much resembled, disliked by their pagan neighbours. They were denounced as atheists, accused of being traitors to the empire, but above all they were hated as peculiar people, who did not join in the social life of their neighbours, but kept themselves to themselves. And since they were disliked, they were popularly believed to indulge in sexual promiscuity at their secret "love feasts" and to practise horrible rites of infant sacrifice. Did not their holy books enjoin upon them to "eat the flesh of the Son of Man and drink His blood"?

Unlike the Jews, the Christians very early, and for reasons which are obscure, incurred the hostility of the imperial government. The two cults had very similar objectionable features, but in the eyes of the Roman government there was one vital difference. The Jews were a race who practised the traditional worship of their ancestors, and had at an early date, while still a political unit, obtained from Rome legal recognition for their peculiar practices. With their great respect for ancestral custom and legal precedent, the Romans therefore tolerated and even privileged Jews. Christians, on the other hand, were innovators, starting a new cult which, on

Anti-Christian graffiti. "Alexamenos worships his god." (Anderson)

the face of it, being devoted to a criminal duly executed by a Roman governor, was undesirable. The government disliked new cults in general as being liable to cause civil disturbances and only too often to introduce immoral practices, and this particular cult was always occasioning riots and lay under grave suspicion of immorality. Whatever the reason, as early as the beginning of the second century Christians who, after due warning, persisted in their cult, were liable to the death penalty.

At first, however, the imperial government took no active steps against the new cult. It was left to informers to denounce Christians, and repressive measures were only sporadically and locally applied, usually under pressure from popular opinion; for the governing classes were in the first

two centuries mainly agnostic, or at any rate did not take religion very seriously. But as during the latter years of the third century religiosity increased in all classes, and as uneducated men of strong religious conviction rose from the lower ranks of society to high administrative or military posts, and to the purple itself, the temper of the government changed. The civil wars and barbarian invasions, the famines and plagues, were surely a sign that the gods were angry with the empire. And it was not difficult to discern the reason for their anger: the number of atheists who refused them worship was steadily growing.

It was the soldier emperor Decius who in 250 made the first systematic attempt to enforce the universal worship of the gods and thus to extirpate Christianity. By his orders all inhabitants of the empire had to sacrifice to the gods before the authorities and obtain certificates that they had done so. The apparent success of this measure was spectacular: thousands of Christians, particularly those in the upper classes who could less easily evade the order, submitted. But very many went into hiding, and a substantial number defied the government, braving imprisonment, torture and death. The courage of the confessors and martyrs roused the enthusiasm of the Christians and impressed the pagans, and so soon as the persecution waned, those who had lapsed petitioned the bishops to be readmitted. Seven years later the emperor Valerian renewed the attack on other lines, ordering the arrest of members of the senatorial and equestrian orders and imperial freedmen who refused to sacrifice, and first deporting and later executing all bishops and priests, and forbidding religious meetings. But Valerian was soon afterwards taken prisoner by the Persians, and his son Gallienus not only released the clergy, but restored their buildings and cemeteries to the churches.

During the intermittent persecutions of the first half of the third century, Christian communities continued to multiply and grow. Christians also began to respond to the arguments advanced against them by their persecutors. Particularly as members of the educated classes accepted the faith, it was natural that they should attempt to get their position better understood by intelligent pagans. The result was a series of apologies designed to counter charges made against them and to assure the Roman authorities that Christians were not in fact seditious and unpatriotic. Among the best known of the apologists was Tertullian (ca. 155–225), a native of Carthage in northern Africa. He had apparently practiced law as an advocate for some time in Rome, for when he was converted

to Christianity, he brought legal language and a mastery of rhetorical pleading into the church. Tertullian was the first Christian theologian to write in Latin, and his vigorously polemical style was a challenge to pagan and Christian alike. When reading his *Apology*, written about 197, consider the following questions: What attitude does Tertullian take toward the Roman state and society? What is the Christian's role in this society? What picture do you get in the *Apology* of the Christian community?

APOLOGY
Tertullian[3]

I. . . . This, . . . is the first plea we lodge with you—the injustice of your hatred of the Christian name. The very excuse that seems to acquit it, at once aggravates and convicts that injustice—to wit, ignorance. For what could be more unjust than for men to hate a thing they do not know, even though it really deserves hatred? It can only deserve hatred when it is known whether it does deserve it. But so long as nothing at all is known of its deserts, how can you defend the justice of the hatred? That must be established, not on the bare fact of its existence, but on knowledge. . . .

II. But now, if it is really certain that we are of all men the most criminal, why do you yourselves treat us otherwise than those like us, the rest of the criminal classes, when the same treatment belongs to the same fault? Whatever you charge against us, when you so charge others, they use their own eloquence, they hire the advocacy of others, to prove their in-

---

[3] Reprinted by permission of the publishers and The Loeb Classical Library from T. R. Glover, translator, Tertullian, *Apology* (Cambridge, Mass.: Harvard University Press, 1931), pp. 5, 9, 13–15, 23–25, 37–39, 47, 53–57, 147–149, 153–161, 173–179, 187–189, 195, 227.

nocence. There is freedom to answer, to cross-question, since in fact it is against the law for men to be condemned, undefended and unheard. But to Christians alone it is forbidden to say anything to clear their case, to defend Truth, to save the judge from being unjust. No! one thing is looked for, one alone, the one thing needful for popular hatred—the confession of the name. Not investigation of the charge! . . .

Then, again, in that matter, you do not deal with us in accordance with your procedure in judging criminals. If the other criminals plead Not guilty, you torture them to make them confess; the Christians alone you torture to make them deny. . . .

A man shouts, "I am a Christian." He says what he is. You, sir, wish to hear what he is *not*. Presiding to extort the truth, you take infinite pains in our case, and ours alone, to hear a lie. "I am," says he, "what you ask if I am; why torture me to twist the fact round? I confess, and you torture me. What would you do if I denied?" Clearly, when others deny, you do not readily believe them; if we have denied, you at once believe us.

IV. So much, then, by way of preface as it were, to assail the injustice that is in the general hatred felt for us. Now I will take my stand on the plea of our innocence. I will not only refute the charges brought against us, but I will turn them against those who bring them; so that, in this too, all may learn that they will not find in Christians what they are unaware of in themselves, and that at the same time they may blush to accuse—no, I will not say that the worst of men are accusing the best, but I will put it, as they would wish, and say—their equals. We will reply in detail as to the crimes we are alleged to commit in secret, but which we find them openly committing—matters in which we are set down as guilty, empty-headed, damnable, ridiculous.

VII. We are said to be the most criminal of men, on the score of our sacramental baby-killing and the baby-eating that goes with it and the incest that follows the banquet, where the dogs are our pimps in the dark, forsooth, and make a sort of decency for guilty lusts by overturning the lamps. That, at all events, is what you always say about us; and yet you take no pains to bring into the daylight what you have been saying about us all this long time. Then, I say, either bring it out, if you believe all this, or refuse to believe it after leaving it uninvestigated. Your habit of looking the other way constitutes a demurrer in the case, a presumption that the thing is not there at all, which not even you yourselves dare to try to bring out. It is quite a different task that you enjoin on the executioner against the Christians—not to make them say what they do, but deny what they are.

IX. To refute these charges still further, I will show that these very things are done by you, sometimes openly, sometimes in secret, and that perhaps is the reason for your having believed them about us also.

In Africa infants used to be sacrificed to Saturn, and quite openly, down to the proconsulate of Tiberius, who took the priests themselves and on the very trees of their temple, under whose shadow their crimes had been committed, hung them alive like votive offerings on crosses; and the soldiers of my own country are witnesses to it, who served that proconsul in that very task. Yes, and to this day that holy crime persists in secret. Christians are not the only people who defy you; no crime is ever wholly rooted out; nor does any of your gods change his ways. . . .

Then again who are more incestuous than the disciples of Jupiter? The Persians according to Ctesias consort with their mothers. And the Macedonians are suspected of it too, because when first they heard the tragedy of *Oedipus*, they laughed at his grief for the incest: "he lay with Jocasta," they said. . . .

From such an event we are guarded by a chastity, supremely careful and faithful; we are safe from random intercourse and from all excess after marriage, and in that degree from the risk of incest. Some indeed, in a much greater security, guard themselves against the violence of this sin by a virgin continence, old in years but still children. If you would realize that these sins are found among yourselves, you would see that they are not to be found among the Christians. The same eyes would assure you of both facts. But two sorts of blindness easily meet, so that those, who do not see what is really there, seem to see what is not. So in all the points at issue, as I will show you. But now of our more conspicuous crimes!

X. "You do not," say you "worship the gods; you do not offer sacrifice for the Emperors." It follows by parity of reasoning that we do not sacrifice for others because we do not for ourselves—it follows from our not worshipping the gods. So we are accused of sacrilege and treason at once. That is the chief of the case against us— the whole of it, in fact; and it in any case deserves investigation, unless the judgement is to be given by prejudice or injustice, the one despairing of the truth, the other refusing it. Your gods, then, we cease to worship, from the moment when we recognize that they are not gods. . . .

"But they are gods for us," you say. Here we lodge an appeal, and carry the case from you to your conscience. Let your conscience judge us, let it condemn us, if it can deny that all these gods of yours were once men. But if your conscience shall contest the point against us, it shall be refuted from the ancient books from which it learnt the gods; and testimony is also given to this day by the cities in which the gods were born, and by the regions in which they left traces of anything they did,—yes, and in which they were demonstrably buried. And now—am I to run over them in detail, in all their number and greatness, new gods and old, barbarian, Greek, Roman, foreign, captive, adoptive, private, public, male, female, rustic, urban, naval, military? It would be idle to list even their titles to make a compendium of them; it would not give you new information but would merely remind you. . . .

XXVIII. . . . So now we have come to the second charge, the charge of treason against a majesty more august. For it is with greater fear and shrewder timidity that you watch Caesar, than Olympian Jove himself. Quite right too, if you only knew it! For who among the living, whoever he be, is not better than a dead man? But it is not reason that makes you do this so much as regard for power that can act on the instant. So that in this too you will be found irreligious to those gods of yours, when you show more fear for the rule of a man. In fact, among you perjury by all the gods together comes quicker than by the genius of a single Caesar.

XXXI. You, sir, then, who fancy we care nothing for Caesar's safety, look into the words of God, into our books, which we do not hide, and which many a chance throws into the hands of outsiders. Learn from them, that the precept is given us (to the point of overflow of kindness) to pray to God even for our enemies, to beseech His blessings for our persecutors. Who are more the enemies and the persecutors of Christians, than those against whose majesty we are accused of treason? But here it is explicitly named and in plain terms. "Pray," he says "for kings, and for princes and powers, that all things may be tranquil for you." For when the empire is shaken, when the rest of its members are shaken, we, too, of course, though we are supposed not to have anything to do with the disorder, are found in some corner of the disaster.

XXXII. There is another need, a greater one, for our praying for the Emperors, and for the whole estate of the empire and the interests of Rome. We know that the great force which threatens the whole world, the end of the age itself with its menace of hideous suffering, is delayed by the respite which the Roman empire means for us. We do not wish to experience all that; and when we pray for its postponement are helping forward the continuance of Rome.

XXXIII. But why need I say more of the religious awe, the piety, of Christians, where the Emperor is concerned? We must needs respect him as the chosen of our Lord. So I have a right to say, Caesar is more ours than yours, appointed as he is by our God. . . .

XXXIV. . . . Augustus, who framed the empire, was unwilling to be called so much as Lord [*Dominus*]; for that also is a name of God. I will frankly call the Emperor Lord, but only in the ordinary way, but only when force is not brought to bear on me to call him Lord in the sense of God. But I am a free man as far as the Emperor is concerned; for my Lord is One, God omnipotent, eternal, who is also the Emperor's Lord. He who is "Father of his Country," how is he its *lord*? But there is more pleasure in the name of affection than in the name of power. Even in the family we say *paterfamilias* rather than lord. So far is it from being right for the Emperor to be called god,—a name incredible save in flattery not merely abject but injurious.

XXXV. So that is why Christians are public enemies,—because they will not give the Emperors vain, false and rash honours; because, being men of a true religion, they celebrate the Emperors' festivals more in heart than in frolic. . . .

XXXVIII. . . . Your public games . . . we renounce, as heartily as we do their

Catacomb inscription. A man praying with outstretched arms, the dove of baptism, and the Chi-Rho monogram of Christ. (Alinari)

origins; we know these origins lie in superstition; we leave on one side the matters with which they are concerned. We have nothing to do, in speech, sight or hearing, with the madness of the circus, the shamelessness of the theatre, the savagery of the arena, the vanity of the gymnasium.

XXXIX. I will now show you the proceedings with which the Christian association occupies itself; I have proved they are not wrong; so now I will make you see they are good. We have a society (*corpus*) with a common religious feeling, unity of discipline, a common bond of hope. We meet in gathering and congregation to approach God in prayer, massing our forces to surround Him. This violence that we do Him pleases God. We pray also for Emperors, for their ministers and those in authority, for the security of the world, for peace on earth, for postponement of the end. We meet to read the books of God—if anything in the nature of the times bids us look to the future or open our eyes to facts. In any case, with those holy words we feed our faith, we lift up our hope, we confirm our confidence; and no less we reinforce our teaching by inculcation of God's precepts. There is, besides, exhortation in our gatherings, rebuke, divine censure. For judgement is passed, and it carries great weight, as it must among men certain that God sees them; and it is a notable foretaste of judgement to come, if any man has so sinned as to be banished from all share in our prayer, our assembly, and all holy intercourse. Our presidents are elders of proved character, men who have reached this honour not for a price, but by character; for nothing that is God's goes for a price.

Even if there is a chest of a sort, it is not made up of money paid in entrance-fees, as if religion were a matter of contract. Every man once a month brings some modest coin—or whenever he wishes, and only if he does wish, and if he can; for nobody is compelled; it is a voluntary offering. You might call them the trust funds of piety. For they are not spent upon banquets nor drinking-parties nor thankless eating-houses; but to feed the poor and to bury them, for boys and girls who lack property and parents, and then for slaves grown old and shipwrecked mariners; and any who may be in mines, islands or prisons, provided that it is for the sake of God's school, become the pensioners of their confession.

Such work of love (for so it is) puts a mark upon us, in the eyes of some. "Look," they say, "how they love one another" (for themselves hate one another); "and how they are ready to die for each other" (for themselves will be readier to kill each other). Yes, their indignation at us for using among ourselves the name of "Brothers" must really, I take it, come from nothing but the fact that among them every name of kinship as far as affection goes is false and feigned. But we are your brothers, too, by right of descent from the one mother, Nature—even if you fall short of being men because you are bad brothers. But how much more fittingly are those both called brothers and treated as brothers who have come to know one Father God, who have drunk of one Spirit of holiness, who from one womb of common ignorance have come with wonder to the one light of Truth! But perhaps the reason for our being thought not quite legitimate brothers may be that no tragedy cries aloud of our brotherhood, or because our brotherhood is upheld by the family substance, which among you as a rule dissolves the fraternal tie.

So we, who are united in mind and soul, have no hesitation about sharing property. All is common among us—except our wives. At that point we dissolve our partnership, which is the one place where the rest of men make it effective. Not only do they use the wives of their friends, but also most patiently yield their own to their friends. They follow (I take it) the example of those who went before them, the wisest of men—Greek Socrates and Roman Cato, who shared with their friends the wives they had taken in marriage, to bear children in other families too. And I don't know whether the wives objected; for why should they care about a chastity, which their husbands gave away so easily? O model of Attic wisdom! O pattern of Roman dignity! The philosopher a pander, and the censor, too!

XL. . . . If we compare ancient disasters, the troubles nowadays are lighter, since the world received the Christians from God. Since that day innocence has tempered the sins of the world, and there have begun to be intercessors with God. . . .

XLI. It is you, then, who are the danger to mankind, it is you who bring upon us public misfortunes—you, by your contempt for God and your worship of statues. In any case it ought to be more credible that He is angry, seeing that He is neglected rather than they who are worshipped. Otherwise, your gods are most unjust, if because of the Christians they injure their own worshippers too, whom they ought to keep clear of the punishment of the Christians.

"But this," you say, "can be retorted upon your God too, since He Himself because of the profane suffers His own worshippers to be injured." First admit His disposition of events, and then you will not turn this against Him. For He who has ordained eternal judgement once for all after the end of the world does not hasten to make that separation (which is the essence of the judgement) before the end of the world. Meantime He treats all mankind equally, both in concession and in warning. He has wished the pleasant things of life to be shared by the profane, the unpleasant by His own, that by an equality of lot we might make trial of His gentleness and His severity. Because we have thus learnt of Him, we love His gentleness, we dread His severity; you, on the other hand, despise both the one and the other. It follows that all the plagues of the world (it may be) come on us for admonition, on you for chastisement, from God.

Yet we are none the worse for it; first, because nothing matters to us in this age but to escape from it with all speed; and next, because, if any trouble is inflicted upon us, we set it down to your sins. But, even if things now and then touch us in passing because we live so close to you, we only rejoice the more to recognize the divine predictions, and they (to be sure) confirm our confidence, our faith in our hope. . . .

XLV. We, then, alone are innocent. What is surprising in that, if it must be so? And it must be. Innocence we have been taught by God; in its perfection we know it, as revealed by a perfect teacher; faithfully we keep it as committed to us by one who reads the heart and cannot be despised.

L. But go to it! my good magistrates; the populace will count you a deal better, if you sacrifice the Christians to them. Torture us, rack us, condemn us, crush us; your cruelty only proves our innocence. That is why God suffers us to suffer all this. . . . There is a rivalry between God's ways and man's; we are condemned by you, we are acquitted by God.

The first and most immediate problem of the Christian Church was popular hostility and official persecution. A second was its own internal development. By the third century the Church had begun to take on some of the characteristics of an organized and continuing institution. This institutional structure, however weak by later standards, helped the church to survive the persecutions of the third century and to maintain some uniformity of belief. But before discussing this structure it would be helpful to consider the problem of institutionalization in general. It has been suggested by many scholars that this problem is inherent in all nontraditional religions. These religions, while based on a spontaneous response to the ultimate and the sacred, must embody this experience in symbolic and organizational structures which are less than ultimate; they are imperfect and worldly. The result is a dilemma for the religious movement which is unavoidable and can never be fully resolved. The following article by a sociologist of religion indicates several aspects of this problem.

Five Dilemmas in the Institutionalization of Religion
Thomas F. O'Dea[4]

It is the great virtue of social institutions from the point of view of the functioning of social systems that they provide stability in a world of inconstancy. The unusual and creative performance of the hero, sage or saint, though of great exemplary and genetic importance, is too unpredictable to become the basis of everyday life. The human world would be an unsteady and incalculable affair indeed were it chiefly dependent upon such phenomena. Yet the achievement of the necessary stability involves a price. It involves a certain loss of spontaneity and creativity, although these are often found operating in some measure

[4] Thomas F. O'Dea, "Five Dilemmas in the Institutionalization of Religion," *Journal for the Scientific Study of Religion*, I, No. 1 (1961), 32–38. Reprinted by permission.

within the expectations of institutional patterns.

The founded religions display this fundamental antinomy in their histories. They begin in "charismatic moments" and proceed in a direction of relative "routinization." This development necessary to give objective form to the religious movement and insure its continuity may in Weber's terms proceed either in a traditional or a rational-legal direction. Such routinization is an unavoidable social process, and as such represents for religious institutions a many-sided and complex paradox.

The charismatic moment is the period of the original religious experience and its corresponding vitality and enthusiasm. Since . . . this experience involves the deep engagement of the person involved with a "beyond" which is sacred, it is unusual in a special sense. It would remain a fleeting and impermanent element in human life without its embodiment in institutional structures to render it continuously present and available. Yet in bringing together two radically heterogeneous elements, ultimacy and concrete social institutions, the sacred and the profane, this necessary institutionalization involves a fundamental tension in which five functional dilemmas take their origin.

In other words, religion both needs most and suffers most from institutionalization. The subtle, the unusual, the charismatic, the supraempirical must be given expression in tangible, ordinary, and empirical social forms. Let us now examine the five dilemmas which express this fundamental antinomy inherent in the relation of religion to normal social processes.

(1) THE DILEMMA OF MIXED MOTIVATION

In the pre-institutionalized stage of a religious movement, the classical type of which is the circle of disciples gathered about a charismatic leader, the motivation of the followers is characterized by single-mindedness. The religious movement does satisfy complex needs for its adherents, but it focuses their satisfaction upon its values and their embodiment in the charismatic leader. The charismatic call receives a wholehearted response. With the emergence of a stable institutional matrix, there arises a structure of offices—of statuses and roles—capable of eliciting another kind of motivation, involving needs for prestige, expression of teaching and leadership abilities, drives for power, aesthetic needs, and the quite prosaic wish for the security of a respectable position in the professional structure of the society. . . .

This dilemma of mixed motivation is found not only among those who occupy important positions in the religious organization. It is also characteristic of changes in the composition of the membership with the passing of the charismatic movement and the founding generation. The passing of the founding generation means that the religious body now contains people who have not had the original conversion experience. Many are born members and their proportion increases with the years. The selection process which voluntary conversion represented often kept out of the organization precisely the kinds of persons who are now brought up within it. Already in the year 150 A.D., Hermas in *The Shepherd* draws a most unflattering picture of some of the lukewarm "born Christians" in the Church.

(2) THE SYMBOLIC DILEMMA: OBJECTIFICA-
    TION VERSUS ALIENATION

Man's response to the holy finds expression not only in community but also in acts of worship. Worship is the fundamental religious response but in order to survive its charismatic moment worship must become stabilized in established forms and procedures. This ritual develops, presenting to the participant an objectified symbolic order of attitude and response to which he is to conform his own interior disposition. Worship becomes something not immediately derivative of individual needs, but rather an objective reality imposing its own patterns upon the participants.

Such objectification is an obvious prerequisite for common and continuous worship, for without it prayer would be individual and ephemeral. The symbolic elements of worship are not simply expressions of individual response, but have an autonomy enabling them to pattern individual response. Yet here too the element of dilemma appears. The process of objectification, which makes it possible for cult to be a genuine social and communal activity, can proceed so far that symbolic and ritual elements become cut off from the subjective experience of the participants. A system of religious liturgy may come to lose its resonance with the interior dispositions of the members of the religious body. In such a case the forms of worship become alienated from personal religiosity, and whereas previously cult had evoked and patterned response and molded personal religiosity after its own image, now such an overextension of objectification leads to routinization. Liturgy then becomes a set of counters without symbolic impact upon the worshippers. It may of course retain its element of sacredness through the very fact of its obscurity and mystery, a situation conducive to the development of a semi-magical or magical attitude. . . .

The alienation of symbolism is one of the most important religious developments and its possibility and likelihood derives from the fact that the religious symbol is in itself an antinomy—an expression *par excellence* of the dilemma of institutionalizing religion. To symbolize the transcendent is to take the inevitable risk of losing the contact with it. To embody the sacred in a vehicle is to run the risk of its secularization. Yet if religious life is to be shared and transmitted down the generations the attempt must be made. . . .

(3) THE DILEMMA OF ADMINISTRATIVE ORDER: ELABORATION VERSUS EFFECTIVENESS

Max Weber showed that charismatic leadership soon undergoes a process of routinization into a traditional or rational-legal structure made up of a chief and an administrative staff. There is an elaboration and standardization of procedures and the emergence of statuses and roles within a complex of offices. One important aspect is the development in many cases of a distinction between the office and its incumbent, which has become characteristic of the bureaucratic structures of the modern world. The Catholic Church has been the chief prototype in this evolution of the concept of office in European society.

It is characteristic of bureaucratic structure to elaborate new offices and new networks of communication and command in the face of new problems. Precedents are established which lead to the precipitation of new rules and procedures. One result may indeed be that the structure tends to complicate itself. This state of affairs evolves in order to cope with new problems effectively. Yet such self-complication can overextend itself and produce an unwieldy organization with blocks and breakdowns in communication, overlapping of spheres of competence, and ambiguous definitions of authority and

related functions. . . . Weber noted that bureaucracy of the rational-legal type was the most effective means for rational purposeful management of affairs. Yet the word bureaucracy has not become a pejorative epithet in the folklore of modern western societies for nothing. The tendency of organization to complicate itself to meet new situations often transforms it into an awkward and confusing mechanism within whose context it is difficult to accomplish anything. . . .

(4) THE DILEMMA OF DELIMITATION: CONCRETE DEFINITION VERSUS SUBSTITUTION OF LETTER FOR SPIRIT

In order to affect the lives of men, the import of a religious message must be translated into terms that have relevance with respect to the prosaic course of everyday life. This translation is first of all a process of concretization. It involves the application of the religious insight to the small and prosaic events of ordinary life as lived by quite ordinary people. In that process the religious ideas and ideals themselves may come to appear to be of limited prosaic significance. Concretization may result in finitizing the religious message itself. For example, ethical insights are translated into a set of rules. Since rules, however elaborate, cannot make explicit all that is implied in the original ethical epiphany, the process of evolving a set of rules becomes a process of delimiting the import of the original message. Translation becomes a betraying transformation. Moreover, the more elaborate the rules become in the attempt to meet real complexities and render a profound and many-sided ethic tangible and concrete, the greater the chance of transforming the original insight into a complicated set of legalistic formulae and the development of legalistic rigorism. Then, as St. Paul put it, the letter killeth but the spirit giveth life.

Yet the fact is that the ethical insight must be given some institutionalized concretization or it will remain forever beyond the grasp of the ordinary man. The high call of the ethical message may well, however, be reduced to petty conformity to rules in the process. . . .

(5) THE DILEMMA OF POWER: CONVERSION VERSUS COERCION

The religious experience exercises a call. In Otto's words, its content "shows itself as something uniquely attractive and *fascinating*." Moreover, the propagation of the religious message in Christianity has involved an invitation to interior change. This interior "turning" or "conversion" is the classical beginning of the religious life for the individual. With institutionalization of the religious movement, such a conversion may be replaced by the socialization of the young so that a slow process of education and training substitutes for the more dramatic conversion experience. . . .

. . . As religion becomes institutionalized it becomes a repository of many of the values from which much of the life of the society derives its legitimation. Thus the preservation of religious beliefs and even the maintenance of the religious organization can come to be intertwined with societal problems of public order and political loyalty. This tends to become the case whether or not there is a legal separation of church and state.

In addition, since religion is dependent upon interior disposition and since that disposition is subject to numerous unexpected shocks and is always weak among those merely nominally religious, there is always the subtle temptation for religious leaders to avail themselves of the close relation between religion and cultural values in order to reinforce the position of religion itself. A society may find itself unable to tolerate religious dissent, since such dissent is seen as threatening the consensus upon which social solidarity rests. Religious leaders may be tempted to utilize the agencies of a society so disposed to reinforce the position of their own organization.

While such an interpenetration of religious adherence and political loyalty may strengthen the position of religion in the society, it may also weaken it in important respects. It may antagonize members of the religious body who are political oppositionists, and it may antagonize political oppositionists who otherwise might have remained religiously neutral. Second it may produce an apparent religiosity beneath which lurks a devastating cynicism. . . .

A genuine dilemma is involved. Religion cannot but relate itself to the other institutions of society since religious values must be worked out to have some relation to the other values of a particular cultural complex. Since religion is concerned with ultimate values which legitimate other values and institutions, a relation with established authority and power structures is unavoidable. Such partial identification of basic values in religion and culture tends to strengthen both religious conformity and political loyalty. Yet with the progressive differentiation of society, the confusion of the two soon tends to be detrimental to both. It weakens the bonds of the religious community by weakening voluntary adherence and thereby diluting the religious ethos and substituting external pressures for interior conviction. It weakens the general society by narrowing the possibility of consensus among the population by insisting on a far greater area of value agreement than would in fact be necessary to the continued life of society. Yet some relation between the functionally necessary values in a society and the ultimate sanction of religion is necessary and it necessarily involves a relation between religious institutions and power and authority structures. . . .

These five dilemmas represent five sides of the central dilemma involved in the institutionalization of religion, a dilemma which involves transforming the religious experience to render it continuously available to the mass of men and to provide for it a stable institutionalized context. The nature of the religious experience tends to be in conflict with the requisites and characteristics of the institutionalization process and the resultant social institutions. From this incompatibility there derive the special problems of the functioning of religious institutions delineated in this paper. Some of these antinomies have their analogues in other social institutions. Yet there is reason to suspect that because of the unique character of the religious experience, its elements of incompatibility with institutionalization are more exaggerated than is the case with other areas of human activity. . . .

The organization of the earliest Christian churches had been based on the Jewish synagogue. Presbyters, analogous to the elders of the synagogue, exercised a judicial and administrative function within the community, establishing an internal discipline distinct from the jurisdiction of the state. There were also leaders, holy men, recognized because of their special spiritual powers, but no particular office was assigned to them. Christianity with its claim to universality, however, had, in addition to the problems of local organization, an ideal of a unity of belief and practice—a unity expressed in the words of St. Paul (Eph. 4:3–6):

> Spare no effort to make fast with bonds of peace the unity which the spirit gives. There is one body and one Spirit, as there is also one hope held out in God's call to you; one Lord, one faith, one baptism; one God and Father of all, who is over all and through all and in all.

Despite this ideal there had been dissensions within and among the various Christian communities which the apostles, travelling from church to church, labored hard to overcome. The churches at Ephesus, Corinth, and Rome, for example, to which Paul addressed his letters, had little formal organization of their own and no central organization uniting them, except perhaps a general recognition of Jerusalem as the mother Church.

A pattern of organization for each individual community had begun to emerge, however, by the end of the second century. The Christian congregations in most urban areas had coalesced under the leadership of a single head, or bishop. The bishop was the only authoritative minister of baptism and the eucharist, and was the person responsible for the welfare of the entire community. Presbyters continued to be recognized as the officers of the Church. They advised the bishop, sometimes acted as teachers and assisted the bishop in his pastoral duties. The official recognition of presbyters as special assistants to the bishop was the origin of the Christian priesthood. Officers called deacons, of lesser status than presbyters, also assisted the bishop, most frequently in the holy offices of worship.

The bishop was the primary unifying agent of the early Church. Cyprian, the third-century bishop of Carthage, stated the claims of the episcopate in uncompromising terms:

> The episcopate is one; the individual members have each a part, and the parts make up the whole. The Church is a unity . . . the

Church is made up of the people united to their priest as the flock that cleaves to the shepherd. Hence you should know that the bishop is in the Church and the Church in the bishop, and that if any one be not with the bishop he is not in the Church . . . the Church is one and may not be rent or sundered, but should assuredly be bound together and united by the glue of the priests who are in harmony one with another.[5]

Cyprian's claim that the unity of the Church rested upon the solidarity of the episcopate as a whole was not far from the actual situation of the third century. While an individual community could select its own bishop, his office was not considered valid until he had been consecrated by a neighboring bishop or group of bishops. The spiritual authority of the priesthood was thus conceived to be transmitted in a continuous line from the apostles. Each bishop at first exercised full powers within his own area (called a see). The occasional meeting of the bishops of a province to decide on matters of doctrine and discipline was the only form of central organization then in existence. The bishops of the provincial capitals, called metropolitans, who presided at these meetings, however, acquired a certain prestige and often exercised authority over the local bishops in their area. Increasingly,

> . . . the ecclesiastical organisation tended to model itself on the civil, and when Diocletian grouped the provinces into dioceses, the cities where the deputy prefects resided became the natural centres for larger meetings, and their bishops acquired a certain authority over the other metropolitans of the diocese. Carthage was recognized as the ecclesiastical capital of Africa, and Antioch of the Orient, except Egypt, where Alexandria occupied an exceptional position; for by analogy with the centralized system which till Diocletian's reforms prevailed in the civil government, its bishop

nominated every bishop in the country. Rome exercised a similar jurisdiction over the suburbicarian diocese of southern Italy and the islands; it had long, whether as the capital of the empire or the see of Peter, enjoyed an undefined primacy throughout the Roman world.[6]

However, the claim made by the bishop of Rome that, as the successor to the apostle Peter, he had a right to settle disputes and decide matters of doctrine was not recognized until late in the fourth century, and then only by some bishops in the West.

Perhaps the surest sign of the institutional development of the Church was the appearance of reactions against this process from within the Christian community itself. Despite the institutionalization of the Church, prophetic voices which claimed to be under the direct influence of the Holy Spirit continued to be heard. One such prophet who gained a considerable following in Asia Minor and in northern Africa was a man named Montanus. The Montanists believed in the imminence of the apocalypse, the continuation of revelation through ecstatic prophecy, and the maintenance of a strict standard of Christian living. The most illustrious convert to Montanism was Tertullian. While he remained orthodox in most aspects of doctrine and rejected much of the ecstatic quality of Montanism as it had originated in the East, Tertullian found in it an assurance that the Holy Spirit was still active in a church growing rigid in organization and doctrine. His most often quoted statement reveals a profound suspicion of the attempts being made in his time to define the Christian faith in terms borrowed from Greek rationalist philosophy.[7]

> What has Atnens to do with Jerusalem? What concord is there between the Academy and the Church? . . . Our instruction comes from

---

[5] Cyprian, *On the Unity of the Catholic Church*, 5; *Epistle*, LXVI, 7, in S. Wolin, *Politics and Vision* (Boston: Little, Brown & Company, 1960), p. 108.

[6] Jones, *Constantine and the Conversion of Europe*, p. 45.

[7] These developments are treated in the next chapter.

the Porch of Solomon who taught that the Lord should be sought in simplicity of heart. Away with all attempts to produce a mottled Christianity of Stoic, Platonic and dialectic composition. We want no curious disputation after possessing Christ Jesus. . . .[8]

Tertullian brought to Montanism an acute opposition to both religious and philosophical paganism and also an exaggerated admiration for martyrdom, both of which attitudes were already in evidence in his earlier writings, such as the *Apology*. The asceticism which Tertullian enjoined continued to have a strong appeal within the Christian tradition, but the apocalyptic movement which inspired it was condemned by the Church. The Montanist books of prophecy were ordered burned by some bishops because they claimed to supersede the New Testament books. The bishops thus excluded the possibility

[8] *Treatise Against the Heretics*, vii, in M. C. D'Arcy, et al., *St. Augustine* (New York: Meridian Books, Inc., 1957), p. 53.

of new revelation by closing the canon of scripture. Montanism was proscribed as heretical at the first recorded gathering of bishops, or synod, shortly after 160.

The eventual defeat of Montanism was inevitable. It is already foreshadowed in the sage advice whispered by the Holy Spirit to Ignatius: "Do nothing without the Bishop." In vain did Tertullian protest that the Church is not a collection of Bishops; in vain did Irenaeus plead against the expulsion of prophecy. From the point of view of the hierarchy the Third Person of the Trinity [the Holy Spirit] had outlived his primitive function. He was too deeply entrenched in the New Testament to be demoted, but he ceased in practice to play any audible part in the counsels of the Church. The old tradition of the inspired *prophetes* who spoke what came to him was replaced by the more convenient idea of a continuous divine guidance which was granted, without their noticing it,

Reconstructed model of St. Peter's Basilica in Rome. It was built in the pontificate of Silvester (314–335) and destroyed by Julius II (1503–1513) to make room for the present cathedral. (Anderson)

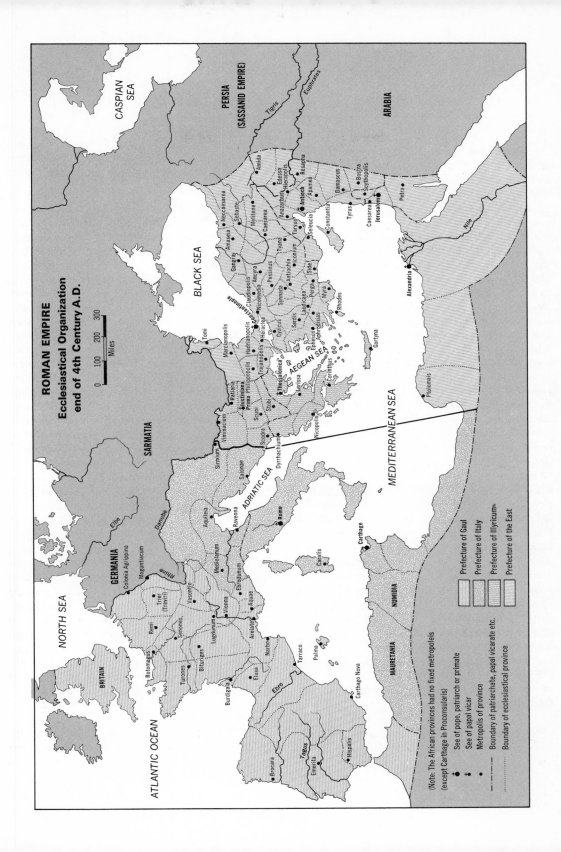

ROMAN EMPIRE
Ecclesiastical Organization
end of 4th Century A.D.

Miles
0   100   200   300

NORTH SEA

BRITAIN

ATLANTIC OCEAN

GERMANIA

SARMATIA

CASPIAN
SEA

PERSIA
(SASSANID EMPIRE)

ARABIA

BLACK SEA

Elbe

Danube

Rhine

Colonia Agrippina
Moguntiacum

Trier
(Treviri)

Remi
Senones

Rotomagus
Turones
Bituriges

Vasontio

Lugdunum
Vienna

Ebrodunum

Aquae

Arelate
Narbo

Burdigala
Elusa

Brocara

Emerita
Hispalis

Tagus

Ebro

Tarraco
Palma

Carthago Nova

Carthago Nova

MAURETANIA

NUMIDIA

Carthage

Caralis

Palma

Aquileia

Ravenna

Mediolanum

Rome

ADRIATIC SEA

MEDITERRANEAN SEA

Salonae

Dyrrhachium

Sirmium

Viminacium

Ratiaria

Justiniana
Prima

Scupi

Stobi

Serdica

Nicopolis

Thessalonica

Larissa

Corinthus

Nicopolis

Gortyna

Ptolemais

AEGEAN SEA

Marcianopolis

Tomi

Hadrianopolis

Heraclea

Constantinople

Cyzicus

Sardis

Ephesus
Aphrodisias

Laodicea

Myra

Rhodes

Perga

Side

Iconium

Tyana

Antiochia

Claudiopolis

Nicomedia

Pessinus

Synnada

Gangra

Amasea

Neocaesarea

Sebaste

Melitene

Caesarea

Amida

Edessa
Hierapolis

Anazarbus

Tarsus

Seleucia

Constantia

Apamea

Antioch

Damascus

Bostra

Scythopolis

Resapha

Tyrus

Caesarea

Jerusalem

Petra

Alexandria

Nile

Tigris

Euphrates

(Note: The African provinces had no fixed metropoleis
(except Carthage in Proconsularis)

●✛ See of pope, patriarch or primate

✛   See of papal vicar

●   Metropolis of province

     Boundary of patriarchate, papal vicarate etc.

     Boundary of ecclesiastical province

     Prefecture of Gaul

     Prefecture of Italy

     Prefecture of Illyricum

     Prefecture of the East

to the principal Church dignitaries. Prophecy went underground, to re-appear in the chiliastic manias of the later Middle Ages.[9]

It seemed toward the end of the third century, following the period of persecution under Decius and Valerian (249–259), that the Christian Church had come a long way in developing a permanent organization and in adjusting its outlook to Roman society. The period of peace during which these changes had taken place was ended abruptly, however, in 298. According to the Christian historian, Lactantius, Diocletian and his Caesar, Galerius, in that year attempted to obtain omens for the Persian campaign, but the sacrificial animals failed to show the usual signs. The chief augur declared that the sacrifice did not work because certain Christians among the officials present had been crossing themselves to ward off demons. Diocletian reacted, perhaps at the instance of Galerius, by requiring all members of the court, the army and the civil service to sacrifice to the state gods on pain of flogging and dismissal. This was followed in 303 by edicts which ordered that all copies of the Christian scriptures be surrendered and burned, churches be dismantled, and Christians be deprived of all legal rank. The Christians were thus placed outside the protection of the courts and made liable to torture. Officials in most parts of the Empire carried out these measures meticulously. Thousands (no accurate estimate of numbers can be made) were imprisoned, tortured, and executed in the ensuing bloodbath. The edicts were strictly enforced for a time by Diocletian, Galerius, and Maximian in their sections of the Empire. In Britain and Gaul under the Caesar Constantius, churches were dismantled, but the surrender of scriptures was not insisted upon. The persecution continued intermittently in the rest of the Empire until 311. In that year Galerius, now senior Augustus following the abdication of Diocletian and Maximian, issued an edict of toleration for the Eastern Empire. In the West Constantius and his son, Constantine, who succeeded him as Caesar in 306, had already allowed the persecution to lapse. Galerius' edict gives a surprisingly frank explanation of the motives for the persecution and for its cessation.

Among all other measures, which we arrange always for the State's advantages and profit, we indeed hitherto had wished to correct all things in accordance with the ancient laws and the public order of the Romans and to provide for this: that also the Christians, who had abandoned the way of life of their fathers, should return to their right minds. For indeed, through some reasoning, such wilfulness had seized and such folly had possessed the said Christians that they followed not their ancestors' well-known institutions, which perchance their own forefathers formerly had established, but they, through their own decision and as it had pleased them, made for themselves laws, which they were observing, and in various places assembled various peoples. Therefore, when our command had ensued to the following effect, that they should betake themselves to the ancient institutions, many have been subjected to danger and many also have been dispossessed. And since very many still persevered in their determined course and because we perceived that the said persons neither were showing veneration and reverence due to the gods nor were worshipping the Christians' god, we, in view of our most kindly Clemency, having regard also for our continual custom, by which we are wont to bestow pardon upon all men, have believed that we ought to extend our promptest indulgence also in these matters, that Christians may exist again and may arrange their own conventicles, yet so as that they do nothing contrary to public order.

Moreover in another letter we shall show the governors what they ought to observe.

Wherefore in accordance with this our indulgence they shall be bound to beseech their own god for our and the State's and their own

[9] E. R. Dodds, *Pagan and Christian in an Age of Anxiety* (Cambridge: Cambridge University Press, 1965), pp. 67–68.

The Milvian Bridge over the Tiber—still standing—first built of stone in 190 B.C. (Alinari)

welfare, that in every way the State may be preserved safely and they may be able to live securely in their own homes.[10]

Galerius died shortly after issuing his edict of toleration. His death added to the already intense rivalry among the Caesars for the senior position in the Tetrarchy. Constantine, operating from the provinces of Britain and Gaul, reached an agreement with Licinius to cooperate against the two senior Caesars. He led his army into Italy in 312, won an important battle near Turin and marched on Rome. At the Milvian Bridge over the Tiber, Constantine met and conquered the forces led by his rival Maxentius. Constantine was left in full control of the Western Empire. Licinius ruled in the East after the last of the imperial rivals was defeated.

Just prior to the battle of Milvian Bridge, Constantine claimed to have seen a vision of the cross and to have received instructions to go into battle with the monogram of Christ on his soldiers' shields. His decisive victory on the fol-

[10] P. R. Coleman-Norton, *Roman State and Christian Church: A Collection of Legal Documents to A.D. 535* (London: S.P.C.K., 1966), vol. I, pp. 19–20.

lowing day was thus interpreted by Christians as a sign of God's judgement in their favor. Whether Constantine himself was converted to the Christian religion at that time is a subject of much speculation. But it is certain that his victory was a decisive event in the history of the Christian Church.

Constantine and Licinius met in Milan in 313 and completed Galerius' last act by joining in a declaration giving complete freedom of worship to the Christians and restoring their property rights. Within a few years, however, tension arose between the two Augusti partly over Licinius' refusal to extend the policy of toleration to open favoritism of the Christians. When war broke out in 324, it was interpreted by Western Christians as a crusade to free their coreligionists in the East. Constantine defeated Licinius at Adrianople in 324 and become sole Augustus of a reunited Empire. Constantine immediately began the construction of a new capital on the site of the old Greek colony of Byzantium not far from Nicomedia, symbolizing the shift of power to the East and the strategic importance of the eastern and Danubian frontiers. For Constantine his new capital, Constan-

Constantine's vision of the cross at the Milvian Bridge—from a Byzantine manuscript. (Bibliotheque National)

tinople, probably also symbolized a break with pagan Rome and the beginning of a new Christian empire.

The following selection considers the significance of Constantine's conversion to Christianity both for the Empire and for the Church. To what extent do the developments in the Church since the second century illustrate the five dilemmas outlined by O'Dea? And what role did the Church play in the maintenance of consensus and stability within the Empire?

The State Church of the Roman Empire
Erwin R. Goodenough[11]

Although only about one-tenth of the citizens of the Empire were Christians, Constantine recognized in the Christian brotherhood a cohesive force with which nothing else in the Empire could compare. For the feeling of Christian brotherhood

[11] From *The Church in the Roman Empire* by Erwin Goodenough. Copyright 1931 by Holt, Rinehart and Winston, Inc. Copyright © 1959 by Erwin Goodenough. Reprinted by permission of Holt, Rinehart and Winston, Inc.

was not only widespread: it had already expressed itself in an organization which claimed a monopoly of this thing which all Christians seemed to prize more than life, the saving grace of Christ which it gave them in the sacraments. In all parts of the Empire were local organizations of this one Catholic Church, and everywhere it was admitted that the local organization had validity only as it remained in organic connection with the Church universal. Could not the loyalty to the Church be so guided as to become loyalty also to the Empire? Constantine thought that this could be done if he tolerated Christianity, and if, by taking an official interest in its discipline, he encouraged the clergy to strengthen its organization. That is, he hoped by making the Church a part of the state that he could tap the abundant Christian store of spiritual strength to supply his sadly enervated Empire. So, unlike Diocletian, Constantine, as has been seen, threw his mantle of protection and favor over the delighted Christians.

With this hope of strengthening the Empire by using the organization of the

Church went another motive in Constantine's toleration of the Church, namely superstition. From earliest times, one of the chief functions of an officer in the Roman state had been to keep the gods favorably disposed toward Rome and her projects. Always the Romans had said that if they were more successful than their enemies in war it was because the Romans were more skilful in attracting the divine favor. At a time when matters went badly for the Romans they had accordingly always turned to religion as the hope for better success, in which case they not only increased their rigor in observing their own traditional rites, but frequently sought out new deities and rites, the recognition of which might "change their luck." Now for a long time matters had indeed been going badly for the Empire, and Constantine seems sincerely to have hoped that by tolerating the Christians he might get the support of their deity and so be more successful. The Christians assured him that it would be so, and when he tried putting their symbol with the symbols of other religions carried by the army he won a great victory [at the Milvian Bridge in 312]. According to the logic of a vigorous and practical Roman of the

The triumphal Arch of Constantine, erected by the Roman Senate in celebration of Constantine's victory over Maxentius. The pagan Senators did not wish to acknowledge the aid Constantine claimed to have received from the Christian god and, therefore, decorated the arch with reliefs from monuments of Trajan, Hadrian, and Marcus Aurelius. (Pan American Airways)

day it would be foolish to antagonize further a people who had such possibilities of support in their organization, and who worshipped a victory-bringing deity.

Yet the Church could serve Constantine's purpose only if it were kept united in organization and spirit. Hence from Constantine's time matters of Christian doctrine and discipline were affairs of state. For with the state and Church co-operating, in so far as heresies or disputes about administration threatened to dismember the Church they would weaken the state also, so that if the state were to be helped rather than injured by her alliance with the Church, the emperors must intervene to settle controversies about orthodoxy and ecclesiastical practice which it is now hard to understand as issues of practical statecraft. At the same time the more the emperors gave their attention to the Church, the more political they made its organization. The result, as will be seen, was quite different in the east from that in the west. In the east the Church finally settled down as a department of the state. In the west, because of the collapse of the state, the Church went forth into the storms of early mediaeval civilization with its head fogged with half-formed dreams of universal political supremacy. In the west, indeed, one is presented with the stupendous spectacle of the death of the greatest organization the world had ever seen, and the reincarnation of its spirit in an organization at least as magnificent. For the spirit of the Empire became the spirit of the Church. . . .

It has already been stated that strong as was the feeling of union among Christians in the face of pagan opposition, and cohesive as their organization appeared in comparison with the weakening bonds of Roman society, the Church as a whole was actually far from being a close-knit organization. In theory there could be but one Church, the seamless robe, the single body of Christ. All admitted this, and yet the immediate difficulty in Constantine's time was that when any difference of opinion arose on which the churches in various regions took different sides there was no way in which the Church as a whole could speak so that all Catholics would at once recognize her decision as final. It was easy to keep the feeling of the one Catholic Church when a generally united sentiment was opposed by scattered heretics. But when whole sections, with their bishops and priests, were convinced that other whole sections were completely in the wrong, what should be done? For the Church had a two-fold obligation: first to transmit the grace of Christ in sacraments through the apostolic succession, and second to preserve the true doctrine. The Church was not the Church at all unless it fulfilled both functions. Consequently large sections tended recurrently to drop away according as they felt that the rest of the faithful were failing in either particular. The Church which Constantine took over was threatened with dismemberment on both accounts, and accordingly he was compelled, if the Church was to be a force for unity, to try to settle the disputes.

In the matter of Church practice, that is in the matter of preserving and administering the sacraments, there had developed a very serious controversy as a result of a disputed election to the office of Bishop of Carthage. Two men claimed to have been properly elected, and local councils or synods were quite unable to settle the matter. One of the claimants, Caecilian, was recognized by the rest of the Church, but his famous rival, Donatus, undaunted, defied the Church as being corrupt if it could recognize one elected by such methods as he thought had put his opponent into office. He said that since he and his followers alone stood for purity of election, and so of apostolic succession, they were the only remnant of the true Church of Christ. It was precisely the sort of argument by which the majority had frequently expelled undesired minorities; now a powerful minority had turned its back upon the majority, and the Church as a whole had no way once and for all to pronounce it wrong. Had there been such a way at the beginning, the whole affair would have amounted to nothing. As it was it had dragged on for some years by the time Constantine began to take official interest in the Church, and was a great source of weakness in all the provinces of North Africa and Spain.

Constantine at once recognized the importance of settling this particular dispute and of getting some sort of machinery by which the Church could act as a whole. His first move was to ask the Bishop of Rome to call a synod to arbitrate the matter. Only a few bishops attended, however, so that its declaration for Caecilian helped not at all. Constantine next tried to get an expression of opinion from the entire Church under his supervision. (He was then Emperor only in the west, with his capital at Milan.) He commanded as an imperial act that the bishops of his realm assemble in Arles. This Council met in 314, and ratified the findings of the previous Synod of Rome, but at its close the bishops dared not return until they had Constantine's permission to do so. The Donatists then appealed to the Court of the Emperor himself, where they finally lost their suit and were threatened with imperial discipline if they continued to resist. But they returned unconvinced to Africa where they survived until extinguished by the Vandals a century and a half later. Apparently nothing had been settled, and yet the results were very real. For under Constantine the entire Christian sentiment of the west had been for the first time brought to bear upon a problem, an official pronouncement had been made, and if the result for the Donatists was not convincing, the effect in uniting the Church as a whole was profound.

From the point of view of doctrine a still greater problem faced Constantine. In the latter part of the third century a new dispute had arisen as a larger number of Christians were men of philosophical training who wanted to fit their worship of Christ into the prevailing philosophical system of the day. The difficulties in doing so centered about the question, "In what sense was Christ divine?" For true deity was, by all accepted definition at the time, best to be thought of as bare Unity, which was utterly different from all the complications of this life. God had no parts, no constitution, no emotions. He was always active in thinking, but in no other way, and indeed He was nothing but Mind in its most abstract form. He seems to have been a glorification of the vanishing point of perspective, the resolution and orientation of everything in the world, and yet completely unrelated to anything outside of Himself.

The problem was, how, if God was such a Unity, could Jesus of Nazareth be divine also. The early solution had been to identify Christ with the Spirit which radiated out of God, and which had created and now governs the world. Practically, Christ was the Christians' God, to whom they prayed as the devotees of Mithra prayed to Mithra, and little attention was paid to the deity of philosophy. Such a solution had satisfied the first two centuries of Christians, but did not answer at all when people of philosophic training were converted. From the middle of the third century the question had been raised with increasing insistence: if Christ was the incarnate Word or Spirit, in what sense was he divine; was he truly God, or demigod? Early in the fourth century the issue was brought out sharply by Arius, a brilliant churchman in Alexandria, who became the protagonist of the philosophical party by openly arguing that if Jesus was the incarnate Word of God he must be subordinate to God, a radiation out from God, divine, but still not true deity. Against him Alexander, the venerable bishop of Alexandria, led the group primarily interested in the religious tradition of Christianity. He was later succeeded by Athanasius as bishop and party leader, so that this party, in contrast to the Arian party, came to be called the Athanasian, or, as it was ultimately victorious, the Orthodox party. . . .

To Constantine, who cared nothing for the merits of the controversy, the situation presented only the problem of how he was to unite the Church on either one side or the other in order to get the support of the Church's unified force. When news of the trouble reached him he drew up an appeal in a letter addressed in common to both Alexander and Arius which he sent by his most intimate clerical friend, Bishop Hosius of Spain. Constantine pointed out that the question in dispute was one which human minds could never settle, and a dispute which was in any case a matter of minor detail, for both sides still agreed in what seemed to him the main points, that is in matters of morality and worship. He reminded them that in philosophical sects the philosophers often disagreed in details,

but still remained together because of what they had in common, while they respected each other's differences of opinion on smaller matters.

Clearly Constantine had no appreciation of the importance of the question in the minds of the disputants at this early stage, so that his letter belittling their dispute only embittered both sides. His next expedient was therefore to try to repeat his success at Arles by again settling a Church controversy at a Council held under the awe of imperial prestige. In 325 he summoned to Nicea all the bishops of the east, including many groups hardly recognized by the orthodox, with a generous representation of western bishops, including, of course, Rome. For two months a fierce battle raged. The extremists on one side, led by Arius, seemed totally given over to the philosophical implications of the terms in question, and openly expressed their unconcern if proof-texts from the Scriptures could be quoted against them. Extremists on the other side were well represented by one loyal, though uneducated Christian who reproved those who relied upon reason, and said that Christ and his apostles did not teach dialectics, cleverness or subtleness, but simple-mindedness as preserved in faith and good works. The majority of the assembly, however, fell between these two extremes, and tried to use both the authority of Scripture and rational argument. The Emperor sat in his golden chair as umpire through the entire two months of argumentation and eventually all but five of the more than three hundred bishops present agreed on a formula. The final settlement was a complete victory for the party of Alexander and Athanasius. A creed was adopted containing their chosen phrase "of the same nature as the Father," and Arius with all his sympathizers was not only condemned by the Church, but banished from the Empire, while an Imperial Decree made it an offense to be punished by immediate death if any man should ever try to harbor in secret a book written by Arius.

Apart from its dogmatic interest, quite apparently the Council marks a definite step beyond Constantine's first attempt at Arles in uniting the Church by imperial discipline. The Council was not only summoned by imperial decree, but the expenses of travel and entertainment were paid from the imperial treasury, and its proceedings were supervised throughout by imperial authority. At the end the decisions of the Council became imperial law by receiving the confirmation of the Emperor. The effect of this precedent was enormous in all future ages of the Church. Whatever the religious origin of the Christian Faith, the Church as a universal corporation was formed deliberately as a branch of secular government and the first expressions of the Church as a whole were

Constantine. The head from a colossal statue of the Christian emperor which sat enthroned in the west apse of the Basilica of Constantine in Rome. The regent of God gazes unperturbed beyond his physical surroundings to the higher sphere from whence he derives his power. The very personification of providence, he expresses the greatly altered view of imperial authority since the fall of the Republic. Compare with the statue of Augustus on page 90. (Anderson)

matters at the same time of faith and of imperial legislation. Thereafter, as the organization of the Church steadily became stronger, it always looked to the forces of government for coercive power.

Constantine also established important precedents in his treatment of the clergy. In pagan Rome, the clergy, what few there were, had certain outstanding privileges. Since their office often involved large personal expenditure, they were exempt from all state financial obligations and from the necessity of military service. These privileges Constantine extended to the great body of Christian clergy, which in fact accorded them official standing as individuals in the Empire. For the basis of exemption of priests in the early days of Rome had been the fact that they were regarded as representatives of the state in its dealings with those gods who had been officially elected as such by the senate. The priests were hence officials of the state, and not to be disturbed in their beneficent public service. In giving to Christian clergy the same privileges, Constantine laid the foundation of the political independence of the clergy which later provoked centuries of controversy. Similarly Constantine recognized as legal the courts of the bishops. During times of persecution, when Christians had a matter to settle, it had rarely been wise to appeal to a Roman court. The custom had arisen, following the earliest Christian advice, of appealing such disputes to the bishop as final judge. The decisions of the bishops Constantine now recognized as of final validity, quite on a par with the decisions of the imperial courts. A case might be taken before either an ecclesiastical or an imperial court according to the desires of the contestants. Also, Constantine recognized the Church as a valid property-hold-ing institution. Legally regarded now as a corporation under the state, each episcopal seat was allowed to hold property, and was frequently given by the state money and land, or former pagan temples, to be kept as Church property. As part of this policy, Constantine permitted people to bequeath their property to the Church, a privilege the clergy were not slow to urge the pious wealthy to exercise. Land once in the possession of the Church practically never left its hands, so that by 370 the landed wealth of the Church had already become a vexing problem and continued so until modern times.

Under Constantine there began also an attempt to fit the Church into the new divisions of the Empire. Diocletian and Constantine had established four great prefectures in the Empire, subdivided into dioceses, each diocese in turn made up of several provinces. At the chief city, or metropolis, of each province it now seemed desirable to establish formally a Metropolitan Bishop, or Metropolitan, who would supervise all the bishops of the province. In turn the bishop in the great capital city of a diocese was to have similar supervision over the metropolitans in the various provinces of the diocese. There was at first no particular title for such Diocesan-Bishops, but they came gradually to be known as Patriarchs. The arrangement was of course an expression of the Roman desire for centralized control by means of a systematic organization, but it was never fully worked out. In places where a political capital of a diocese, such as Alexandria, had already been associated with episcopal prestige over all provincial bishops and metropolitans, the system could at once be installed, as was done in the case of Alexandria by the Nicene Council. Antioch, Rome, Carthage, and soon Constantinople, were also obvious ecclesiastical capitals. But though the system could never he put into operation as a whole, the very fact that it was regarded as the ideal did much to bind the state and Church together in men's minds.

So much space has been given to the treatment of the Church by Constantine because the generation flourishing in the first half of the fourth century saw a transition in the Christian Church comparable in its importance only to that change from a Palestinian sect to a mystery religion of salvation witnessed by the first generation of Christians. During the first three hundred years, Christianity had flourished as a religious body made up of people who at considerable risk to themselves joined an organization held together only by the devotion of its members. But Constantine's desire to use the organization for his own political ends had introduced problems totally unknown to the earlier Christians. Church discipline had now become a matter of legal enforcement. Heresy was a crime against the state, to be punished by banishment or even execution. The decrees of the Church councils were made into formal imperial law by the sanction of the Emperor. Accordingly, where the Church had formerly been, in its relation to paganism at least, interested in religious liberty, this interest now turned into active persecution by Christians of those, at first especially the heretics, who did not accept her decrees. And almost at once the Emperor came to be regarded as having the final word even in matters of doctrine. The new spirit went down through every part of the Church. Whereas a bishop had heretofore been, with few exceptions, one who held his office with slight financial return, and often great risk, he was now an important Roman official, conducting a recognized law court, frequently managing large financial estates, and prone to dispute his rights step by step against the other officials of the state. It was thus natural that in a period of steady decline of state power the Church would take over more and more of the business of government, until, at the complete collapse of the state it would begin to dream of being itself the ideal rulership for the world, though such a thought was utterly foreign to the Church of the first three centuries.

CHAPTER 6

THE CHRISTIAN FOUNDATIONS OF SPIRITUAL AND POLITICAL AUTHORITY:
Saint Augustine's Synthesis of the Greco-Roman and Judeo-Christian Traditions

Understanding is the reward of faith. Therefore seek not to understand that thou mayest believe, but believe that thou mayest understand.

St. Augustine, On the Gospel of John

While the spirit of the classical culture lies close to the spatiality of objects, it has little affinity with the temporality of the inner life. Selfhood as such, cut off from the matrix of civil society, is hardly a category for Greek thought. Autobiography as a literary form simply does not appear among the Greeks, and it is from the basic spirit of autobiography that the tradition of the psychological novel takes its origin. It is not until the establishment of Christian eschatology with its emphasis upon sin and repentance, the inward searchings of the individual soul in its quest for salvation, and the confessional act which is the culmination of this search, that inwardness becomes a climate of opinion and that confession, autobiography, and interior monologue alike become established as experiences upon which much later the modern novel can draw.

Albert William Levi, Literature, Philosophy and the Imagination

[Augustine's] transvaluation of classicism began with the ruthless excision of every human pretension of absoluteness. The wisdom of the ancient world had foundered on the dilemma of ideals that had to be imposed by force. Vergil's soaring vision of the Augustan principate had given way to a chronic anxiety over survival. Augustine confronted a shattered idealism with the Christian message of creation and redemption, of God's sovereign grace diffused in every event, effective in every dimension of existence. If grace is valued foremost, then nature may be valued in consequence. If faith is primary, then the quest for understanding becomes a legitimate enterprise. When men are bedeviled to absolutize some person or creaturely thing, they fall into tragic confusion and disorder. When they are converted to God, their interest in "things" falls into right proportion. Thus, pagan literature, philosophy and history can be transvalued and conserved, provided only that they abandon every claim to ultimacy.

Albert C. Outler, "Augustine and the Transvaluation of the Classical Tradition,"
The Classical Journal, 54 *(February, 1959)*

The union of Empire and Church seemed to many partisans of the Christian cause to usher in a new age. The biographer of Constantine wrote:

> . . . By the express appointment of the same God, two roots of blessing, the Roman empire and the doctrine of Christian piety, sprang up together for the benefit of men. . . . [With the reign of Constantine] a new and fresh era of existence had begun to appear, and a light heretofore unknown suddenly dawned from the midst of darkness of the human race: and all must confess that these things were entirely the work of God, who raised up this pious emperor to withstand the multitude of the ungodly.[1]

But, as we have seen, this attempt to regenerate the Empire with the spirit of Christianity was not without consequences for both Church and state—for both Christianity and classical culture.

The measure of these consequences is to be found in the writings of Saint Augustine. Augustine's mind ranged over the whole of classical culture; he was both an educated pagan and a converted Christian, and he was a bishop of the Church at a time when the foundations of society were being shaken. He thus drew from a vast reservoir of accumulated knowledge and immediate experience. In so far as Western civilization can be seen as a fusion of the Greco-Roman and Judeo-Christian traditions, Saint Augustine is the "key" figure. But there is no single "key" to Augustine's thought. He must be understood in context, in relation to his age.

Augustine was born in 354 and died in 430. His lifetime coincided with the most critical years in the history of the late Empire. Formal unity was maintained until the end of the fourth century, but the policy established under the Tetrarchy of dividing power to meet the threat of military invasion reasserted itself immediately after the death of Constantine. The Empire re-

mained in the hands of members of Constantine's family until 364, when the army again became the determining factor in imperial succession. The political arrangements reached between Rome and the German tribes in eastern Europe were upset by the migration of the Huns out of central Asia. Bands of refugees from the destroyed Germanic kingdoms moved across the Danube into Thrace. At the Battle of Adrianople in 378, the army of the Emperor Valens was annihilated by the Goths, who then formed a virtually independent enclave within the borders of the Empire. The Emperor Theodosius (379–395) struggled to maintain the unity of the Empire against barbarian incursions, rebellious generals, and rivals to the throne. When he died, the Empire was divided, as the future was to demonstrate, permanently between East and West.

In the West, Theodosius' successor, Honorius (395–423), moved the court and administration to Ravenna on the Adriatic for the natural protection it afforded against the threatened invasion of a large and mixed group of barbarians gathering in the Alps. His general, Stilicho, prevented complete disaster by defeating the invaders near Florence, but after his death the Visigothic chieftain, Alaric, subjected the city of Rome itself to three days of plundering in 410. The Vandals in the meantime moved across Gaul and Spain and in 429 crossed to North Africa, taking Carthage in 439 and establishing an independent kingdom. The Western Empire was further fragmented in the course of the century into a number of independent Germanic kingdoms, some maintaining a continuity with the Roman tradition. In Italy, Roman administration continued under Germanic kings, Odoacer (476–493) and Theodoric the Ostrogoth (493–526).

In the Eastern Empire, with its capital at Constantinople, unity was preserved. In the sixth century, the Emperor Justinian I (527–565), under whose direction the Roman law was codified, attempted to reunite the Empire. He succeeded in reconquering Italy by 554, but the experiment was short-lived. Italy, with the ex-

---

[1] Eusebius, *Life of Constantine,* in S. Wolin, *Politics and Vision* (Boston: Little, Brown & Company, 1960), p. 121.

ception of Rome, Ravenna, and the extreme southern portions, fell to the Lombards in the next century. The Eastern Empire continued for another 900 years, and a form of classical culture, known as Byzantine, persisted until the area was conquered by the Turks in 1453.

The religious institutions developed during Constantine's reign proved stronger than the political ones. Though Christianity was growing in numbers and importance in the fourth century, it was far from being a universal faith. In a brief three-year reign the Emperor Julian (Julian the Apostate, 361–363) attempted to return Rome to pagan religion and philosophy. He did not proscribe Christianity but deprived the Church of its privileges. He removed Christian teachers from Greek and Latin schools, returned land previously confiscated from pagan temples, and eliminated Christians from the imperial administration. Julian's attempt to revive paganism was short-lived, and the Church was restored to its position of influence by his suc-

cessors. But the degree to which he had succeeded was a measure of the fact that paganism was still an active force in the Empire. Most of the Christian emperors of the fourth century tolerated pagan religious practices which were particularly strong in the rural areas and among the remaining old Roman aristocracy. Only in the last decade of the fourth century did the Emperor Theodosius prohibit pagan worship, proclaim Christianity the official religion of the Empire, and, with the assistance of Ambrose, Bishop of Milan, actively persecute all deviation from the Nicene orthodoxy.

During the fourth century there began to emerge differences between the East and West in the relationship between Church and state. The emperors who resided in Constantinople tended to continue Constantine's close supervision of ecclesiastical affairs. Constantinople was officially recognized as the chief see of the East in 381, thereafter owing a loose allegiance only to Rome. In the West, the absence of the

A procession of saints from San Apollinare Nuovo in Ravenna (sixth century). The individualized portraits of classical antiquity here give place to the meaningful stereotypes of the middle ages. The figures are disembodied spirits identifiable only by their symbols of martyrdom and sainthood. (The Bettmann Archive)

emperor from Rome, and the almost total pre-occupation of the Western rulers with military defense, enhanced the prestige of the Bishop of Rome and enabled the Church to establish relative independence from the state. Bishops in the West were often chosen by popular acclamation and thus became secular leaders with strong local support. They were often the only mediator between the people and the stringent demands of the imperial bureaucracy. Some Western bishops exerted a considerable degree of political influence. Saint Ambrose, for instance, made Bishop of Milan by popular acclamation in 374, was on one occasion able to force the Emperor Theodosius to perform public penance for ordering the slaughter of 7000 rebellious inhabitants of Thessalonica. In the East, municipal bishops also attained considerable local secular power, but the Eastern Church as a whole lacked the able administrators who appeared in the West and remained under the power and influence of the Eastern emperor.

The world into which Augustine was born and in which he grew up was, thus, a time of unprecedented perplexities. The men of his age could not discern the clear pattern of political and ecclesiastical division between East and West which historians now record, but the quarrels and open fighting produced by these tendencies were evident enough. The economic burdens produced by taxation and inflation were yet more real, and military disasters like those which occurred at Adrianople in 378 and at Rome in 410 indicated to any perceptive observer that the Empire no longer had the physical means to defend itself. For an intellectual, these times of confusion were compounded by the tremendous variety of philosophical schools and religious sects which continued to compete for his attention. Even the "official" Christian religion left wide room for theological and philosophical speculation. Saint Augustine's own life exemplifies some of the confusions confronting a young man in the late Empire and also illustrates how Christianity was for him, as for so many, a way out of that confusion.

The future churchman and theologian was born in Thagaste, a small town in North Africa not far from Carthage, in the ancient province of Numidia. This part of the Empire was relatively prosperous in the fourth century. It had escaped the turbulence produced by the barbarian incursions in Europe and the East and continued to supply grain and olive oil for the Italian market. But the economic boom of the second and third centuries, which had laced the province with roads and produced towns like Timgad far into the interior, had given way to a more sedate, rural, and truly "provincial" atmosphere. Augustine's father was a minor town official in Thagaste who worked hard to provide an education for his promising son. He was not a Christian, but his wife Monica was fanatically so, and enrolled her son as a catechumen in the Catholic Church shortly after his birth. Augustine did not receive baptism, however, since it was the practice in the African Church to postpone this rite until adulthood.

Augustine received the usual precise and meticulous elementary education in Thagaste. He proved an unusually bright pupil, although he developed an intense dislike for the Greek language which he never succeeded in mastering. His parents sent him away to school for three years to the neighboring city of Madaura where he was drilled in the few Latin texts—Vergil, Cicero, Sallust, Terence—which constituted the entire curriculum of the standard school of rhetoric. Augustine returned home for a year—most probably because his parents did not have the money to keep him in school—but at the age of seventeen, was able to go to Carthage to continue the study of rhetoric.

Carthage was the largest urban center in northern Africa and offered to the young provincial all the allurements of big city life. Augustine, according to his own testimony, enjoyed himself immensely with a large group of student friends. It was at this time that he took a nameless concubine with whom he lived for the next thirteen years. She bore him a son, Adeodatus. However, Augustine's libertine life was of short duration. His father died in the second year of his studies at Carthage, and his pious Christian mother continued to press him to mend his ways. The profligate youth became an intense young student in search of truth and spiritual solace. His search for wisdom began with a reading of Cicero's *Hortensius,* a text now lost, but one which hit Augustine with the intensity of a religious experience. His quest led him at about this same time to the Manichaeans, whose strongly dualistic belief appealed to Augustine as an answer to his question; "From what cause do we do evil?" The Manichaeans believed in the separate existence of a force of darkness or evil and a force of light, identified with the material and spiritual worlds, respectively. They taught a purely rationalist philosophy and an ascetic practice by which the initiate could release the particles of light embedded in his soul and thus take part in the cosmic struggle between good and evil. A series of prophets, beginning with Adam, including Jesus and Paul, and ending with Mani himself, had been sent by God to reveal the nature of truth and to aid man in liberating the light in his soul. Manichaeism, as Augustine knew it, was a sect with a priesthood and a class of apprentices. Augustine soon joined a cell in Carthage and began to train in the faith.

All the while he was developing his religious life, Augustine was training to be a teacher of rhetoric, and in 375 at the age of twenty-one he

Aerial diagram of Timgad in North Africa. In these fortified cities the Romans imposed on the rough landscape the regular pattern of the army camp. Compare with the diagram on page 47. (Rev. Raymond V. Schoder)

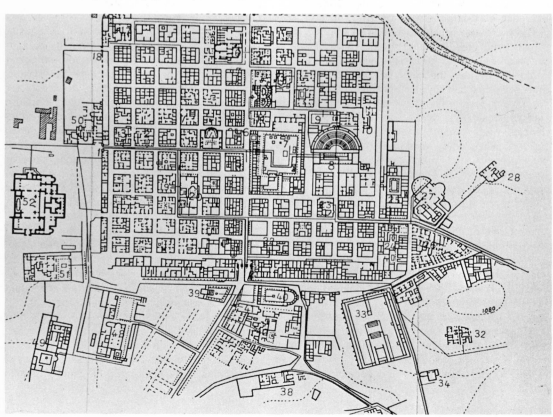

Crossing of main streets, in town center of Timgad. (Rev. Raymond V. Schoder)

embarked on his chosen career, first at Thagaste, then at Carthage. Here he taught the sons
of aristocrats and administrative officials that
smattering of Latin letters which was a mark of
their status. In his profession he began to move
in social circles which would take him to Rome
and Milan in pursuit of worldly success. His
closest friend, Alypius, had gone to Rome in
382 as an administrative lawyer; Augustine,
beginning to be disillusioned with Manichaeism
and the unruliness of his Carthaginian pupils,
resolved to follow. He lied to his mother about
his intentions and embarked for Rome in 383.

By this time Augustine had gained some reputation as a young scholar and orator and accordingly became a protégé of Symmachus, the
prefect of Rome and leading pagan scholar of
his day. It was Symmachus who secured for
Augustine the important post of professor of
rhetoric at Milan, then the imperial capital in
the West, whence he journeyed in 384, only a
year after arriving in Rome. Augustine's intention was to acquire wealth and achieve eminence

in his profession. His mother joined him in Milan
and did her part to further her son's ambition.
She found him a suitable wife, although the marriage was postponed for two years until the girl
came of age. Augustine summarily dismissed
the woman with whom he had lived for thirteen
years and sent her back to Africa, keeping their
son with him in Milan.

Despite his considerable worldly success,
Augustine was a disillusioned man. The Manichaeans' fanatical adherence to their own
version of the truth now seemed to him to
be intellectually indefensible. He temporarily
adopted the more sophisticated skeptical attitude of the New Academy which he found in the
works of Cicero. His position as chief rhetor at
Milan also brought him into contact with a circle
of intellectuals—some Christian, some pagan—
who were consciously cultivating a revival of
Platonism. Most important of all, Augustine
came under the influence of Ambrose, the
Bishop of Milan, whose dominating personality,
political position, and superior learning (Am-

brose knew Greek) worked powerfully on the African provincial thrust into the center of imperial court life. For the next two years Augustine was tormented by doubts and spiritual anxieties. He came more and more under the influence of the Platonists and of Ambrose. In 386, he reached the decision to join the Catholic Church as a catechumen, and shortly thereafter underwent an intense religious experience which he later recorded in his *Confessions*. All his doubts were dissolved and he entered a life in the Church.

Thus began the career of Saint Augustine, the most influential father of the Western Church. As a bishop, polemicist, and theologian he left an indelible mark on the religious life of succeeding generations. He was not a systematic theologian, but his writing ranged over the whole of Christian belief, doctrine, and practice, and the particular structure which he gave to them had a profound and lasting influence on Western Christianity.

A long history of doctrinal controversy lay behind Saint Augustine. Tertullian's paradox, "I believe it because it is absurd," had for the most part been rejected by the church as its apologists engaged in internal theological controversies and defended the faith against a still-active paganism. Because this process of defining doctrine began in the East, it was inevitable that the influence of Greek philosophical thought should be felt. Many learned men began to make a serious effort to understand the doctrines of Christianity. The hostility toward pagan culture expressed by Tertullian in his famous question, "What has Athens to do with Jerusalem?" gave way among these writers to a synthesis of Biblical and Hellenic thought which left a permanent mark on the development of Christian doctrine.

It is important to note that the pagan intellectual atmosphere in which church doctrine was formulated was itself undergoing change. We have already noted the increasingly religious and introspective quality of later Stoicism. A general tendency known as gnosticism, of which Manichaeism was one manifestation, was evident in most contemporary religions. Gnostics of all varieties were in search of knowledge (*gnosis*) of the mysteries of the universe—knowledge which would yield personal victory over fate and demonic powers. And when Platonism was revived as a distinct and disciplined school of philosophy in the second century, it was the religious element, particularly the Pythagorean element, in Plato's thought which came into prominence. The so-called Middle Platonists systematized Platonic thought, arranging all elements into a hierarchical order headed by a Supreme Mind regarded as the author of all other forms of being. The Forms thus became the "thoughts" in the mind of the Supreme Being or One.

Neoplatonism, a further development of Plato's thought, associated with the name of Plotinus (205–270), was frankly religious and mystical.

For Plotinus the first substantial principle or hypostasis is the One or the Good. The double title reflects the influence of both Neo-Pythagoreanism and Middle Platonism, and ultimately of Plato himself, whose preoccupations were both ethical and mathematical. This first principle is also termed God and is beyond Being (following the *Republic* 509B).

Next, by a process of necessary emanation, comes Nous or Intellect, also referred to as divine, in which the whole world of Ideas or Forms is contained. It is on this level that Being, which always entails some multiplicity, and Life appear. From Intellect, in turn, comes Soul, which at its highest level belongs to the world of Intellect. The World Soul forms and rules the material universe, and at its lower level, where it acts as a principle of life and growth, receives the name of Nature, which is almost a distinct fourth hypostasis. Each of these principles has proceeded from the previous, and then turned back in contemplation of it in order to be fully constituted, according to a law of abiding, procession, and reversion. But the last principle is too weak to produce anything further than the forms immanent in bodies, beneath which exists only formless matter.

This material visible world is therefore good, as emanating ultimately from the Good, but unformed matter is evil, in the ontological sense of lacking form, definition, or shape. Moral evil consists in the assimilation of the soul to matter, with all that this entails in terms of deficiency. Evil is simply the complete lack of good.

Individual human souls are one with the Universal Soul, but with distinct identity, and descend by destiny into the body. Plotinus harmonizes the seemingly opposed views that the soul's entry into the body is somehow a fall, and yet at the same time for the benefit of the universe. But human souls are only expressions on the level of Soul of particular intellects within the sphere of Intellect, and so man's highest and most real point never descends into union with the body. Each human soul has three levels—the transcendent intellect, the intermediate soul, and the lowest soul that immediately gives life to the body. Whether one's life is to be virtuous or not depends upon the decision of the intermediate soul, either to return in contemplation to the sphere of Intellect, or to devote itself to the needs and cravings of the body.

The process of return to contemplation is much as Plato described it, the most suitable souls being those of the musician, the lover, and the philosopher. The first two still need to learn detachment from particular images of Beauty, but the last can go straight on to the study of mathematics and then dialectic—the complete knowledge of the world of Forms within the unity of Intellect. One is led to this state of intellectual contemplation by the practice of the virtues—practical wisdom, courage, moderation, and justice. In their normal exercise these are civic virtues, but as specially directed toward detachment from the body they become higher virtues or purifications. The purified soul can rise still

higher and be united to the One by the Intellect, although only intermittently while it is still in this life. This union is beyond thought or expression in word; it is a unity of love in which the lover is no longer conscious of any distinction between him and the beloved. It is the simplicity of a single glance, and once attained all else seems worthless in comparison with it.[2]

The whole emphasis in Neoplatonism on the unity of being in the One was thus an elaboration of Plato's first principle of the Good. After Plato, the Good had become a Cosmic God or High God, and this transformation was part of a general tendency in later classicism to establish an authoritative principle of unity in a pluralistic and syncretic world. Neoplatonism's special contribution was in providing a formula by which man could attain unity with that increasingly transcendent being. Yet its rigorous intellectual prerequisites confined the popularity of this philosophy to a relatively small number of intellectuals.

The study of Plato was not exclusively a pagan concern. Many Christian writers of the second and third centuries found in Platonism a rational basis for their faith. The Platonic philosophy which Plotinus first learned in Alexandria was also a source of inspiration for Clement of Alexandria (ca. 150–219) and Origen (ca. 180–255), the best known among the Christian Platonists. Alexandria with its famous libraries was the leading intellectual center and one of the wealthiest cities of the late Roman Empire. It had long been a center of Hellenistic Judaism, and it was here that the Greek translation of the Old Testament, the Septuagint, was made. Alexandria was the city of Philo Judaeus (20 B.C.–A.D. 40) who had led the process of interpreting Jewish culture in the light of Greek philosophy; it was also an early center of gnostic Christianity. In

---

[2] From *New Catholic Encyclopedia*, vol. XI. Copyright © 1967 by The Catholic University of America, Washington, D.C. Used with permission of McGraw-Hill Book Company.

such an atmosphere the uncompromising theology of the African Church, as represented by Tertullian, was rejected in favor of a more speculative approach. Clement and Origen, as teachers in a school of Christian catechism, began the process by which the leading ideas of Greek philosophy were incorporated into Christian theology.

The greatest fascination for these early Christian theologians was the Greek concept of unity.

In the Platonic tradition the ideal form of unity, the idea of the One, which has so supreme a role in the world of the ideas, is a unity without parts, a unity without differentiation or division of any kind. It is a unity of this absolute kind that Christians claimed to be characteristic of the God whom they affirmed. "God is simple, uncompounded being," says Irenaeus of Lyons (c. A.D. 180); "no parts are to be ascribed to God; for the One is indivisible," says Clement of Alexandria (c. A.D. 200); "God is one and altogether simple," says Origen.

The Bible also speaks in emphatic terms of God as one. But the concern of the biblical tradition is to declare the falsity of all forms of polytheism and idol-worship. It is the fact that there is only one and not many Gods that is there taught. This is not necessarily the same thing as to say that God is one in the sense of being a simple undifferentiated unity. The Fathers thought themselves to be doing no more than giving full and worthy expression to the biblical teaching about the divine unity. In fact they were doing something more than that. They were developing that teaching in terms of a particular conception of unity. That conception, the idea of a simple undifferentiated unity, is a mathematical ideal. The development was natural enough; it happened unconsciously without deliberate intent. But its implications for Christian doctrine are enormous. The idea of one who is in a full sense Son of God sharing

the divine nature is a difficult enough idea to work out and to express in terms of Jewish monotheistic faith. But once transform the biblical conception of the one God into the Platonic concept of God as a simple undifferentiated unity, and the already existing difficulty is raised to the level of logical impossibility.[3]

But such was the difficulty with which the Church fathers from Clement to Augustine struggled.

Clement taught that philosophy, and particularly Platonism, could be used as an aid in understanding Biblical faith, for he believed that all truth is one and that the faculty of reason could not lead to results which contradicted revelation. "There is but one river of truth," he wrote, "but many streams pour into it from this side and from that." Indeed he argued that the elements of truth to be found in Greek philosophy had been borrowed from the Old Testament and that "the law is for the Jew what philosophy is for the Greek, a schoolmaster to bring them to Christ."

While Faith remained the foundation of Christianity, the enlightened Christian advanced from Faith towards knowledge, the deeper understanding and imitation of the Word, not arrived at through any single act, but by a daily obedience to the divine command. Like his Gnostic opponents, Clement saw spiritual perfection in intellectual terms attainable by an *élite,* though he stressed the need for a visible Church and rejected the determinism which characterized the Gnostics. Even so, while Tertullian's ideal for the Christian was martyrdom, Clement's was that of the Gnostic ascetic. For him the joys of Paradise lay in no material benefits but in "becoming like God," enjoying a freedom

[3] From *The Christian Fathers* by Maurice Wiles. Copyright © 1966 by Maurice Wiles. Reprinted with permission from J. B. Lippincott Company and Hodder and Stoughton Limited.

from all passions which might hinder the soul from attaining this end.[4]

Origen, the most influential of the early Church fathers, went much further in working out a synthesis of Christianity and Platonism than had Clement. As Clement's pupil in the Catechetical School and as a fellow student with Plotinus at the lectures of the Platonist, Ammonius Saccas, Origen embraced the concept of God as an undifferentiated unity. In the first systematic statement of Christian doctrine ever to be undertaken, he attempted to reach an understanding of the nature of God as pure spirit, who, through the Word (*Logos* or Christ), generated all being which had existed from eternity. The *Logos* was, according to Origen, an agent of creation, a teacher of divine truth in the person of Jesus, and of divine nature but subordinate to God. Origen regarded faith in the accepted doctrines of the Church as necessary for salvation; but, like Clement before him, he praised knowledge which is the demonstration of faith as a higher stage of Christian life, available only to a spiritual elite.

One of the most difficult problems confronting Christian philosophers was how to make the crude and obscure, yet authoritative, scriptures yield moral and spiritual meaning. Origen provided the solution most usually followed.

[His] method was based on allegory. To the agreed tradition among orthodox exegetes that incidents in the Old Testament directly pre-figured the promises of the New, Origen added a new factor derived from his Platonist studies. All things, even the simplest, in the Bible reflected the real and spiritual order beyond the visible world. It was the duty of the exegete to find the clue to this spiritual truth in a given text, and by analogy and comparison with other texts to work out the message. Thus, Jerusalem, Sion, Carmel, Beer-sheba and hundreds of other places ceased to be geographical expressions, but under Origen's imaginative erudition became the mirrors of heavenly truth. Every word of Scripture meant something, otherwise it would not have been written, he argued. Today much of this can be dismissed as irrelevant, but for the time, it established the Bible as a consistent whole, all equally important to the Christian as the word of God.[5]

Origen's writings were instrumental in raising Christian theology and Biblical scholarship to an intellectual level where they could compete with pagan and Jewish philosophy, though his enthusiasm for Platonism sometimes led him into heterodox positions later condemned by the Church.

It was the rationalist tendencies of Christian theology which gave rise to the bitter controversy within the Church over the divinity of Jesus and his relationship to God the Father. We have already seen how this issue was raised by Arius of Alexandria in the early fourth century and how his view was finally condemned at the Council of Nicaea in 325.[6] The creed drawn up at Nicaea, nevertheless, represented the official recognition by the Church of the necessity of employing the terminology of pagan philosophy to define faith. The original Nicene Creed read as follows:

We believe in one God, the Father All-sovereign, maker of all things visible and invisible. And in one Lord Jesus Christ, the Son of God, begotten of the Father, only begotten, that is from the substance of the Father. . . . God of God, Light of Light, true God of true God, begotten, not made, of one substance with the Father, through whom all

---

[4] From *The Early Church* by W. H. C. Frend. Copyright © 1965 by W. H. C. Frend. Published in the United States by J. B. Lippincott Company and outside the USA by Hodder and Stoughton Limited. Reprinted by permission of J. B. Lippincott Company and Hodder and Stoughton Limited.

[5] Frend, *The Early Church*, pp. 103–104. Reprinted by permission.

[6] See pp. 159–161.

things were made, things in heaven and things on earth: who for us men and for our salvation, came down and was made flesh, and became man, suffered, and rose on the third day, ascended into the heavens; is coming to judge the living and dead. And in the Holy Spirit. And those who say, "There was when he was not," and "Before he was begotten he was not," and that "He came into being from what is not, . . . or those that allege, that the son of God is "of another substance or essence," or "created," or "changeable," or "alterable," these the Catholic and Apostolic Church anathematizes.[7]

The Trinitarian formula worked out at Nicaea became the test of orthodoxy, but it did not put an end to theological controversy. Speculation continued in the Eastern part of the Church over the exact relationship of the persons of the Trinity. In the West, however, reaction against the speculative tendencies of theology set in. The emphasis in Western theology shifted to the redemptive aspect of religion and away from the philosophical speculation inaugurated by the Alexandrian school. In the West, orthodoxy had the added support of a strong ecclesiastical organization.

One other aspect of the life of the Church needs to be mentioned before moving on to a consideration of Augustine's own intellectual and spiritual development. Asceticism had always been a part of Eastern religions; in the fourth century, asceticism in the form of a Christian monastic movement gained considerable importance first in Egypt and then in other parts of the Empire. As the era of persecution and martyrdom waned and the Church became socially and politically more acceptable, monasticism emerged as an alternative to martyrdom as an ideal for the perfect Christian life. The earliest Christian monastic movement was stimulated by the example of Antony (251–356), an Egyptian farmer who retired into the desert to

[7] Frend, *The Early Church*, p. 154. Reprinted by permission.

fast, pray, discipline the flesh, study the Bible, and thus to seek a more intimate union with God. Antony's asceticism was primarily individual, but he gained many followers and monastic communities grew up rapidly in Egypt and elsewhere throughout the East. In Asia Minor, Saint Basil established a monastic organization, combining communal living with service in the Church, which became the model for monasticism in the Eastern Church. Monasticism was not so fully developed in the West in the fourth century, but the example set by many Eastern ascetics attracted considerable attention.

Rich heiresses like the Roman aristocrat Melania went out and visited Antony's hermitage at Pispir as tourists. Jerome's friend, Rufinus, went to Scete and Nitria and others went to Palestine. By 350 there was a regular pilgrim route from Bordeaux to Jerusalem with hospices on the way. The story of Etheria, a noble and observant lady from north-western Spain who travelled as far as the Thebaid and then via the Sinai desert first to Jerusalem and then to Constantinople, reads like a modern travelogue. She was determined to see everything from monastic cells to the rock which Moses struck. The ancient world was gradually being transformed into the Middle Ages with its pilgrimages, its monastic sagas and elaborate cult of saints. In northern Gaul the 370's were to see the first and brilliantly successful piece of monastic missionary enterprise in the West, that of Martin of Tours among Celts at a time when Christianity had been still an unknown faith to most of them.

Jerome's career (345–420) fits into the current pattern of intellectual asceticism. His wanderings in the East early in his life, his curiosity and enthusiasm combined with ignorance of Eastern habits of mind and theological problems, represented a prevalent outlook among the new generation of aristocratic Roman Christians. His salon, centered on the household of the rich matron Paula and her daughter Eustochion, on the Aventine was a real centre of religious life and learning.[8]

It was here that Jerome, at the behest of Pope Damasus, began to translate the Hebrew and Greek scriptures into Latin. The resulting Vulgate became the authoritative text for the Roman Catholic Church and was unrivalled as a scholarly translation until the sixteenth century.

When in 385, disappointed of succeeding Pope Damasus, the translator of the Vulgate sailed away to Palestine and his "cave" at Bethlehem he left an example of asceticism combined with scholarship which the Benedictines of the early Middle Ages were to take to heart. Even so, the centre of his activity as a monk was the East. Another generation was to go by before John Cassian provided the Western provinces with a monastic order which they could accept, and which was to prepare the way for the Benedictine Order.[9]

This rich mixture of theological controversy, still vital paganism, ecclesiastical development, and examples of spiritual asceticism form the background for Augustine's intellectual and spiritual development. His long search for certain belief in Manichaeism and pagan philosophy ended in a surrender to the authoritative doctrine of the Trinity and the orthodox Catholic Church of Saint Ambrose. Yet in embracing Christian orthodoxy, Saint Augustine did not abandon Platonism. Indeed, he brought Platonism, and particularly Neoplatonism, into a relationship with the Christian religion by which it was transmitted into the West. In reading the following selection from the Confessions, written some ten years after Augustine's conversion, keep in mind the basic tenets of Neoplatonism and of orthodox Christian belief. The ways in which Saint Augustine attempts to find a firm yet logical faith by blending elements of the Greco-Roman and Judeo-Christian traditions

should become clear. The importance of asceticism, both Manichaean and orthodox, in Augustine's own spiritual development should also become evident. The Confessions is an introspective and subjective document, the first of its kind in the Western tradition. What significance do you attach to the fact that Augustine chose to discuss his religious and philosophical beliefs in the form of a personal confession? In the Confessions, Saint Augustine also reveals other and more specific elements of his theology and philosophy, but these will be considered separately later.

THE CONFESSIONS
Saint Augustine[10]

BOOK ONE

vii. He shows by example that even infancy is prone to sin

Hearken, O God! Alas for the sins of men! Man saith this, and Thou dost have mercy on him; for Thou didst create him, but didst not create the sin that is in him. Who bringeth to my remembrance the sin of my infancy? For before Thee none is free from sin, not even the infant which has lived but a day upon the earth. Who bringeth this to my remembrance? Doth not each little one, in whom I behold that which I do not remember of myself? In what, then, did I sin? Is it that I cried for the breast? If I should now so cry—not indeed for the breast, but for the food suitable to my years—I should be most justly laughed at and rebuked. What I then did deserved rebuke; but as I could not understand those who rebuked me, neither

[8] Frend, *The Early Church*, pp. 208–209. Reprinted by permission.

[9] Frend, *The Early Church*, p. 209. Reprinted by permission.

[10] Saint Augustine, *The Confessions*, translated by J. G. Pilkington, in Whitney J. Oates, ed., *Basic Writings of Saint Augustine*, vol. I (New York: Random House, 1948), pp. 8–15, 17–24, 29–34, 42–43, 55, 59–60, 64–66, 68–72, 99–102, 104–106, 118–121, 124–127.

An early representation of St. Augustine from Cefalú Cathedral in Sicily. (Alinari)

custom nor reason suffered me to be rebuked. . . . In the weakness of the infant's limbs, and not in its will, lies its innocence. I myself have seen and known an infant to be jealous though it could not speak. It became pale, and cast bitter looks on its foster-brother. Who is ignorant of this? Mothers and nurses tell us that they appease these things by I know not what remedies; and may this be taken for innocence, that when the fountain of milk is flowing fresh and abundant, one who has need should not be allowed to share it, though needing that nourishment to sustain life? Yet we look leniently on these things, not because they are not faults, nor because the faults are small, but because they will vanish as age increases. For although you may allow these things now, you could not bear them with equanimity it found in an older person.

viii. That when a boy he learned to speak, not by any set method, but from the acts and words of his parents

Did I not, then, growing out of the state of infancy, come to boyhood, or rather did it not come to me, and succeed to infancy? Nor did my infancy depart (for whither went it?); and yet it did no longer abide, for I was no longer an infant that could not speak, but a chattering boy. I remember this, and I afterwards observed how I first learned to speak, for my elders did not teach me words in any set method, as they did letters afterwards; but I myself, when I was unable to say all I wished and to whomsoever I desired, by means of the whimperings and broken utterances and various motions of my limbs, which I used to enforce my wishes, repeated the sounds in my memory by the mind, O my God, which Thou gavest me. When they called anything by name, and moved the body towards it while they spoke, I saw and gathered that the thing they wished to point out was called by the name they then uttered; and that they did mean this was made plain by the motion of the body, even by the natural language of all nations expressed by the countenance, glance of the eye, movement of other members, and by the sound of the voice indicating the affections of the mind, as it seeks, possesses, rejects, or avoids. So it was that by frequently hearing words, in duly placed sentences, I gradually gathered what things they were the signs of; and having formed my mouth to the utterance of these signs, I thereby expressed my will. Thus I exchanged with those about me the signs by which we express our wishes, and advanced deeper into the stormy fellowship of human life, depending the while on the authority of parents, and the beck of elders.

ix. Concerning the hatred of learning, the love of play, and the fear of being whipped noticeable in boys; and of the folly of our elders and masters

O my God! what miseries and mockeries did I then experience, when obedience to my teachers was set before me as proper to my boyhood, that I might flourish in this world, and distinguish myself in the science of speech, which should get me honor amongst men, and deceitful riches! After that I was put to school to get learning, of which I (worthless as I was) knew not what use there was; and yet, if slow to learn, I was flogged! For this was deemed praiseworthy by our forefathers; and many before us, passing the same course, had appointed beforehand for us these troublesome ways by which we were compelled to pass, multiplying labor and sorrow upon the sons of Adam. But we found, O Lord, men praying to Thee, and we learned from them to conceive of Thee, according to our ability, to be some Great One, who was able (though not visible to our senses) to hear and help us. For as a boy I began to pray to Thee, my help and my refuge, and in invoking Thee broke the bands of my tongue, and entreated Thee though little, with no little earnestness, that I might not be beaten at school. And when Thou heardest me not, giving me not over to folly thereby, my elders, yea, and my own parents too, who wished me no ill, laughed at my stripes, my then great and grievous ill.

. . . For we were no less afraid of our pains, nor did we pray less to Thee to avoid them; and yet we sinned, in writing, or reading, or reflecting upon our lessons less than was required of us. For we wanted not, O Lord, memory or capacity—of which, by Thy will, we possessed enough for our age—but we delighted only in play; and we were punished for this by those who were doing the same things themselves. But the idleness of our elders they call business, while boys who do the like are punished by those same elders, and yet neither boys nor men find any pity. For will any one of good sense approve of my being whipped because, as a boy, I played ball, and so was hindered from learning quickly those lessons by means of which, as a man, I should play more unbecomingly? And did he by whom I was beaten do other than this, who, when he was overcome in any little controversy with a co-tutor, was more tormented by anger and envy than I when beaten by a playfellow in a match at ball?

xii. Being compelled, he gave his attention to learning; but fully acknowledges that this was the work of God

In this my childhood (which was far less dreaded for me than youth) I had no love of learning, and hated to be forced to it, yet was I forced to it notwithstanding; and this was well done towards me, but I did not well, for I would not have learned had

I not been compelled. For no man does well against his will, even if that which he does be good. Neither did they who forced me do well, but the good that was done to me came from Thee, my God. . . .

xiii. *He delighted in Latin Studies and the empty fables of the Poets, but hated the elements of literature and the Greek language*

But what was the cause of my dislike of Greek literature, which I studied from my boyhood, I cannot even now understand. For the Latin I loved exceedingly—not what our first masters, but what the grammarians teach; for those primary lessons of reading, writing, and ciphering, I considered no less of a burden and a punishment than Greek. Yet whence was this unless from the sin and vanity of this life? For I was but flesh, a wind that passeth away and cometh not again. For those primary lessons were better, assuredly, because more certain; seeing that by their agency I acquired, and still retain, the power of reading what I find written, and writing myself what I will; whilst in the others I was compelled to learn about the wanderings of a certain Aeneas, oblivious of my own, and to weep for Dido dead, because she slew herself for love; while at the same time I brooked with dry eyes my wretched self dying far from Thee, in the midst of those things, O God, my life.

xiv. *Why he despised Greek literature, and easily learned Latin*

But why, then, did I dislike Greek learning, which was full of like tales? For Homer also was skilled in inventing similar stories, and is most sweetly vain, yet was he disagreeable to me as a boy. I believe Virgil, indeed, would be the same to Greek children, if compelled to learn him,

as I was to Homer. The difficulty, in truth, the difficulty of learning a foreign language mingled as it were with gall all the sweetness of those fabulous Grecian stories. For not a single word of it did I understand, and to make me do so, they vehemently urged me with cruel threatenings and punishments. There was a time also when (as an infant) I knew no Latin; but this I acquired without any fear or tormenting, by merely taking notice, amid the blandishments of my nurses, the jests of those who smiled on me, and the sportiveness of those who toyed with me. I learnt all this, indeed, without being urged by any pressure of punishment, for my own heart urged me to bring forth its own conceptions, which I could not do unless by learning words, not of those who taught me, but of those who talked to me; into whose ears, also, I brought forth whatever I discerned. . . .

xviii. *Men desire to observe the rules of learning, but neglect the eternal rules of everlasting safety*

. . . Behold, O Lord God, and behold patiently, as Thou art wont to do, how diligently the sons of men observe the conventional rules of letters and syllables, received from those who spoke prior to them, and yet neglect the eternal rules of everlasting salvation received from Thee, insomuch that he who practices or teaches the hereditary rules of pronunciation, if, contrary to grammatical usage, he should say, without aspirating the first letter a *uman* being, will offend men more than if, in opposition to Thy commandments, he, a human being, were to hate a human being. . . .

These were the customs in the midst of which, I, unhappy boy, was cast, and on that arena it was that I was more fearful of perpetrating a barbarism than, having done so, of envying those who had not. These things I declare and confess unto Thee, my God, for which I was applauded by them whom I then thought it my whole duty to please, for I did not perceive the gulf of infamy wherein I was cast away from Thine eyes. . . .

But yet, O Lord, to Thee, most excellent and most good, Thou Architect and Governor of the universe, thanks had been due unto Thee, our God, even hadst Thou willed that I should not survive my boyhood. For I existed even then; I lived, and felt, and was solicitous about my own wellbeing—a trace of that most mysterious unity from whence I had my being; I kept watch by my inner sense over the wholeness of my senses, and in these insignificant pursuits, and also in my thoughts on things insignificant, I learnt to take pleasure in truth. I was averse to being deceived, I had a vigorous memory, was provided with the power of speech, was softened by friendship, shunned sorrow, meanness, ignorance. In such a being what was not wonderful and praiseworthy? But all these are gifts of my God; I did not give them to myself; and they are good, and all these constitute myself. Good, then, is He that made me, and He is my God; and before Him will I rejoice exceedingly for every good gift which, as a boy, I had. For in this lay my sin, that not in Him, but in His creatures—myself and the rest—I sought for pleasures, honors, and truths, falling thereby into sorrows, troubles, and errors. Thanks be to Thee, my joy, my pride, my confidence, my God—thanks be to Thee for Thy gifts; but preserve Thou them to me. For thus wilt Thou preserve me; and those things which Thou hast given me shall be developed and perfected, and I myself shall be with Thee, for from Thee is my being.

BOOK TWO

i. He deplored the wickedness of his youth

I will now call to mind my past foulness, and the carnal corruptions of my soul, not because I love them, but that I may love Thee, O my God. For love of Thy love I do it, recalling, in the very bitterness of my remembrance, my most vicious ways, that Thou mayest grow sweet to me—Thou sweetness without deception! Thou sweetness happy and assured!—and re-collecting myself out of my dissipation, in which I was torn to pieces, while, turned away from Thee the One, I lost myself among many vanities. For I even longed in my youth formerly to be satisfied with worldly things, and I dared to grow wild again with various and shadowy loves; my form consumed away, and I became corrupt in Thine eyes, pleasing myself, and eager to please in the eyes of men.

ii. Stricken with exceeding grief, he remembers the dissolute passions in which, in his sixteenth year, he used to indulge

But what was it that I delighted in save to love and to be loved? But I held it not in moderation, mind to mind, the bright path of friendship, but out of the dark concupiscence of the flesh and the efferverscence of youth exhalations came forth which obscured and overcast my heart, so that I was unable to discern pure affection from unholy desire. Both boiled confusedly within me, and dragged away my unstable youth into the rough places of unchaste desires, and plunged me into a gulf of infamy. . . .

. . . Where was I, and how far was I exiled from the delights of Thy house, in that sixteenth year of the age of my flesh, when the madness of lust—to which human shamelessness granted full freedom, although forbidden by Thy laws—held complete sway over me, and I resigned myself entirely to it? Those about me meanwhile took no care to save me from ruin by marriage, their sole care being that I should learn to make a powerful speech, and become a persuasive orator.

iii. Concerning his father, a freeman of Thagaste, the assister of his son's studies, and on the admonitions of his mother on the preservation of chastity

. . . But while, in that sixteenth year of my age, I resided with my parents, having holiday from school for a time (this idleness being imposed upon me by my parents' necessitous circumstances), the thorns of lust grew rank over my head, and there was no hand to pluck them out. Moreover when my father, seeing me at the baths, perceived that I was becoming a man, and was stirred with a restless youthfulness, he, as if from this anticipating future descendants, joyfully told it to my mother; rejoicing in that intoxication wherein the world so often forgets Thee, its Creator, and falls in love with Thy creature instead of Thee, from the invisible wine of its own perversity turning and bowing down to the most infamous things. But in my mother's breast Thou hadst even now begun Thy temple, and the commencement of Thy holy habitation, whereas my father was only a catechumen as yet, and that but recently. She then started up with a pious fear and trembling; and, although I had not yet been baptized, she feared those crooked ways in which they walk who turn their back to Thee, and not their face.

. . . She desired, and I remember privately warned me, with great solicitude, not to commit fornication; but above all things never to defile another man's wife. These appeared to me but womanish counsels, which I should blush to obey. But they were Thine, and I knew it not, and I thought that Thou heldest Thy peace, and that it was she who spoke, through whom Thou heldest not Thy peace to me, and in her person wast despised by me, her son, the son of Thy handmaid, Thy servant. But this I knew not; and rushed on headlong with such blindness, that amongst my equals I was ashamed to be less shameless, when I heard them pluming themselves upon their disgraceful acts, and glorying all the more in proportion to the greatness of their baseness; and I took pleasure in doing it, not for the pleasure's sake only, but for the praise. What is worthy of dispraise but vice? But I made myself out worse than I was, in order that I might not be dispraised; and when in anything I had not sinned as the abandoned ones, I would affirm that I had done what I had not, that I might not appear abject for being more innocent, or of less esteem for being more chaste.

iv. He commits theft with his companions, not urged on by poverty, but from a certain distaste of well-doing

Theft is punished by Thy law, O Lord, and by the law written in men's hearts, which iniquity itself cannot blot out. For what thief will suffer a thief? Even a rich thief will not suffer him who is driven to it by want. Yet had I a desire to commit robbery, and did so, compelled neither by hunger, nor poverty, but through a distaste for well-doing, and a lustiness of iniquity. For I pilfered that of which I had already sufficient, and much better. Nor did

I desire to enjoy what I pilfered, but the theft and sin itself. There was a pear-tree close to our vineyard, heavily laden with fruit, which was tempting neither for its color nor its flavor. To shake and rob this some of us wanton young fellows went, late one night (having, according to our disgraceful habit, prolonged our games in the streets until then), and carried away great loads, not to eat ourselves, but to fling to the very swine, having only eaten some of them; and to do this pleased us all the more because it was not permitted. Behold my heart, O my God; behold my heart, which Thou hadst pity upon when in the bottomless pit. Behold, now, let my heart tell Thee what it was seeking there, that I should be gratuitously wanton, having no inducement to evil but the evil itself. It was foul, and I loved it. I loved to perish. I loved my own error—not that for which I erred, but the error itself. Base soul, falling from Thy firmament to utter destruction—not seeking aught through the shame but the shame itself!

BOOK THREE

i. Deluded by an insane love, he, though foul and dishonorable, desires to be thought elegant and urbane

To Carthage I came, where a cauldron of unholy loves bubbled up all around me. I loved not as yet, yet I loved to love; and, with a hidden want, I abhorred myself that I wanted not. I searched about for something to love, in love with loving, and hating security, and a way not beset with snares. For within me I had a dearth of that inward food, Thyself, my God, though that dearth caused me no hunger; but I remained without all desire for incorruptible food, not because I was already filled thereby, but the more empty

I was the more I loathed it. For this reason my soul was far from well, and, full of ulcers, it miserably cast itself forth, craving to be excited by contact with objects of sense. Yet, had these no soul, they would not surely inspire love. To love and to be loved was sweet to me, and all the more I succeeded in enjoying the person I loved. I befouled, therefore, the spring of friendship with the filth of concupiscence, and I dimmed its lustre with the hell of lustfulness; and yet, foul and dishonorable as I was, I craved, through an excess of vanity, to be thought elegant and urbane. I fell precipitately, then, into the love in which I longed to be ensnared. My God, my mercy, with how much bitterness didst Thou, out of Thy infinite goodness, besprinkle for me that sweetness! For I was both beloved, and secretly arrived at the bond of enjoying; and was joyfully bound with troublesome ties, that I might be scourged with the burning iron rods of jealousy, suspicion, fear, anger, and strife.

ii. In public spectacles he is moved by an empty compassion. He is attacked by a troublesome spiritual disease

Stage-plays also drew me away, full of representations of my miseries and of fuel to my fire. Why does man like to be made sad when viewing doleful and tragical scenes, which yet he himself would by no means suffer? And yet he wishes as a spectator, to experience from them a sense of grief, and in this very grief his pleasure consists. What is this but wretched insanity? . . .

But I, wretched one, then loved to grieve, and sought out what to grieve at, as when, in another man's misery, though feigned and counterfeited, that delivery of the actor best pleased me, and attracted me the most powerfully, which moved me to tears. What marvel was it that an un-happy sheep, straying from Thy flock, and impatient of Thy care, I became in-fected with a foul disease? And hence came my love of griefs—not such as should probe me too deeply, for I loved not to suffer such things as I loved to look upon, but such as, when hearing their fictions, should lightly affect the surface; upon which, like as with empoisoned nails, fol-lowing burning, swelling, putrefaction, and horrible corruption. Such was my life! But was it life, O my God?

iii. Not even when at church does he sup-press his desires. In the school of rhetoric he abhors the acts of the subverters

And Thy faithful mercy hovered over me afar. Upon what unseemly iniquities did I wear myself out, following a sacrilegious curiosity, that, having deserted Thee, it might drag me into the treacherous abyss, and to the beguiling obedience of devils, unto whom I immolated my wicked deeds, and in all which Thou didst scourge me! I dared, even while Thy solemn rites were being celebrated within the walls of Thy church, to desire, and to plan a business sufficient to procure me the fruits of death; for which Thou chastisedst me with griev-ous punishments, but nothing in com-parison with my fault, O Thou my great-est mercy, my God, my refuge from those terrible hurts, among which I wandered with presumtuous neck, receding farther from Thee, loving my own ways, and not Thine—loving a vagrant liberty.

Those studies, also, which were ac-counted honorable, were directed towards the courts of law; to excel in which, the more crafty I was, the more I should be praised. Such is the blindness of men, that they even glory in their blindness. And now I was head in the School of Rhetoric,

whereat I rejoiced proudly, and became inflated with arrogance, though more se-date, O Lord, as Thou knowest, and alto-gether removed from the subvertings of those "subverters" (for this stupid and diabolical name was held to be the very brand of gallantry) amongst whom I lived, with an impudent shamefacedness that I was not even as they were. And with them I was, and at times I was delighted with their friendship whose acts I ever ab-horred, that is, their "subverting," where-with they insolently attacked the modesty of strangers, which they disturbed by un-called for jeers, gratifying thereby their mischievous mirth. Nothing can more nearly resemble the actions of devils than these. By what name, therefore, could they be more truly called "subverters"?—being themselves subverted first, and altogether perverted—being secretly mocked at and seduced by the deceiving spirits, in what they themselves delight to jeer at and de-ceive others.

iv. In the nineteenth year of his age (his father having died two years before) he is led by the "Hortensius" of Cicero to "Philosophy," to God, and a better mode of thinking

Among such as these, at that unstable period of my life, I studied books of elo-quence, wherein I was eager to be eminent from a damnable and inflated purpose, even a delight in human vanity. In the ordinary course of study, I lighted upon a certain book of Cicero, whose language, though not his heart, almost all admire. This book of his contains an exhortation to philosophy, and is called *Hortensius*. This book, in truth, changed my affections, and turned my prayers to Thyself, O Lord, and made me have other hopes and de-sires. Worthless suddenly became every vain hope to me; and with an incredible warmth of heart, I yearned for an immortality of wisdom, and began now to arise that I might return to Thee. Not, then to improve my language—which I appeared to be purchasing with my mother's means, in my nineteenth year, my father having died two years before—not to improve my language did I have recourse to that book; nor did it persuade me by its style, but its matter.

How ardent was I then, my God, how ardent to fly from earthly things to Thee! Nor did I know how Thou wouldst deal with me. For with Thee is wisdom. In Greek the love of wisdom is called philosophy, with which that book inflamed me. There are some who seduce through philosophy, under a great, and alluring, and honorable name coloring and adorning their own errors. And almost all who in that and former times were such, are in that book censured and pointed out. There is also disclosed that most salutary admonition of Thy Spirit, by Thy good and pious servant: "Beware lest any man spoil you through philosophy and vain deceit, after the tradition of men, after the rudiments of the world, and not after Christ: for in Him dwelleth all the fulness of the Godhead bodily." And since at that time (as Thou, O Light of my heart, knowest) the words of the apostle were unknown to me, I was delighted with that exhortation, in so far only as I was thereby stimulated, and enkindled, and inflamed to love, seek, obtain, hold, and embrace, not this or that sect, but wisdom itself, whatever it were; and this alone checked me thus ardent, that the name of Christ was not in it. For this name, according to Thy mercy, O Lord, this name of my Saviour Thy Son, had my tender heart piously drunk in, deeply treasured even

with my mother's milk; and whatsoever was without that name, though never so erudite, polished, and truthful, took not complete hold of me.

v. He rejects the sacred scriptures as too simple, and as not to be compared with the dignity of Tully

I resolved, therefore, to direct my mind to the Holy Scriptures, that I might see what they were. And behold, I perceive something not comprehended by the proud, not disclosed to children, but lowly as you approach, sublime as you advance, and veiled in mysteries; and I was not of the number of those who could enter into it, or bend my neck to follow its steps. For not as when now I speak did I feel when I turned towards those Scriptures, but they appeared to me to be unworthy to be compared with the dignity of Tully; for my inflated pride shunned their style, nor could the sharpness of my wit pierce their inner meaning. Yet, truly, were they such as would develop in little ones; but I scorned to be a little one, and, swollen with pride, I looked upon myself as a great one.

vi. Deceived by his own fault, he falls into the errors of the Manichaeans, who glorified in the true knowledge of God and in a thorough examination of things

Therefore I fell among men proudly raving, very carnal, and voluble, in whose mouths were the snares of the devil—the birdlime being composed of a mixture of the syllables of Thy name, and of our Lord Jesus Christ, and of the Paraclete, the Holy Ghost, the Comforter. These names departed not out of their mouths, but so far forth as the sound only and the clatter of the tongue, for the heart was empty of truth. Still they cried, "Truth, Truth," and spoke much about it to me, yet was it not in them; but they spake falsely not of Thee only—who, verily, art the Truth—but also of these elements of this world, Thy creatures. . . . But I hungered and thirsted not even after those first works of Thine, but after Thee Thyself, the Truth, with whom is no variableness, neither shadow of turning; yet they still served up to me in those dishes glowing phantasies, than which better were it to love this very sun (which, at least, is true to our sight), than those illusions which deceive the mind through the eye. And yet, because I supposed them to be Thee, I fed upon them; not with avidity, for Thou didst not taste to my mouth as Thou art, for Thou wast not these empty fictions; neither was I nourished by them, but was rather exhausted.

BOOK FOUR

ii. He teaches rhetoric, the only thing he loved, and scorns the soothsayer, who pomised him victory

In those years I taught the art of rhetoric, and overcome by cupidity, put to sale a loquacity by which to overcome. Yet I preferred—Lord, Thou knowest—to have honest scholars (as they are esteemed); and these I, without artifice, taught artifices, not to be put in practise against the life of the guiltless, though sometimes for the life of the guilty. And Thou, O God from afar sawest me stumbling in that slippery path, and amid much smoke sending out some flashes of fidelity, which I exhibited in my guidance of such as loved vanity and sought after leasing, I being their companion. In those years I had one (whom I knew not in what is called lawful wedlock, but whom my wayward passion, void of understanding, had discovered),

yet one only, remaining faithful even to her; in whom I found out truly by my own experience what difference there is between the restraints of the marriage bonds, contracted for the sake of issue, and the compact of a lustful love, where children are born against the parents' will, although, being born, they compel love. . . .

xvi. He very easily understood the liberal arts and the categories of Aristotle, but without true fruit

And what did it profit me that, when scarce twenty years old, a book of Aristotle's, entitled *The Ten Categories*[11] fell into my hands—on whose very name I hung as on something great and divine, when my rhetoric master of Carthage, and others who were esteemed learned, referred to it with cheeks swelling with pride—I read it alone and understood it? And on my conferring with others, who said that with the assistance of very able masters—who not only explained it orally, but drew many things in the dust—they scarcely understood it, and could tell me no more about it than I had acquired in reading it by myself alone? And the book appeared to me to speak plainly enough of substances, such as man is, and of their qualities—such as the figure of a man, of what kind it is; and his stature, how many feet high; and his relationship, whose brother he is; or where placed, or when born; or whether he stands or sits, or is shod or armed, or does or suffers anything; and whatever innumerable things might be classed under these nine categories—of which I have given some examples—or under the chief category of substance. . . .

And what did it profit me that I, the

[11] Aristotle's categories are: substance, quantity, quality, relation, place, time, position, possession, activity, and passivity.

base slave of the vile affections, read un-aided, and understood, all the books that I could get of the so-called liberal arts? And I took delight in them, but knew not whence came whatever in them was true and certain. For my back then was to the light, and my face towards the things en-lightened; whence my face, with which I discerned the things enlightened, was not itself enlightened. Whatever was written either on rhetoric or logic, geometry, music, or arithmetic, did I, without any great difficulty, and without the teaching of any man, understand, as Thou knowest, O Lord my God, because both quickness of comprehension and acuteness of per-ception are Thy gifts. Yet did I not there-upon sacrifice to Thee. So then, it served not to my use, but rather to my destruc-tion, since I went about to get so good a portion of my substance into my own power; and I kept not my strength for Thee, but went away from Thee into a far country, to waste it upon harlotries. For what did good abilities profit me, if I did not employ them to good uses? For I did not perceive that those arts were acquired with great difficulty, even by the studious and those gifted with genius, until I en-deavored to explain them to such; and he was the most proficient in them who fol-lowed my explanations not too slowly. . . .

BOOK FIVE

iii. Having heard Faustus, the most learned bishop of the Manichaeans, he discerns that God, the author both of things animate and inanimate, chiefly has care for the humble

Let me lay bare before my God that twenty-ninth year of my age. There had at this time come to Carthage a certain bishop of the Manichaeans, by name Faus-tus, a great snare of the devil, and many were entangled by him through the allure-ment of his smooth speech; which, al-though I did command it, yet could I sep-arate from the truth of those things which I was eager to learn. Nor did I esteem the small dish of oratory so much as the sci-ence, which this their so praised Faustus placed before me to feed upon. Fame, in-deed, had before spoken of him to me, as most skilled in all becoming learning, and pre-eminently skilled in the liberal sci-ences. . . .

For with their understanding and the capacity which Thou hast bestowed upon them they search out these things; and much have they found out, and foretold many years before—the eclipses of those luminaries, the sun and moon, on what day, at what hour, and from how many particular points they were likely to come. Nor did their calculation fail them; and it came to pass even as they foretold. And they wrote down the rules found out, which are read at this day; and from these others foretell in what year, and in what month of the year, and on what day of the month, and at what hour of the day, and at what quarter of its light, either moon or sun is to be eclipsed, and thus it shall be even as it is foretold. And men who are ignorant of these things marvel and are amazed, and they that know them exult and are exalted; and by an impious pride, departing from Thee, and forsaking Thy light, they foretell a failure of the sun's light which is likely to occur so long be-fore, but see not their own, which is now present. For they seek not religiously whence they have the ability wherewith they seek out these things. And finding that Thou has made them, they give not themselves up to Thee, that Thou mayest preserve what Thou hast made, nor sacrifice themselves to Thee, even such as they have made themselves to be; nor do they slay their own pride, as fowls of the air, nor their own curiosities, by which (like the fishes of the sea) they wander over the unknown paths of the abyss, nor their own extravagance, as the beasts of the field, that Thou, Lord, a consuming fire, mayest burn up their lifeless cares and renew them immortally. . . .

vii. Clearly seeing the fallacies of the Manichaeans, he retires from them, being remarkably aided by God

My eagerness after the writings of Manichaeus having thus received a check, and despairing even more of their other teachers—seeing that in sundry things which puzzled me, . . . [Faustus], so famous amongst them, had thus turned out —I began to occupy myself with him in the study of that literature which he also much affected, and which I, as Professor of Rhetoric, was then engaged in teaching the young Carthaginian students, and in reading with him either what he expressed a wish to hear, or I deemed suited to his bent of mind. But all my endeavors by which I had concluded to improve in that sect, by acquaintance with that man, came completely to an end; not that I separated myself altogether from them, but, as one who could find nothing better, I determined in the meantime upon contenting myself with what I had in any way lighted upon, unless, by chance, something more desirable should present itself. . . .

viii. He sets out for Rome, his mother in vain lamenting it

Thou dealedst with me, therefore, that I should be persuaded to go to Rome, and teach there rather what I was then teach-ing at Carthage. And how I was persuaded to do this, I will not fail to confess unto Thee; for in this also the profoundest workings of Thy wisdom, and Thy ever present mercy to me, must be pondered and avowed. It was not my desire to go to Rome because greater advantages and dignities were guaranteed me by the friends who persuaded me into this—although even at this period I was influenced by these considerations—but my principal and almost sole motive was, that I had been informed that the youths studied more quietly there, and were kept under by the control of more rigid discipline, so that they did not capriciously and imprudently rush into the school of a master not their own, into whose presence they were forbidden to enter unless with his consent. At Carthage, on the contrary, there was amongst the scholars a shameful and intemperate license. They burst in rudely, and, with almost furious gesticulations, interrupt the system which any one may have instituted for the good of his pupils. Many outrages they perpetrate with astounding stupidity, which would be punishable by law were they not sustained by custom; that custom showing them to be the more worthless, in that they now do, as according to law, what by Thy unchangeable law will never be lawful. . . .

But the cause of my going thence and going thither, Thou, O God, knewest, yet revealedst it not, either to me or to my mother, who grievously lamented my journey, and went with me as far as the sea. But I deceived her, when she violently restrained me either that she might retain me or accompany me, and I pretended that I had a friend whom I could not quit until he had a favourable wind to set sail. And I lied to my mother—and such a mother!— and got away. . . . Like all mothers—though even more than others—she loved to have me with her, and knew not what joy Thou wert preparing for her by my absence. Being ignorant of this, she did weep and mourn, and in her agony was seen the inheritance of Eve—seeking in sorrow what in sorrow she had brought forth. And yet, after accusing my perfidy and cruelty, she again continued her intercessions for me with Thee, returned to her accustomed place, and I to Rome.

x. When he had left the Manichaeans, he retained his depraved opinions concerning sin and the origin of the Saviour

. . . And even then at Rome I joined those deluding and deluded "saints"; not their "hearers" only . . . but those also whom they designate "The Elect." For it still seemed to me that it was not we that sin, but that I know not what other nature sinned in us. And it gratified my pride to be free from blame, and, after I had committed any fault, not to acknowledge that I had done any. . . .

But now, hopeless of becoming proficient in that false doctrine, even those things with which I had decided upon contenting myself, providing that I could find nothing better, I now held more loosely and negligently. For I was half inclined to believe that those philosophers whom they call "Academics" were more sagacious than the rest, in that they held that we ought to doubt everything, and ruled that man had not the power of comprehending any truth; for so, not yet realizing their meaning, I also was fully persuaded that they thought just as they are commonly held to do. And I did not fail frankly to restrain in my host that assurance which I observed him to have in those fictions of which the works of Manichaeus are full. Notwithstanding, I was on terms of more intimate friendship with them than with others who were not of this heresy. Nor did I defend it with my former ardor; still my familiarity with that sect (many of them being concealed in Rome) made me slower to seek any other way—particularly since I was hopeless of finding the truth, from which in Thy Church, O Lord of heaven and earth, Creator of all things visible and invisible, they had turned me aside—and it seemed to me most unbecoming to believe Thee to have the form of human flesh, and to be bounded by the bodily lineaments of our members. And because, when I desired to meditate on my God, I knew not what to think of but a mass of bodies (for what was not such did not seem to me to be), this was the greatest and almost sole cause of my inevitable error.

For hence I also believed evil to be a similar sort of substance, and to be possessed of its own foul and misshapen mass—whether dense, which they denominated earth, or thin and subtle, as is the body of the air, which they fancy some malignant spirit crawling through that earth. And because a piety—such as it was—compelled me to believe that the good God never created any evil nature, I conceived two masses, the one opposed to the other, both infinite, but the evil the more contracted, the good the more expansive. And from this mischievous commencement the other profanities followed on me. For when my mind tried to revert to the Catholic faith, I was cast back, since what I had held to be the Catholic faith was not so. . . .

xii. Professing rhetoric at Rome, he discovers the fraud of his scholars

Then I began assiduously to practise that for which I came to Rome—the teaching of rhetoric; and first to bring together at my home some to whom, and through whom, I had begun to be known; when, behold, I learnt that other offences were committed in Rome which I had not to bear in Africa. For those subvertings by abandoned young men were not practised here, as I had been informed; yet, suddenly, said they, to evade paying their master's fees, many of the youths conspire together, and remove themselves to another—breakers of faith, who, for the love of money, set a small value on justice. These also my heart hated, though not with a perfect hatred; for, perhaps, I hated them more in that I was to suffer by them, than for the illicit acts they committed. . . .

xiii. He is sent to Milan, that he, about to teach rhetoric, may be known by Ambrose

When, therefore, they of Milan had sent to Rome to the prefect of the city, to provide them with a teacher of rhetoric for their city, and to despatch him at the public expense, I made solicitations through those identical persons, drunk with Manichaean vanities, to be freed from whom I was going away—neither of us, however, being aware of it—that Symmachus, the then prefect, having proved me by proposing a subject, would send me. And to Milan I came, to Ambrose the bishop, known to the whole world as among the best of men, Thy devout servant; whose eloquent discourse did at that time strenuously dispense unto Thy people the flour of Thy wheat, the gladness of Thy oil, and the sober intoxication of Thy wine. To him was I unknowingly led by Thee, that by him I might knowingly be led to Thee. That man of God received me like a father, and looked with a benevolent and episcopal kindliness on my change of abode. And I began to love him, not at first, indeed,

as a teacher of the truth—which I entirely despaired of in Thy Church—but as a man friendly to myself. And I studiously hearkened to him preaching to the people, not with the motive I should, but, as it were, trying to discover whether his eloquence came up to the fame thereof, or flowed fuller or lower than was asserted; and I hung on his words intently, but of the matter I was but as a careless and a contemptuous spectator; and I was delighted with the pleasantness of his speech, more erudite, yet less cheerful and soothing in manner, than that of Faustus. Of the matter, however, there could be no comparison; for the latter was straying amid Manichaean deceptions, while the former was teaching salvation most soundly. But salvation is far from the wicked, such as I then stood before him; and yet I was drawing nearer gradually and unconsciously.

xiv. Having heard the bishop, he perceives the force of the Catholic faith, yet doubts, after the manner of the modern academics

For although I took no trouble to learn what he spoke, but only to hear how he spoke (for that empty care alone remained to me, despairing of a way accessible for man to Thee), yet, together with the words which I prized, there came into my mind also the things about which I was careless; for I could not separate them. And whilst I opened my heart to admit how skilfully he spoke, there also entered with it, but gradually, and how truly he spoke! For first, these things also had begun to appear to me to be defensible; and the Catholic faith, for which I had fancied nothing could be said against the attacks of the Manichaeans, I now conceived might be maintained without presumption; especially after I had heard one or two parts of the Old Testament explained, and often allegorically—which when I accepted literally, I was killed spiritually. . . .

Hereupon did I earnestly bend my mind to see if in any way I could possibly prove the Manichaeans guilty of falsehood. Could I have realized a spiritual substance, all their strongholds would have been beaten down, and cast utterly out of my mind; but I could not. But yet, concerning the body of this world, and the whole of nature, which the senses of the flesh can attain unto, I now more and more considering and comparing things, judged that the greater part of the philosophers held much the more probable opinions. So, then, after the manner of the Academics (as they are supposed), doubting of everything and fluctuating between all, I decided that the Manichaeans were to be abandoned; judging that, even while in that period of doubt, I could not remain in a sect to which I preferred some of the philosophers; to which philosophers, however, because they were without the saving name of Christ, I utterly refused to commit the cure of my fainting soul. I resolved, therefore, to be a catechumen in the Catholic Church, which my parents had commended to me, until something settled should manifest itself to me wither I might steer my course.

BOOK SEVEN

ix. He compares the doctrine of the Platonists concerning the Logos *with the much more excellent doctrine of Christianity*

And Thou, willing first to show me how Thou resistest the proud, but givest grace unto the humble, and by how great an act of mercy Thou hadst pointed out to men the path of humility, in that Thy Word was made flesh and dwelt among men— Thou procuredst for me, by the instrumentality of one inflated with most monstrous pride, certain books of the Platonists, translated from Greek into Latin. And therein I read, not indeed in the same words, but to the selfsame effect, enforced by many and varied reasons, that, In the beginning was the Word, and the Word was with God and the Word was God. The same was in the beginning with God. All things were made by Him; and without Him was not anything made that was made. That which was made by Him is life; and the life was the light of men. And the light shineth in darkness; and the darkness comprehendeth it not. And that the soul of man, though it bears witness of the light, yet itself is not that light; but the Word of God, being God, is that true light that lighteth every man that cometh into the world. And that He was in the world, and the world was made by Him, and the world knew Him not. But that He came unto His own, and His own received Him not. But as many as received Him, to them gave He power to become the sons of God, even to them that believe on His name. This I did not read there.

In like manner, I read there that God the Word was born not of flesh, nor of blood, nor of the will of man, nor of the will of the flesh, but of God. But that the Word was made flesh, and dwelt among us, I read not there. For I discovered in those books that it was in many and varied ways said, that the Son was in the form of the Father, and thought it not robbery to be equal with God, for that naturally He was the same substance. But that He emptied Himself, and took upon Him the form of a servant, and was made in the likeness of men: and being found in fashion as a man, He humbled Himself, and became obedient unto death, even the death of the cross. Wherefore God also hath highly exalted Him from the dead, and given Him a name above every name; that at the name of Jesus every knee should bow, of things in heaven, and things in earth, and things under the earth; and that every tongue should confess that Jesus Christ is Lord, to the glory of God the Father; those books have not. For that before all times, and above all times, Thy only-begotten Son remaineth unchangeably co-eternal with Thee; and that of His fulness souls receive, that they may be blessed; and that by participation of the wisdom remaining in them they are renewed, that they may be wise, is there. But that in due time Christ died for the ungodly, and that Thou sparedst not Thine only Son, but deliveredst Him up for us all, is not there. . . .

x. Divine things are the more clearly manifested to him who withdraws into the recesses of his heart.

And being thence warned to return to myself, I entered into my inward self, Thou leading me on; and I was able to do it, for Thou wert become my helper. And I entered, and with the eye of my soul (such as it was) saw above the same eye of my soul, above my mind, the Unchangeable Light. Not this common light, which all flesh may look upon, nor, as it were, a greater one of the same kind, as though the brightness of this should be much more resplendent, and with its greatness fill up all things. Not like this was that light, but different, very different from all these. Nor was it above my mind as oil is above water, nor as heaven above earth; but above it was, because it made me, and I below it, because I was made by it. He who knows the Truth knows that Light; and he that knows it knoweth eternity. Love

knoweth it. O Eternal Truth, and true love, and loved Eternity! Thou art my God; to Thee do I sigh both night and day. When I first knew Thee, Thou liftedst me up, that I might see there was that which I might see, and that yet it was not I that did see. And Thou didst beat back the infirmity of my sight, pouring forth upon me most strongly Thy beams of light, and I trembled with love and fear; and I found myself to be far off from Thee, in the region of dissimilarity, as if I heard this voice of Thine from on high: "I am the food of strong men; grow, and thou shalt feed upon me; nor shalt thou convert me, like the food of thy flesh, into thee, but thou shalt be converted into me." And I learned that Thou for iniquity dost correct man, and Thou dost make my soul to consume away like a spider. And I said, "Is Truth, therefore, nothing because it is neither diffused through space, finite, nor infinite?" And Thou criedst to me from afar, "Yea, verily, 'I Am That I Am.' " And I heard this, as things are heard in the heart, nor was there room for doubt; and I should more readily doubt that I live than that Truth is not, which is clearly seen, being understood by the things that are made.

xi. That creatures are mutable and God alone immutable

And I viewed the other things below Thee, and perceived that they neither altogether are, nor altogether are not. They are, indeed, because they are from Thee; but are not, because they are not what Thou art. For that truly is which remains immutably. It is good, then, for me to cleave unto God, for if I remain not in Him, neither shall I in myself; but He, remaining in Himself, reneweth all things. And Thou art the Lord my God, since Thou standest not in need of my goodness.

xii. Whatever things the good God has created are very good

And it was made clear to me that those things are good which yet are corrupted, which, neither were they supremely good, nor unless they were good, could be corrupted; because if supremely good, they were incorruptible, and if not good at all, there was nothing in them to be corrupted. For corruption harms, but, unless it could diminish goodness, it could not harm. Either, then, corruption harms not, which cannot be; or, what is most certain, all which is corrupted is deprived of good. But if they be deprived of all good, they will cease to be. For if they be, and cannot be at all corrupted, they will become better, because they shall remain incorruptibly. And what more monstrous than to assert that those things which have lost all their goodness are made better? Therefore, if they shall be deprived of all good, they shall no longer be. So long, therefore, as they are, they are good; therefore whatsoever is, is good. That evil, then, which I sought whence it was, is not any substance; for were it a substance, it would be good. For either it would be an incorruptible substance, and so a chief good, or a corruptible substance, which unless it were good it could not be corrupted. I perceived, therefore, and it was made clear to me, that Thou didst make all things good, nor is there any substance at all that was not made by Thee; and because all that Thou hast made are not equal, therefore all things are; because individually they are good, and altogether very good, because our God made all things very good.

xvi. Evil arises not from a substance, but from the perversion of the will

And I discerned and found it no marvel, that bread which is distasteful to an unhealthy palate is pleasant to a healthy one; and that the light, which is painful to sore eyes, is delightful to sound ones. And Thy righteousness displeaseth the wicked; much more the viper and little worm, which Thou hast created good, fitting in with inferior parts of Thy creation; with which the wicked themselves also fit in, the more in proportion as they are unlike Thee, but with the superior creatures, in proportion as they become like to Thee. And I inquired what iniquity was, and ascertained it not to be a substance, but a perversion of the will, bent aside from Thee, O God, the Supreme Substance, towards these lower things, and casting out its bowels, and swelling outwardly.

xvii. Above his changeable mind, he discovers the unchangeable author of truth

And I marvelled that I now loved Thee, and no phantasm instead of Thee. And yet I did not merit to enjoy my God, but was transported to Thee by Thy beauty, and presently torn away from Thee by mine own weight, sinking with grief into these inferior things. This weight was carnal custom. Yet was there a remembrance of Thee with me; nor did I any way doubt that there was one to whom I might cleave, but that I was not yet one who could cleave unto Thee; for the body which is corrupted presseth down the soul, and the earthly dwelling weigheth down the mind which thinketh upon many things. And most certain I was that Thy invisible things from the creation of the world are clearly seen, being understood by the things that are made, even Thy eternal power and Godhead. For, inquiring whence it was that I admired the beauty of bodies whether celestial or terrestrial, and what supported me in judging correctly on things mutable, and pronouncing, "This should be thus, this not,"—

inquiring, then, whence I so judged, seeing I did so judge, I had found the unchangeable and true eternity of Truth, above my changeable mind. And thus, by degrees, I passed from bodies to the soul, which makes use of the senses of the body to perceive; and thence to its inward faculty, to which the bodily senses represent outward things, and up to which reach the capabilities of beasts; and thence, again, I passed on to the reasoning faculty, to which whatever is received from the senses of the body is referred to be judged, which also, finding itself to be variable in me, raised itself up to its own intelligence, and from habit drew away my thoughts, withdrawing itself from the crowds of contradictory phantasms; that so it might find out that light by which it was besprinkled, when, without all doubting, it cried out, that the unchangeable was to be preferred before the changeable; whence also it knew that unchangeable, which, unless it had in some way known, it could have had no sure ground for preferring it to the changeable. And thus, with the flash of a trembling glance, it arrived at that which is. And then I saw Thy invisible things understood by the things that are made. But I was not able to fix my gaze thereon; and my infirmity being beaten back, I was thrown again on my accustomed habits, carrying along with me naught but a loving memory thereof, and an appetite for what I had, as it were, smelt the odor of, but was not yet able to eat.

xviii. Jesus Christ, the mediator, is the only way of safety

And I sought a way of acquiring strength sufficient to enjoy Thee; but I found it not until I embraced that Mediator between God and man, the man Christ Jesus, who is over all, God blessed forever, calling unto me, and saying, I am the way, the truth, and the life, and mingling that food which I was unable to receive with our flesh. For the Word was made flesh, that Thy Wisdom, by which Thou createdst all things, might provide milk for our infancy. For I did not grasp my Lord Jesus— I, though humbled, grasped not the humble One; nor did I know what lesson that infirmity of His would teach us. For Thy Word, the Eternal Truth, pre-eminent above the higher parts of Thy creation, raises up those that are subject unto Itself; but in this lower world built for Itself a humble habitation of our clay, whereby He intended to abase from themselves such as would be subjected and bring them over unto Himself, allaying their swelling, and fostering their love; to the end that they might go on no further in self-confidence, but rather should become weak, seeing before their feet the Divinity weak by taking our coats of skins; and wearied, might cast themselves down upon It, and It rising, might lift them up.

BOOK EIGHT

vi. Pontitianus' account of Antony, the founder of Monachism, and of some who imitated him

Upon a certain day . . . there came to the house to see Alypius and me, Pontitianus, a countryman of ours, in so far as he was an African, who held high office in the emperor's court. What he wanted with us I know not, but we sat down to talk together, and it fell out that upon a table before us, used for games, he noticed a book; he took it up, opened it, and, contrary to his expectation, found it to be the Apostle Paul—for he imagined it to be one of those books which I was wearing myself out in teaching. At this he looked up at me smilingly, and expressed his delight and wonder that he had so unexpectedly found this book, and this only, before my eyes. For he was both a Christian and baptized, and often prostrated himself before Thee our God in the church, in constant and daily prayers. When, then, I had told him that I bestowed much pains upon these writings, a conversation ensued on his speaking of Antony, the Egyptian monk, whose name was in high repute among Thy servants, though up to that time not familiar to us. When he came to know us, he lingered on that topic, imparting to us a knowledge of this man so eminent, and marvelling at our ignorance. But we were amazed, hearing Thy wonderful works most fully manifested in times so recent, and almost in our own, wrought in the true faith and the Catholic Church. We all wondered—we, that they were so great, and he, that we had never heard of them.

From this his conversation turned to the companies in the monasteries, and their manners so fragrant unto Thee, and of the fruitful deserts of the wilderness, of which we knew nothing. And there was a monastery at Milan full of good brethren, without the walls of the city, under the fostering care of Ambrose, and we were ignorant of it. He went on with his relation, and we listened intently and in silence. He then related to us how on a certain afternoon, at Triers, when the emperor was taken up with seeing the Circensian games, he and three others, his comrades, went out for a walk in the gardens close to the city walls, and there, as they chanced to walk two and two, one strolled away with him, while the other two went by themselves; and these, in their rambling, came upon a certain cottage inhabited by some of Thy servants, poor in spirit, of whom is the kingdom of heaven, where they found a book in which was written the life of Antony. This one of

them began to read, marvel at, and be inflamed by it; and in the reading, to meditate on embracing such a life, and giving up his worldly employments to serve Thee. And these were of the body called Agents for Public Affairs. Then, suddenly being overwhelmed with a holy love and a sober sense of shame, in anger with himself, he cast his eyes upon his friend, exclaiming, "Tell me, I entreat thee, what end we are striving for by all these labors of ours. What is our aim? What is our motive in doing service? Can our hopes in court rise higher than to be ministers of the emperor? And in such a position, what is there not brittle, and fraught with danger, and by how many dangers arrive we at greater danger? And when arrive we thither? But if I desire to become a friend of God, behold, I am even now made it." Thus he spoke, and in the pangs of the travail of the new life, he turned his eyes again upon the page and continued reading, and was inwardly changed where Thou sawest, and his mind was divested of the world, as soon became evident; for as he read, and the surging of his heart rolled along, he raged awhile, discerned and resolved on a better course, and now, having become Thine, he said to his friend, "Now have I broken loose from those hopes of ours, and am determined to serve God; and this, from this hour, in this place, I enter upon. If thou art reluctant to imitate me, hinder me not." The other replied that he would cleave to him, to share in so great a reward and so great a service. Thus both of them, being now Thine, were building a tower at the necessary cost—of forsaking all that they had and following Thee. Then Pontitianus, and he who had walked with him through other parts of the garden, came in search of them to the same place, and having found them, reminded them to return as the day had declined. But they, making known to him their resolution and purpose, and how such a resolve had sprung up and become confirmed in them, entreated them not to molest them, if they refused to join themselves to them. But the others, no whit changed from their former selves, did yet (as he said) bewail themselves, and piously congratulated them, recommending themselves to their prayers; and with their hearts inclining towards earthly things, returned to the palace. But the other two, setting their affections upon heavenly things, remained in the cottage. And both of them had affianced brides, who, when they heard of this, dedicated also their virginity to Thee.

vii. He deplores his wretchedness, that having been born thirty-two years, he had not yet found out the truth

Such was the story of Pontitianus. But Thou, O Lord, whilst he was speaking, didst turn me towards myself, taking me from behind my back, where I had placed myself while unwilling to exercise self-scrutiny; and Thou didst set me face to face with myself, that I might behold how foul I was, and how crooked and sordid, bespotted and ulcerous. And I beheld and loathed myself; and whither to fly from myself I discovered not. And if I sought to turn my gaze away from myself, he continued his narrative, and Thou again opposedst me unto myself, and thrustedst me before my own eyes, that I might discover my iniquity, and hate it. I had known it, but acted as though I knew it not—winked at it, and forgot it.

But now, the more ardently I loved those whose healthful affections I heard of, that they had given up themselves wholly to Thee to be cured, the more did I abhor myself when compared with them.

For many of my years (perhaps twelve) had passed away since my nineteenth, when, on the reading of Cicero's *Hortensius,* I was roused to a desire for wisdom; and still I was delaying to reject mere worldly happiness, and to devote myself to search out that of which not the finding alone, but the bare search, ought to have been preferred before the treasures and kingdoms of this world, though already found, and before the pleasures of the body, though encompassing me at my will. But I, miserable young man, supremely miserable even in the very outset of my youth, had entreated chastity of Thee, and said, "Grant me chastity and continency, but not yet." For I was afraid lest Thou shouldest hear me soon, and soon deliver me from the disease of concupiscence, which I desired to have satisfied rather than extinguished. . . .

. . . Thus was I inwardly consumed and mightily confounded with a horrible shame, while Pontitianus was relating these things. And he, having finished his story, and the business he came for, went his way. And to myself, what said I not within myself? With what scourges of rebuke lashed I not my soul to make it follow me, struggling to go after Thee! Yet it drew back; it refused, and exercised not itself. All its arguments were exhausted and confuted. There remained a silent trembling; and it feared, as it would death, to be restrained from the flow of that custom whereby it was wasting away even to death.

viii. The conversation with Alypius being ended, he retires to the garden, whither his friend follows him

In the midst, then, of this great strife of my inner dwelling, which I had strongly raised up against my soul in the chamber of my heart, troubled both in mind and countenance, I seized upon Alypius, and exclaimed: "What is wrong with us? What is this? What heardest thou? The unlearned start up and 'take' heaven, and we, with our learning, but wanting heart, see where we wallow in flesh and blood! Because others have preceded us, are we ashamed to follow, and not rather ashamed at not following?" Some such words I uttered, and in my excitement flung myself from him, while he gazed upon me in silent astonishment. For I spoke not in my wonted tone, and my brow, cheeks, eyes, color, tone of voice, all expressed my emotion more than the words. There was a little garden belonging to our lodging, of which we had the use, as of the whole house; for the master, our landlord, did not live there. Thither had the tempest within my breast hurried me, where no one might impede the fiery struggle in which I was engaged with myself, until it came to the issue that Thou knewest, though I did not. But I was mad that I might be whole, and dying that I might have life, knowing what evil thing I was, but not knowing what good thing I was shortly to become. Into the garden, then, I retired, Alypius following my steps. For his presence was no bar to my solitude; or how could he desert me so troubled? We sat down at as great a distance from the house as we could. I was disquieted in spirit, being most impatient with myself that I entered not into Thy will and covenant, O my God, which all my bones cried out to me to enter, extolling it to the skies. And we enter not therein by ships, or chariots, or feet, no, nor by going so far as I had come from the house to that place where we were sitting. For not to go only, but to enter there, was naught else but to will to go, but to will it resolutely and thoroughly; not to stagger and sway about this way and that, a changeable and half-wounded will, wrestling, with one part falling as another rose. . . .

xi. In what manner the spirit struggled with the flesh, that it might be freed from the bondage of vanity

Thus was I sick and tormented, accusing myself far more severely than was my wont, tossing and turning me in my chain till that was utterly broken, whereby I now was but slightly, but still was held. And Thou, O Lord, pressedst upon me in my inward parts by a severe mercy, redoubling the lashes of fear and shame, lest I should again give way, and that same slender remaining tie not being broken off, it should recover strength, and enchain me the faster. For I said mentally, "Lo, let it be done now, let it be done now." And as I spoke, I all but came to a resolve. I all but did it, yet I did it not. Yet I fell not back to my old condition, but took up my position hard by, and drew breath. And I tried again, and wanted but very little of reaching it, and somewhat less, and then all but touched and grasped it; and yet came not at it, nor touched, nor grasped it, hesitating to die to death, and to live to life; and the worse, to which I had been habituated, prevailed more with me than the better, which I had not tried. And the very moment in which I was to become another man, the nearer it approached me, the greater horror did it strike into me; but it did not strike me back, nor turn me aside, but kept me in suspense.

The very toys of toys, and vanities of vanities, my old mistresses, still enthralled me; they shook my fleshly garment, and whispered softly, "Dost thou part with us? And from that moment shall we no more be with thee for ever? And from that moment shall not this or that be lawful for thee for ever?" And what did they suggest to me in the words "this or that?" What is it they suggested, O my God? Let Thy mercy avert it from the soul of Thy servant. What impurities did they suggest! What shame! And now I far less than half heard them, not openly showing themselves and contradicting me, but muttering, as it were, behind my back, and furtively plucking me as I was departing, to make me look back upon them. Yet they did delay me, so that I hesitated to burst and shake myself free from them, and to leap over wither I was called—an unruly habit saying to me, "Dost thou think thou canst live without them?"

But now it said this very faintly; for on that side towards which I had set my face, and whither I trembled to go, did the chaste dignity of Continence appear to me, cheerful, but not dissolutely gay, honestly alluring me to come and doubt nothing, and extending her holy hands, full of a multiplicity of good examples, to receive and embrace me. There were there so many young men and maidens, a multitude of youth and every age, grave widows and ancient virgins, and Continence herself in all, not barren, but a fruitful mother of children of joys, by Thee, O Lord, her Husband. And she smiled on me with an encouraging mockery, as if to say, "Canst not thou do what these youths and maidens can? Or can one or other do it of themselves, and not rather in the Lord their God? The Lord their God gave me to them. Why standest thou in thine own strength, and so standest not? Cast thyself upon Him; fear not, He will not withdraw that thou shouldest fall; cast thyself upon Him without fear, He will receive thee, and heal thee." And I blushed beyond measure, for I still heard the muttering of

those toys, and hung in suspense. And she again seemed to say, "Shut up thine ears against those unclean members of thine upon the earth, that they may be mortified. They tell thee of delights, but not as doth the law of the Lord thy God." This controversy in my heart was naught but self against self. But Alypius, sitting close by my side, awaited in silence the result of my unwonted emotion.

xii. *Having prayed to God, he pours forth a shower of tears, and, admonished by a voice, he opens the book and reads the words in Romans XIII:13; by which, being changed in his whole soul, he discloses the divine favor to his friend and his mother*

But when a profound reflection had, from the secret depths of my soul, drawn together and heaped up all my misery before the sight of my heart, there arose a mighty storm, accompanied by as mighty a shower of tears. Which, that I might pour forth fully, with its natural expressions, I stole away from Alypius; for it suggested itself to me that solitude was fitter for the business of weeping. So I retired to such a distance that even his presence could not be oppressive to me. Thus it was with me at that time, and he perceived it; for something, I believe, I had spoken, wherein the sound of my voice appeared choked with weeping, and in that state had I risen up. He then remained where we had been sitting, most completely astonished. I flung myself down, how, I know not, under a certain fig-tree, giving free course to my tears, and the streams of mine eyes gushed out, an acceptable sacrifice unto Thee. And, not indeed in these words, yet to this effect, spake I much unto Thee—"But Thou, O Lord, how long?" "How long, Lord? Wilt Thou be angry for ever? Oh, remember not against us former iniquities;" for I felt that I was enthralled by them. I sent up these sorrowful cries—"How long, how long? To-morrow, and to-morrow? Why not now? Why is there not this hour an end to my uncleanness?"

I was saying these things and weeping and in the most bitter contrition of my heart, when, lo, I heard the voice as of a boy or girl, I know not which, coming from a neighboring house, chanting, and oft repeating, "Take up and read; take up and read." Immediately my countenance was changed, and I began most earnestly to consider whether it was usual for children in any kind of game to sing such words; nor could I remember ever to have heard the like. So, restraining the torrent of my tears, I rose up, interpreting it no other way than as a command to me from Heaven to open the book, and to read the first chapter I should light upon. For I had heard of Antony, that, accidentally coming in while the gospel was being read, he received the admonition as if what was read were addressed to him, "Go and sell that thou hast, and give to the poor, and thou shalt have treasure in heaven; and come and follow me." And by such oracle was he forthwith converted unto Thee. So quickly I returned to the place where Alypius was sitting; for there had I put down the volume of the apostles, when I rose thence. I grasped, opened, and in silence read that paragraph on which my eyes first fell—"Not in rioting and drunkenness, not in chambering and wantonness, not in strife and envying; but put ye on the Lord Jesus Christ, and make not provision for the flesh, to fulfil the lusts thereof." No further would I read, nor did I need; for instantly, as the sentence ended—by a light, as it were, of security

infused into my heart—all the gloom of doubt vanished away.

Closing the book, then, and putting either my finger between, or some other mark, I now with a tranquil countenance made it known to Alypius. And he thus disclosed to me what was wrought in him, which I knew not. He asked to look at what I had read. I showed him; and he looked even further than I had read, and I knew not what followed. This it was, "Him that is weak in the faith, receive ye;" which he applied to himself, and discovered to me. By this admonition was he strengthened; and by a good resolution and purpose, very much in accord with his character (in which, for the better, he was always far different from me), without any restless delay he joined me. Thence we go in to my mother. We make it known to her—she rejoices. We relate how it came to pass—she leaps for joy, and triumphs, and blesses Thee, who art able to do exceeding abundantly above all that we ask or think; for she perceived Thee to have given her more for me than she used to ask by her pitiful and most doleful groanings. For Thou didst so convert me unto Thyself, that I sought neither a wife, nor any other of this world's hopes—standing in that rule of faith in which Thou, so many years before, had showed me unto her in a vision. And thou didst turn her grief into a gladness, much more plentiful than she had desired, and much dearer and chaster than she used to crave, by having grandchildren of my body.

Saint Augustine's spiritual odyssey had ended in a surrender to the authority of Christian faith. His wandering spirit had found its true home. The experience in the Milanese garden led Augustine to abandon his plans for an advantageous marriage and his official position as rhetor in Milan, and to go with his mother, some cousins, and a few other young friends, including Alypius, to Cassiciacum, a retreat on Lake Como in sight of the Alps. There Augustine began his life as a Christian scholar and teacher, sketching out a program for continued philosophical speculation in the light of the gospel. After a year at Cassiciacum, and following his baptism by Saint Ambrose, Augustine decided to return to his home town in North Africa. On the way there, his mother Monica died, but Augustine and a group of friends continued their journey and arrived in Thagaste in 388. Augustine was now a *Servus Dei,* a Servant of God, one of many such men set apart from the rest of society by their black robes and dedication to a life in the service of the Church. Augustine and his friends had no special functions to perform, but were honored by pious Christians wherever they travelled. Alypius soon became the bishop of Thagaste, and Augustine engaged his intellectual powers by writing as a defender of orthodoxy against the Manichaean sect which he knew so intimately and which was still popular in North Africa.

Soon Augustine and a number of other *Servi Dei* felt the need to provide a more regular life for themselves. They sought a place where they could carry on their theological discussions and practice an ascetic life. In 381 Augustine went to Hippo Regius, the second greatest city in North Africa after Carthage, in search of a suitable monastic retreat. This he was successful in finding, but at the same time he was drafted as a priest by the local bishop and the popular acclamation of his congregation. Augustine continued to live in monastic seclusion with his fellow *Servi Dei,* but worked actively in the affairs of the Church and soon gained a considerable reputation as a preacher. This became the pattern for others in the monastic community at Hippo. Rather than an ascetic retreat from the world, it became in effect a seminary from which young men were sent out to become priests and bishops in the African Church.

Within four years Augustine was made bishop of Hippo, the position he held for the remainder of his life. The duties of a Catholic bishop in a bustling port city were varied and often arduous, and Augustine must have often regretted the series of events which had led him to this position. As bishop, he was responsible for the effective operations of the church in his district and constantly had to travel to small backward towns as well as to the metropolitan see at Carthage. A bishop in the late Roman Empire often found himself looked upon much as the head of a large family or as a patron for his clients. He had to act as an arbitrator of lawsuits which arose between members of his congregation, and as a special pleader before the secular authorities on behalf of his parishoners. These were in addition to his duties as preacher, counselor, and priest.

Life as bishop of Hippo was far different from the life of Christian scholarship Augustine had first envisioned at Cassiciacum. He was, nonetheless, able to find time to lead a full and creative intellectual life. His sermons were taken down by scribes and distributed throughout the Christian Church. He wrote long and carefully composed letters to other churchmen on matters of doctrine and Church policy. He became a leading defender of the faith against heretical sects which continued to plague the African Church. Augustine also found time for more scholarly writing. He produced several studies on scripture, and the great theological treatises which have made him the single most important father of the Western Church.

It is evident from the many works which came from Augustine's pen in the next several years that the personal struggle which he had reported in the *Confessions* was as much an intellectual as a spiritual affair. His affirmation of the Christian faith had not resulted in the abandonment of reason. He could not, like Tertullian, believe it because it was absurd. On the contrary, Saint Augustine found in the Christian faith a resolution of the many philosophical problems which had disturbed him all his life. He had found certainty—the *Truth.* His many theologicial writings and sermons are all in one way or another an elaboration and explanation of this insight which he had first gained in the Milanese garden.

As such they are a searching examination of the relationship between the contemplative and spiritual life—between knowledge and faith.

KNOWLEDGE AND FAITH
Karl Löwith[12]

To inquire into the relation between knowledge and faith may seem to presuppose that philosophical knowledge has necessary and intrinsic relation to faith. This presupposition, however, finds no warrant in the history of Greek thought, from which our later philosophy is derived. It holds only for philosophy in the Christian Era. Both the separation of knowledge and faith and the attempt to harmonize them are peculiar to Christianity. For this reason we must start by seeking to determine how the Greeks understood the relation of faith to knowledge.

Classical philosophy does not confine itself to the either-or of knowledge and faith in the Christian sense, but addresses itself to the difference between *episteme* and *doxa*. *Doxa* may be translated as opinion as well as belief. The latter is at stake when we speak of "orthodoxy." Measured against *episteme* as true knowledge, *doxa* is but belief in the sense of a simple acceptance of some truth, not faith in the New Testament sense of *pistis*. What *doxa* holds to be true is in reality but a semblance, a seeming truth. One thinks or believes that one knows what is true, but does not really know the truth.

This difference between *doxa* and *episteme* is fundamental for all philosophical

[12] From pp. 197–202 "Knowledge and Faith: From the Pre-Socratics to Heidegger" by Karl Löwith in *Religion and Culture: Essays in Honor of Paul Tillich*, edited by Walter Leibrecht. Copyright © 1959 by Walter Leibrecht. By permission of Harper & Row, Publishers. Footnotes have been omitted.

reflection. There is for antiquity no transition from faith in the invisible to knowledge of the empirical and demonstrable. There is instead the possibility of ascending from opinion to true knowledge. All his life Socrates did nothing else but question the unexamined opinions of his contemporaries in order to bring them gradually to real knowledge, or at least to the admission of their lack of knowledge. Faith in the Christian sense, which is no mere taking-to-be-true and not-yet-knowing, allows no similar transition to evident knowledge, because Christian faith is not conceived as an initial step to demonstrable knowledge. . . .

The Christian view of the relation of Faith to knowledge receives its decisive expression in the theology of St. Paul. Paul distinguishes philosophical knowledge, as the wisdom of this world, from the true wisdom of faith, by comparison with which the wisdom of this world is folly before God. Faith itself is characterized in the New Testament as certainty, not certainty on the basis of theoretical evidence but certainy on the basis of an unconditional trust in things which cannot be seen and understood. Paul's alternative between worldly, evident insight and faithful trust in the invisible and uncertain survives not only in theology and its concept of faith but in philosophy and its concept of knowledge as well. Until the eighteenth century, philosophy described itself as "worldly wisdom," in contrast to an entirely different wisdom which is not of this world.

But pre-Christian, classical thought does not move within this alternative of worldly knowledge and otherworldly faith. Greek philosophy wants to know what is, even what God or the divine is. And where there is knowledge there are supposed to be proofs, even proofs of the existence of

God. These proofs do not presuppose any faith; but demonstrate the divine in its relation to the visible world, or as directly known in the cosmos. Thus ancient theology is par excellence theological ontology and cosmology, but not a theology of faith. The Greeks did not ask so much about the *existence* but rather about the *essence* of the divine, about the nature of the gods. The existence of the gods was generally taken for granted. The nature of the gods seemed to manifest itself in the ancient natural world and consequently could be proved by natural theology.

All Christian proofs of God, from Paul to Anselm, ask primarily about God's *existence*. Because the Christian God is an otherworldly, invisible Creator of all that is, His existence must be proved, since it cannot be shown from that which already is. The Biblical God cannot be seen simply in His creation. In order to see the whole visible world, heaven and earth, as creation, one would have first to know about its Creator, and one knows of Him only through faith in His Word in Scripture. The really *Christian* proofs of God have no intention of somehow establishing faith in God; rather, they take faith for granted, in order to make it intelligible to natural reason. To the extent that they try to prove more, they are justly subjected to philosophical criticism. Both the proofs of God by the believing theologians and their critique by philosophers presupposed that philosophical knowledge and Christian faith are two different things.

So far is Greek theology from being in conflict with philosophy that theology was thought to be philosophy's most characteristic product, the highest knowledge of the highest being, particularly in its contrast to the popular religion of the *polis*. The question is not: Can one know God or must one first believe in Him? but rather: Does philosophic wisdom provide a more satisfactory understanding of the divine than popular religion? Greek philosophy, which had to come to terms with popular stories of the gods and with myths, therefore has an entirely different attitude toward knowledge than Christian philosophy, which has to come to terms with the dogmatic claim of a revealed faith. Yet, because knowledge in the Christian Era finds itself in this awkward relation to faith, it cannot avoid looking about to see if there is not a reasonable way, in spite of everything, in which fallible knowledge can approach self-confident faith.

Such a way was broached by Augustine with exemplary clarity in his work, *Concerning the Usefulness of Faith*. Augustine follows the Epistle to the Hebrews in his definition of faith: unconditional trust in things which one cannot see or know as one can visible things. His first question bears upon the priority of faith to knowing insight. He wishes to show that, far from being contrary to reason, preliminary subjection to faith is demonstrably reasonable: it is rational for one to believe *before* one knows. If the decision to believe were against reason, *fides* would be but *credulitas*. Augustine illustrates the difference between genuine faith and mere credulity by the difference between being *studiosus* and being *curious*. Both the merely curious and the earnestly industrious person want to know something, just as the credulous and the faithful person both believe something. The difference, however, is that the curious person wants to know much that does not concern him, whereas the faithful person seeks to know only that which is useful and profitable to him, because it serves the salvation of his soul. But admitting that the *credulity* and *faith* of these people are not the same thing, it is still possible that both sorts of belief are false paths, if we are concerned with nothing less than knowing with unconditional certainty what is helpful to the eternal salvation of the soul, because it is the truth of the Christian religion. How sad it would be for the welfare of the soul if *credulitas* and *fides* differ only as do occasional intoxication and habitual alcoholism? If this were the case, Augustine says, then it would not only be impossible to have faith in the religious sense but one could not even have a friend or trust one's parents nor simply engage in business with others. All of human life, most notably community life, is based on mutual trust, loyalty, and faith in things which cannot be seen and known.

As an example of the usefulness and reasonableness of belief *before* all perception, knowledge, and insight, Augustine gives the following instance: one cannot love and trust one's parents unless one believes that they are one's parents. But whether they really are one's parents can never be known with certainty, in the case of the father not at all and of the mother not with complete certainty. One accepts the mother's word, or that of relatives, servants, and doctors, but if someone should draw the conclusion, since this is not certain, I am likewise not obliged to love and obey my presumed parents, one would act not only foolishly but highly immorally. In contrast, he who fulfills his filial duties faithfully, even if it should later be discovered that his presumed parents are not really his parents at all, would have acted in a morally right manner. If, then, trust, faith in something unseeable and unknowable, is found rationally justifiable in merely human relationships in which unconditional, unrestrained trust might seem out of place, how much more will it be

necessary first of all to trust God, in order to come into any relationship with Him at all?

In the same way, Augustine says, the natural relationship of trust between individuals is necessary to and basic for access to Christian faith and its proclamation in the Church. A man learns of the Christian message only through hearing it preached by others who already believe. If one is to believe, one must first of all be willing to listen to others who already believe; one must be willing to learn and let oneself be instructed in the Christian religion by a teacher. In this initial relationship of teacher and pupil, we must reasonably presuppose that the pupil will trust his teacher and, conversely, that the teacher will trust the pupil. The teacher believes that the pupil will really allow himself to be instructed in the Christian faith and is not merely curious or out to dupe the teacher. Whoever first critically tests the trustworthiness of the one he is supposed to trust, putting him on trial, only shows thereby that he has no confidence and also mistrusts his own trust. Trust will never follow from mistrust.

Here a great difficulty arises, which Augustine examines in detail. How shall the unbelieving fool, who indeed seeks after truth but has not yet found it in faith, ever find the religiously informed or wise man, who already is well acquainted with Christianity? The fool would have to be a sage himself in order to be able to recognize the wise man as such. While seeking for the right teacher, how can one keep from falling prey to a teacher of falsehood, especially when so many philosophical schools and religious sects claim the same authority and maintain that they possess the truth? How can one be certain that *fides* in an *auctoritas* is no mere *credulitas* in a false authority? This, says Augustine, is an exceptionally difficult question, which gets one into the greatest perplexity. Even visible signs of Christian truth, such as conversions or miracles, are of little avail. How is one supposed to recognize such manifestations of God as signs, without knowing beforehand what they are signs of? A waymarker cannot be recognized as a waymarker if one does not already know what a way is.

The difficulty, says Augustine, is so great that only God Himself can solve it, when He brings foolish man into the way to faith and thus to believing insight into the truth of the Christian religion. We are unable to ask inquiringly about the true religion if God does not exist and come to our help even in our seeking. The divine authority, to which I am to give faith, must give me that very faith. Even when faith is no mere decision and no mere leap but is inspired by God Himself, it is still a daring wager, the wager of letting oneself go. Faith does not presume knowledge of the outcome of the undertaking.

If we analyze what is existentially a wager, we have a *circle,* in which what is to be proved is already assumed, namely, God, His revelation and faith in it. Augustine's last word on the relation between faith and knowledge is a sort of cyclical movement which turns back upon itself. He sees no contradiction between emphasizing against the Manichaeans that faith must precede insight and stressing against an irrational leap into faith that it is *reasonable* for faith to precede reason.

Thus Augustine set the pattern for subsequent orthodox Christian theology—belief, faith, and the authority of Church doctrine must precede intellectual curiosity. "Understanding is the reward of faith," Augustine wrote, "there-

fore seek not to understand that thou mayest believe, but believe that thou mayest understand."[13] There is still room for speculative philosophy, but it is given purpose and indeed the possibility of fulfillment only by theology. Speculation without faith is idle because it is not speculation about truth.

In the pages that follow we will attempt to treat in some detail six areas in which Augustine's writings were of critical importance in the transmission of the Judeo-Christian and Greco-Roman traditions and in the formulation of a Western Christian culture. These areas are: Christian education, speculative philosophy, the theology of grace, ethics, the relationship between Church and state, and the philosophy of history.

The Authority of Scripture and Church Doctrine in Christian Education

The relationship between religion and philosophy worked out in detail by Saint Augustine became the basis for Christian education in the West. It must be recalled that before his conversion to Christianity, Augustine had been a teacher by profession—a rhetorician, and that as a Christian he was a teacher and pastor as well as a theologian. In a treatise, *On Christian Education,* he took up what had been his professional concerns and interpreted them in the light of the Christian faith. The authoritative text on which Christian education must be based is, of course, Holy Scripture. One learns intellectual skills primarily in order to be able to discover God's truth as revealed in the Bible. In *On Christian Doctrine,* Augustine considers the uses of scripture, beginning in the first section with the allegorical method of interpretation first developed by Clement and Origen.

If the allegorical method fails to produce a single "correct" interpretation for each passage but leads instead to the perception of a diversity of meanings, some of which may not

[13] *On the Gospel of John,* xxix, 6.

have been intended by the author, this fact is regarded by St. Augustine not as a shortcoming but as a virtue, provided that all of these meanings are supported in other parts of the Scriptures. For although the Scriptures are the work of a variety of human authors, they have a single divine inspiration and may hence be considered as a work of unified intention. When we discover a meaning consistent with the whole but not intended by the human author, that meaning may be thought of as intended by the Divine Author, "who undoubtedly foresaw that this meaning would occur to the reader or listener." . . . In short, St. Augustine's method is based on that faith, hope, and charity which he so masterfully describes in Book I, and on a wholehearted trust in Providence rather than in science. . . .

Finally, *On Christian Doctrine* illustrates and describes a literary aesthetic which has much to do with the general character of early Western art and literature. The relevant passage is that in 2. 6. 7–8 where the assertion that the obscurity of Scripture is both pleasant and useful is illustrated by an analysis of a passage from the Canticle. Several features of this illustration deserve comment. St. Augustine says, "I contemplate the saints more pleasantly when I envisage them as the teeth of the Church," and again, "I recognize them most pleasantly as shorn sheep." It will be seen at once that the idea of saints as "teeth" or as "shorn sheep" does not belong to the same order of phenomena as the feeling conveyed by "my love is like a red, red rose." There is no spontaneous emotional appeal in St. Augustine's comparisons of the kind we expect in modern poetry. They do not, to use a phrase from Godwin, "awaken the imagination, astound the fancy, or hurry away the soul." Indeed, if we read what St. Augustine says about these figures with either modern romantic expectations or modern rationalistic expectations, it seems ridiculous. However, we should realize that romantic metaphor would have appeared laughable, or, perhaps, lamentable, to him and that he would have

regarded the modern scientific conscience as a form of slavery. The appeal of the Augustinian comparison lies in an intellectual recognition of an abstraction beneath the surface of the language. The "teeth" are admired as they function "cutting off men from their errors," and the "shorn sheep" are pleasantly, but intellectually, envisaged as "those who have put aside the burdens of the world like so much fleece." The passage from the Canticle is seen to conform, as it were, to the abstract pattern of behavior expected of holy men, and the discovery of this abstract pattern is experienced as a pleasing intellectual revelation. Much of the figurative material in medieval writing, and, in fact, much of the symbolism in medieval art, was designed to have exactly this kind of appeal; the function of figurative expression was not to arouse spontaneous emotional attitudes based on the personal experience of the observer, but to encourage the observer to seek an abstract pattern of philosophical significance beneath the symbolic configuration.[14]

This method of deriving understanding from Scripture was available to the educated churchman. But it was not his private possession; he was to communicate his understanding to others. In the second part of *On Christian Doctrine*, Augustine deals with the arts of persuasion, relying heavily on Cicero.

The tone is serene and uncontroversial. There is no hostility to rhetoric, which is recognised to be not without its uses. "It is true that the art of rhetoric is used for the purpose of commending both truth and falsehood, yet who would venture to say that truth should remain defenceless in the hands of its cham-

[14]From D. W. Robertson, Jr., introduction to *Saint Augustine: On Christian Doctrine*, translated by D. W. Robertson, Jr. Copyright © 1958 by The Liberal Arts Press, Inc. Reprinted by permission of the Liberal Arts Press Division of The Bobbs-Merrill Company, Inc. Footnotes have been omitted.

pions . . . ? The faculty of eloquence is something neutral, which has great persuasive effect whether for good or for evil; why then should not the good acquire it for use in the championship of truth, if the bad use it to win their perverse and vain causes in the interests of wickedness and error?" Or, as he says elsewhere, "The rules of rhetoric are none the less true, although they can be used in the interests of falsehood; but because they can also be used in the interests of truth, rhetorical skill is not in itself to be blamed, but rather the perversity of those who misuse it." . . .

So far Augustine follows Ciceronian doctrine. But the differences from Cicero are as remarkable as the resemblances. Augustine has freed himself more completely than Cicero ever did from the school tradition, and more than Cicero he emphasises the supreme importance of clarity and truth. Moreover Augustine's orator is a very different person from Cicero's; he is not the orator of the forum and the senate house, but the interpreter of the Scriptures and the defender of the faith. He is thus a sort of combination of the *grammaticus,* the philosopher and the orator of the pagan world. He studies his texts like the *grammaticus,* he teaches his doctrine like the philosopher and he persuades his hearers like the orator. His texts are of course the Scriptures, and this brings Augustine up against the question whether eloquence is to be found in the sacred writings. His answer is interesting. We have seen how many saw in them nothing but uncouthness. Augustine finds in the sacred authors an eloquence of their own, one which does not avoid the methods of rhetoric, but does not consciously make use of them. The words are not a detachable ornament, but arise spontaneously from the matter. . . .

In pointing to the formal beauties of scriptural passages Augustine seems to be accepting the standards of pagan culture, and bringing the biblical writings as it were into the canon of stylistic models accepted by the secular tradition. But this was not his purpose. It is clear that for him the Scriptures are to take the place of the pagan writers. The cultural background of the Christian teacher is to be completely different from that of the pagan. The Scriptures and the Christian Fathers provide the models to be studied and imitated, and if any non-Christian writers are to be studied, it is only to assist in understanding the Scriptures. Pagan learning is of use, so far as it is not connected with falsehood and superstition, but its usefulness is very limited. It is small compared with the learning of the Scriptures. "Whatever a man has learned outside is, if it is harmful, condemned in the Scriptures; if it is useful, it is found in them."[15]

The program of *On Christian Doctrine* is at first sight narrow, subordinating as it does all branches of learning to the canon of Scripture and the doctrines of the Church. But it was also a justification in the face of much hostile criticism for the retention of pagan learning in the educational curriculum. So long as the true purposes of learning were kept in mind and due regard paid to the authority of Church doctrine, the Christian was invited to speculate about the deepest mysteries of divine truth. Augustine thus established the necessity for the educated Christian to acquire the basic intellectual tools of pagan culture. In the form of the seven liberal arts (grammar, rhetoric, logic, arithmetic, geometry, music, astronomy), these classical disciplines became the basis for Christian education for the next thousand years. Augustine himself wrote treatises on grammar and music, but the authority of his defense of a liberal education was more important in the long run than his treatises. The most important texts in which a much-condensed version of the classical arts curriculum was preserved, were written by Boethius (480–524), a Roman scholar of the

[15] M. L. Clarke, *Rhetoric at Rome: A Historical Survey* (New York: Barnes & Noble, 1953), pp. 151, 153–154. Footnotes have been omitted. Reprinted by permission of Barnes & Noble, Inc. and Routledge & Kegan Paul Ltd.

The richly carved sarcophagus of Junius Bassus, a Christian prefect of Rome, who died in 359. A classical format is followed, but the subject matter is drawn from the Old and New Testaments: upper row (left to right)—the sacrifice of Isaac, St. Peter taken prisoner, Christ enthroned between Saints Peter and Paul, two scenes of Jesus before Pontius Pilate; lower row—Job and the Tempters, Adam and Eve, Christ's entry into Jerusalem, Daniel in the Lion's Den, and St. Paul led to his martyrdom. (Alinari)

sixth century. These were copied many times over and found their way, along with the writings of the Church fathers, into the monastic schools of the Middle Ages.

Augustine's Philosophy

It was within the framework determined by the authority of Scripture and Church doctrine that Augustine worked out the elements of his philosophy. As a Christian with a metaphysical bent, Augustine's specific philosophical concerns were the nature of God and His creation. Who, or what, is God, and how is the imperfect creature to know Him—to arrive at knowledge of the only true reality, the only worthy object of his faith? These metaphysical and epistemological problems, which Augustine examined autobiographically in the Confessions, are found in others of his philosophical writings and can be understood schematically in his doctrines of self-knowledge, divine illumination, the soul, and the Trinity. His epistemology had much in common with the skeptical Platonism of the New Academy.

St. Augustine's sceptical trait is seen in his dismissal of the fleeting world of things as unable to give us certain knowledge. Not that he denies the validity of the things we encounter there; in themselves they are true, but they do not allow us to pass from the individual facts to the general laws. In the case of refraction, for example, an oar in water appears bent. This is quite correct so far as its *appearance* is concerned, but *false* for the actual state of the oar. This failure to deduce the general from the particular means that we must look elsewhere for truth. For this, St. Augustine turns to self-knowledge. Here, unlike the external world, our very doubts lead to certainty; for by doubting we become aware of ourselves: "You, who wish to know, know you that you are? I know. Whence know you? I know not. . . . Know you that you think? I know. Therefore it is true that you think. It is true" (*Soliloquies,* II, I). "Everyone who is aware that he doubts, knows the truth and is certain of it . . . and should not doubt that he has the truth within him" (*De Trinitate,* x, 10).

The starting-point, then, for knowledge lies in our own thoughts. This remains constant, even though we know nothing else. From this primary awareness of our own existence through thought, we can advance to awareness of certain ideas in our soul. These, unlike the fleeting objects of the real world, remain constant and universal: number, colour, goodness, being, are all concepts that we possess and which are quite independent of external circumstances. They enable us to formulate certain laws such that, say, 2 + 2 = 4, without needing to deal with actual numbers. Such truths are common to all men; they are eternal and immutable, transcending not only the material world but our

own experience. They are signs of a higher Truth which we call God. He is the "interior master," the light which illumines the truth in our soul.

This doctrine was the foundation of the Augustinian outlook which was to prevail throughout the middle ages. It took the Platonic emphasis upon the immaterial nature of knowledge as its starting-point; it identified the Platonic concept or Idea with truth and therefore equated mental images with intelligible reality. But St. Augustine moved beyond Platonism and Neoplatonism in three important respects. The first was to harness these Ideas or concepts in the soul to their source in God. Unlike the Neoplatonists, they were not simply remote manifestations of the One; they were the direct result of God's own action. In this way, St. Augustine is able to see God as first, immutable being—the He-who-is of the Old Testament. In God's own infinite immaterial nature reside the archetypes, or Ideas, of all that exists in the real world: they are indivisible from His own essence and are the signs of it. That which is distinct in this world is one in God. . . .

The second consequence of St. Augustine's view concerned the way in which the soul grasped these Ideas. This was by illumination, an inner light which enabled the soul to recognize them. In the *City of God* St. Augustine referred to this incorporeal light as the means by which the soul reaches sure knowledge. Elsewhere he shows how all truth and understanding are part of the divine light, with God our master. The soul of itself is unable to see intelligible truth; it is therefore dependent upon an illumination from God. This is one more aspect of St. Augustine's belief in the insufficiency of natural powers to transcend the natural; it is in keeping with his whole assumption that God can only be reached through the supernatural aid of His grace. . . .

The third aspect of St. Augustine's view of knowledge was the nature of the soul itself.

Here, again, there are clear signs of Platonic and Neoplatonic influence. Unlike many Christian thinkers, including Tertullian, St. Augustine affirmed that the soul was an immaterial substance. In keeping also with the Platonists, he regarded the soul as indestructible and as the ruler of the body. He differed, however, in giving these concepts a Christian interpretation. The Neoplatonists had regarded the soul as imprisoned in the body. For St. Augustine this was to fly in the face of the Christian belief in a divine providence whose creation was essentially good. The body, no less than the soul, was God's work; it was good in itself and only became bad when disfigured by sin. Similarly, where both the Platonists, and some Christian Fathers, believed that the soul, as an immaterial intelligence, had pre-existed from eternity, St. Augustine upheld instantaneous creation. Although St. Augustine does not specify at what stage the soul was created, he denies that it ever existed separately from the body.

In developing his own theory of the soul, St. Augustine was concerned to stress two points: firstly that the soul, located throughout the body, not in any one place, is its active ruler. Not only does it guide the body in all questions of will and knowledge, but it also informs the body of its own state. Hence, St. Augustine will not even allow that sensation is from the body; to do so would mean that the inferior could act upon the superior, an assertion that went against the whole Augustinian concept of hierarchy. On the contrary, sensation derives from the soul's own awareness of what the body is undergoing. St. Augustine compares it with verse or music: although the physical sounds of the words are from the senses, their meaning and shape are provided by the soul's awareness. Thus through sensation the soul interprets the body's needs.

Secondly, the nature of the soul provides the strongest evidence of its contact with God. It is the mirror of the divine nature: it is immaterial (though not, of course, eternal), immortal, and its faculties correspond to the divine Trinity; its being (*essentia*) is the foundation for its understanding (*intelligentia*) and love (*amor*), just as the being of the Father is the foundation for the Word and the Holy Spirit. Moreover, it is by reminiscence that the soul gains contact with the higher truth; it does not so much learn the truth as recognize it in the light of eternal ideas. This is a further indication of its divine origin and is one more piece of evidence for the way in which Augustine turned a Platonic concept to Christian advantage. The Platonists regarded reminiscence as the soul's link with its spiritual source from which matter (its body) had separated it. It constituted a reminder of the free state of the soul before it had become imprisoned in the body; by turning away from the world of the senses and directing its attention to its inner being, the soul could catch faintly rays of truth and once more tread the path back towards the One. St. Augustine had no need for this contradiction between the body and truth, but reminiscence enabled him to place the soul close to God.

In his view of God and the nature of the Trinity, St. Augustine insists upon the utter simplicity of the divine nature; it allows of no categories or description: He is "good without quality, great without quantity, the creator without need to create . . . everywhere without place, eternal without time . . ." (*De Trinitate,* v, i). He cannot be described save than by saying He is Being. We know with certainty only what He is not: this negative theology was to have great influence for the future. On the Trinity, too, St. Augustine asserted the indivisible unity of the Godhead: his teaching in the *De Trinitate,* one of his most profound works, defined God as a unity subsisting in three persons. This was in marked contrast to the Greek view which by starting with the One saw the three persons as distinct, with the Word and the Holy Spirit subsequent to the Father. St. Augustine's teaching on the Trinity formed the basis of subsequent Catholic faith.[16]

Augustine's Theology of Grace

One can see in his epistemology, his doctrines of the soul, and the Trinity the way in which Augustine tried to reconcile Greek philosophy and Church dogma. These philosophical concerns, however different his conclusions, he shared with the fathers of the Eastern Church. Yet Augustine was also the theologian of redemptive Christianity. The overriding question for him and for many of his generation was the question of man's sinfulness and need for salvation. How does one obtain this salvation? This is the most difficult question in Christian theology and posed in this way cannot lead to an orthodox answer. Man cannot obtain his own salvation; salvation comes only through the giving of God's free grace through Jesus Christ. Only in this way is man reprieved from the just punishment for his sin, which is death. Augus-

[16] Gordon Leff, *Medieval Thought: St. Augustine to Ockham* (Baltimore: Penguin Books, Inc., 1958), pp. 39–43. Reprinted by permission.

tine's elaboration of this essentially Pauline formula is of particular significance in the history of Christian theology.

Augustine's formulation hinges on his understanding of the human personality.

> Recognize in thyself something within, within thyself. Leave thou abroad both thy clothing and thy flesh; descend into thyself; go to thy secret chamber, thy mind. If thou be far from thine own self, how canst thou draw near unto God? For not in the body but in the mind was man made in the image of God. In his own similitude let us seek God: in his own image recognize the Creator.[17]

But man, when he looks inward, discovers not only his likeness to God but also discovers his sinfulness. He not only possesses the divine spark of reason but also an emotional faculty—a will—which is the source of his unhappiness.

> There is nothing that I feel more certainly and more personally than that I have a will, and that it moves me to enjoy this or that. I know nothing I could call my own if the will by which I will "yea" or "nay" is not my own.

[17] *On the Gospel of John,* xxiii.

The death of Judas and the Crucifixion—an ivory panel ca. A.D. 420. (British Museum)

If I use it to do evil, to whom is the evil to be attributed if not to myself?[18]

This understanding of the will is a significant development from the Stoic idea in which the will functioned as the ally of reason against the passions or against external perturbations. In Augustine's view the will is fully capable of choosing evil. It is indeed the only source of evil in the world. Adam's original sin had been an act of will, the result of a wicked desire to be self-sufficient.

> Our first parents fell into open disobedience because already they were secretly corrupted; for the evil act had never been done had not an evil will preceded it. And what is the origin of our evil will but pride? For "pride is the beginning of sin." And what is pride but the craving for undue exaltation? And this is undue exaltation, when the soul abandons Him to whom it ought to cleave as its end, and becomes a kind of end to itself.[19]

Despite the fact that man's sinfulness is determined by the very fact of his being a son of Adam, he is nonetheless responsible for his actions because they continue to be a result of his conscious will. Augustine emphasized this freedom of the will to choose good or evil in his early writings against the Manichaeans who, because of their attribution of evil to an independent demonic force, tended to absolve human beings from moral responsibility.

The sense of personal responsibility for moral acts obliged the Christian to adopt a confessional attitude. Augustine made that abundantly clear when he wrote his own *Confessions* ten years after his conversion. He did not merely recite his past errors in order to contrast them with his new life as a Christian; in addition, he went on to reveal his continuing sense of inadequacy even as a bishop of the Church. The *Confessions* are thus testimony to his belief that the Christian did not wholly erase his past upon conversion, nor did he cease being a person with a will free to choose evil as well as good.

By locating evil in the perverted will of free moral agents, Augustine rejected the Platonic attribution of evil to the nature of the flesh. He nevertheless continued to be influenced by Platonic and Neoplatonic thought. His theology of grace owed much to the Neoplatonic idea of the aspiration of the soul to be reunited with the One. In the *Confessions*, Augustine tells how he was first turned away from a life steeped in material things by reading Cicero's *Hortensius.*

> With an incredible fervour of heart I yearned for the immortal wisdom, and I began to arise in order to return to Thee. . . . How did I burn, O my God, how did I burn with desire to soar from earth to Thee, and I knew not what Thou wouldest do with me. For with Thee is wisdom. But love of wisdom is in Greek called philosophy, and with this that book inflamed me.[20]

Indeed, Augustine's entire life, through his Manichaean and Neoplatonic phases, and even after his conversion to Christianity, was dominated by this essentially Neoplatonic love for the divine—by Eros. But for a Christian this kind of love was deficient in one thing: it lacked staying power. Augustine, through his own love of the divine, was unable to remain fixed and at rest in God. His own Eros-love presupposed a deficiency, an unfulfilled need. This deficiency was supplied by the unsolicited love of God—by Christian Agape.[21]

> What is the difference between . . . Eros and Agape? Augustine seems to be well aware that God's love to us must be distinguished from Eros-love. *God's love is a love of mercy and of the fulness of goodwill.* Eros-love ascends and seeks the satisfaction of its needs;

---

[18] *On Free Will*, III, 3 in Neal W. Gilbert, "The Concept of Will in Early Latin Philosophy," *Journal of the History of Philosophy*, I (October, 1963), p. 31.

[19] *The City of God*, XIV, 13.

[20] As quoted in *Agape and Eros* by Anders Nygren, translated by Philip S. Watson. Published in the USA by The Westminster Press, 1953. Used by permission.

[21] See *Western Man*, vol. II, *The Judeo-Christian Heritage.*

Agape-love descends in order to help and to give. Just because of its unmotivated and spontaneous character—or, in Augustine's own words, because God loves "ultro"—God's love has so much more power to kindle the response of love in man. Man can make no claim to God's love. If it is given to him, that rests upon a Divine miracle. God, the highest Judge, condescends to sinful man. . . . *Neoplatonism had been able to show him* [Augustine] *the object for his love and longing, but not the way to gain it.* Between God and man is a gulf which man cannot bridge. In Eros man is bound to God but cannot reach Him. The wings of yearning are not strong enough to bear him up to the Eternal. Augustine has no doubt that Eros is the way to God, but he has begun to doubt whether we, as we actually are, can gain access to Him by that way. If we are to find God, He must Himself come to meet us—but of that Neoplatonism knew nothing. Of God and His nature, of man's Eros for Him, indeed, of the Word of God which in the beginning was with God—of all these he could read in the writings of the Neoplantonists. "But that the Word became flesh, and dwelt among us, I read not there," says Augustine. These writings might tell him that the Son was in the form of God, but that He emptied Himself and took the form of a servant, that He humbled Himself and became obedient unto death, that God spared not His own Son but delivered Him up for us all—"those books do not contain." *In Neoplatonism he finds human Eros which tries to take heaven by storm, but he misses God's Apage which descends, and without which Eros cannot attain to God.*[22]

In Augustine's Latin, the word which we translate as love, and which carries the meaning of both Eros and Agape, is *caritas.* Augustine makes *caritas* the very center of his theology of grace, and through his writing both the Hel-

lenic and Christian concepts of love enter the Western tradition.

Love, in the sense of desire, in Augustine's understanding is the foundation of all human life. To love is to direct one's longing toward an object which, when possessed, will make one happy. Love is thus acquisitive; it seeks happiness, and is common to all men alike. In itself love is morally neutral. It becomes right love or wrong love according to the object which is desired. For Augustine there are in any true sense only two choices, love of the eternal or the temporal, love of God or love of the world. Only the love of God is truly *caritas.* Its opposite is *cupiditas* (cupidity), love of the world.

> What makes this choice so serious is that we ourselves are transformed into conformity with that which we love. Love binds us to the beloved object, which enters as our "bonum" into us and sets its stamp upon our self; we become like the object we love. By loving God, we become as gods; by loving the world, we ourselves become merely a bit of world, and so the Scripture rightly calls evil men quite simply, "the world."[23]

Only *caritas* is right love. This is true not only because we are commanded by God's law to love Him only, but also because of the very nature of the situation. Only the love of God is capable of fulfillment because in its object alone is to be found eternal rest (*quies*), perfection, peace, and true happiness. *Cupiditas,* which seeks its good in something temporal and transient, is incapable of giving complete satisfaction. So in cupidity one not only transgresses God's law but engages in a futile enterprise.

Caritas is a real option for man only because God has come to man's aid. "He who asserts that we can possess God's Caritas without God's aid, what else does he assert than that we possess God without God?"[24] Love is made possible through grace.

[22] From Nygren, *Agape and Eros,* pp. 469, 471. Reprinted by permission. Footnotes have been omitted.

[23] From Nygren, *Agape and Eros,* pp. 483–484. Reprinted by permission.

[24] *On Endurance,* xviii, 15 in Nygren, *Agape and Eros,* p. 521. Reprinted by permission.

Since the love of God, that is, faith, is possible only through divine grace, the initiative in the process of salvation is God's. Man can do nothing to earn his own redemption. While Augustine never rejected his belief in the human being as a free moral agent, fully responsible for his actions, in his later writings against the Pelagians he became more and more insistent upon man's utter incapacity to take even the first step in his own salvation.

Pelagius, a British monk horrified at the dissolute life being led by so many of his contemporaries, rejected the doctrine of original sin which seemed to him to serve only as an excuse for moral laxity. He emphasized instead the ability of man through the exercise of his own free will to lead a moral life, aided only by proper instruction and sufficient exhortation. Pelagius particularly objected to what seemed to be a passive state of mind in Augustine's prayer in the *Confessions:* "Give what thou commandest and command what thou wilt." This prayer was for Augustine, however, an expression of his subservience to and faith in an all-knowing and all-powerful God. Against the Pelagians, Augustine developed this idea into an uncompromising doctrine of God's predestination of an elect to salvation and the condemnation of the rest of mankind to their just punishment.

> Within that number of the elect and the predestinated, even those who have led the worst lives are by the goodness of God led to repentance. . . . Of these our Lord spoke when He said, "This is the Father's will which hath sent me, that of all He hath given me I should lose nothing" (John vi. 39). But the rest of mankind who are not of this number, but who, out of the same lump of which they are, are made vessels of wrath, are brought into the world for the advantage of the elect. God does not create any of them without a purpose [ac fortuito]. He knows what good to work out of them: He works good in the very fact of creating them human beings, and carrying on by means of them

this visible system of things. But none of them does He lead to a wholesome and spiritual repentance. . . . All indeed do, as far as themselves are concerned, out of the same original mass of perdition treasure up to themselves after their hardness and impenitent heart, wrath against the day of wrath; but out of that mass God leads some in mercy and repentance, and others in just judgment does not lead.[25]

The choice is entirely God's own; it is a just choice but inscrutable. God's justice is forever hidden.

> As to the reason why he wills to convert some, and to punish others for turning away . . . the purpose of his more hidden judgment is in His own power.[26]

Augustine's Moral Teachings

It should be clear from what has been said about Augustine's doctrines concerning human depravity and divine grace that his moral teachings fall within that larger theological framework. Because of man's utter dependence on God's grace, doing good works or keeping the moral law were not in themselves sufficient for salvation. What then was the motive for leading a good life? To this question Augustine gave the definitive Christian answer. The measure of what is truly a good act is the disposition of the individual Christian soul. The Christian leads a good life because he loves God, and he loves God because God has loved him.

> He who lives according to the justice which is in the law, without the faith of the grace of Christ, . . . must be accounted to have no true justice; not because the law is not true and holy, but because to wish to obey the letter which commands without the quickening

[25] *Against Julian the Pelagian,* v, 14 in John Hick, *Evil and the God of Love* (New York: Harper & Row, Publishers, 1966), pp. 72–73.

[26] *Merits and Remission of Sins,* II, 32 in Hick, *Evil and the God of Love,* pp. 74–75.

Spirit of God, as if by the strength of free will, is not true justice.[27]

Augustine's reorientation of the motives for ethical behavior marks a significant departure from the dominant ideas of Greco-Roman culture.

> Where the practice of virtue produces well-being as its natural consequence, as in the Greek view, virtue carries with it its own reward in accordance with the causal processes of nature, so that causal necessity and moral desert are not merely compatible; they normally coincide. But in the Christian view, causal necessity and moral responsibility seem incompatible, for the choice between good and evil is made by the soul, independently of natural processes, and its reward or punishment is independent of the natural effects of human actions. Man is punished or rewarded to the degree to which he voluntarily obeys or disobeys the commands of God. In the Greek view, man suffers from the natural consequences of his mistakes, but in the Christian view, no matter what the natural consequences of his actions, he is held to account for the state of his soul. It is his motives and not his actions that count in assessment of his moral responsibility, and the primary motive is his desire for, or his turning away from, God.
> Responsibility is thus transferred from the consequences of a person's actions to the state of his soul.[28]

And for Augustine, the state of one's soul must be an ordered state; one must have his priorities in order.

> Bodily loveliness, made by God, is nevertheless temporal, carnal, and a lesser good; it is wrongly loved if it is loved above God, the eternal, inward and lasting good. Just as the covetous man subordinates justice to his love of gold—through no fault in the gold but in himself—so it is with all things. They are all good in themselves, and capable of being loved either well or badly. They are loved well when the right order is kept, badly when this order is upset. . . . Hence it seems to me that the briefest and truest definition of virtue is that it is the order of love.[29]

Behind this idea of virtue as the order of love "stands the classical world-picture of the ordered cosmic hierarchy, with its conviction that some things are more worthy of being loved than others, and that man's task is to conform himself to this order in his actions."

> [Augustine] thought that behind human law stands an eternal law, to which we appeal when we criticize particular enactments of human laws. Unlike human law, this eternal law is necessarily just, and it is all-embracing, in that it covers the whole range of human action; unlike it, too, in that it is unchanging, whereas human laws can be and often are changed to suit the circumstances of time and place.[30]

Augustine wrote little about the specific content of the law—little about what specific actions the virtuous man should take. The whole thrust of his ethics was against legalism. He did, however, accept the moral law of the Old and New Testaments as a firm basis for moral instruction. Following the lead of earlier Christian apologists, he found nothing in these moral injunctions that was incompatible with the best teaching of the pagan philosophers. Augustine thus continued

---

[27] *On Christian Doctrine,* III, vii, 23 in Erich Przywara, ed., *An Augustine Synthesis* (New York: Harper & Row, Publishers, 1958), p. 312.

[28] "Ethics," *The Encyclopedia of Philosophy,* vol. III (New York: The Macmillan Company and Free Press, 1967), p. 88.

[29] From *The City of God,* 22, quoted in R. A. Markus, "Marius Victorinus and Augustine" in A. H. Armstrong, ed., *The Cambridge History of Later Greek and Early Medieval Philosophy* (London: Cambridge University Press, 1967), p. 386.

[30] From "Marius Victorinus and Augustine" by Marcus in Armstrong, ed., *The Cambridge History of Later Greek and Early Medieval Philosophy,* p. 387.

the process begun in the second century of incorporating Greek and Roman ethics into the Christian framework. In this effort he followed the lead of Saint Ambrose who had written the first systematic Christian treatise on ethics. Ambrose, following very closely the organization and style of Cicero's *On Duties*, attempted to interpret the four cardinal virtues of classical literature in accordance with Christian ideas. Augustine completed the Christian reinterpretation by placing faith, hope, and love, the three "theological virtues" (derived from I Cor. 13:13), clearly in the forefront and reducing the four classical virtues to aspects of the love of God.

> As to virtue leading us to a happy life, I hold virtue to be nothing else than perfect love of God. For the fourfold division of virtue I regard as taken from four forms of love. For these four virtues . . . I should have no hesitation in defining them: that temperance is love giving itself entirely to that which is loved; fortitude is love readily bearing all things for the sake of the loved object; justice is love serving only the loved object; and therefore ruling rightly; prudence is love distinguishing with sagacity between what hinders it and what helps it. The object of this love is not anything, but only God, the chief good, the highest wisdom, the perfect harmony. So we may express the definition thus; that temperance is love keeping itself entire and incorrupt for God; fortitude is love bearing everything readily for the sake of God; justice is love serving God only, and therefore ruling well all else, as subject to man; prudence is love making a right distinction between what helps it towards God and what might hinder it.[31]

Due in large measure to Augustine's influence the four cardinal virtues of the classical tradition

plus the three theological virtues (together comprising the seven Christian virtues) became the accepted scheme for systematic treatment of Christian ethics throughout the Middle Ages.

Augustine's Doctrine of the Church

Taken as a whole, Augustine's ethical teachings were broad-minded and concentrated on motive rather than conduct. He avoided the legalistic tendency, found in a great many contemporary Christian writings, to catalogue virtues to be pursued and vices to be avoided. Yet it must be remembered as well that Augustine was a bishop of the Church and as such a supporter of its role as moral teacher and disciplinarian. He was well aware that his own congregation at Hippo was not composed solely of elected saints who would live moral lives out of gratitude for the love of God. As a part of the universal Church, it also contained reprobate sinners in need of instruction and guidance. Even the elect, so long as they lived in the temporal world, needed to live within a framework of authority. For the most part, Augustine was content to leave matters of moral discipline to the family and to the constituted authorities of the state. But in the social and political upheaval of his day, the Church and the clergy were beginning to take on more and more tasks of administration. It was rapidly becoming the single most important institution in the Empire, replacing even the imperial bureaucracy.

This increasingly powerful Catholic Church owed much to the hard work and exceptional talents of bishops such as Augustine, who fought for unity within the Church and an increasingly independent role for the Church in relationship to the secular authorities. As bishop of Hippo, Augustine was instrumental in establishing the Catholic Church as the dominant force in Africa. When he became bishop in 395, a rival branch of the Church, the Donatists, still outnumbered the Catholics. The Donatists, it will be recalled, had arisen as the result of a disputed election to the see of Carthage and had withstood the opposition of Constantine and

---

[31] *The Morals of the Catholic Church*, XV in John A. Mourant, *Introduction to the Philosophy of Saint Augustine: Selected Readings and Commentaries* (University Park, Pa.: The Pennsylvania State University Press, 1964), pp. 281–282.

the councils of the Church.[32] At stake in the rivalry between Donatists and Catholics was the attitude which the Church would take toward the world around them.

The problem was acutely relevant. Christianity was the only religious group that had expanded in Roman society. Both churches had played a dramatic role in bringing about the end of paganism in Africa. They were faced by the fundamental problem of the relationship of any group to the society in which it lives. Briefly, the Donatists thought of themselves as a group which existed to preserve and protect an alternative to the society around them. They felt their identity to be constantly threatened: first by persecution, later, by compromise. Innocence, ritual purity, meritorious suffering, predominate in their image of themselves. They were unique, "pure": "the Church of the righteous who are persecuted and do not persecute."

The Catholicism of Augustine, by contrast, reflects the attitude of a group confident of its powers to absorb the world without losing its identity. This identity existed independently of the quality of the human agents of the Church: it rested on "objective" promises of God, working out magnificently in history, and on the "objective" efficacy of its sacraments. This Church was hungry for souls: let it eat, indiscriminately if needs be. It is a group no longer committed to defend itself against society; but rather, poised, ready to fulfil what it considered its historic mission, to dominate, to absorb, to lead a whole Empire. "*Ask Me, and I shall give the uttermost parts of the earth as Thy possession.*" It is not surprising, therefore, that Africa, which had always been the home of articulate and extreme views on the nature of the Church as a group in society, should, once again, in the age of Augustine, become the "cockpit of Europe," for this, the last great debate, whose outcome would determine the form taken by

the Catholic domination of the Latin world until the Reformation.[33]

The Donatists and the Catholics professed the same creed and celebrated the same liturgy but existed under separate administration with rival congregations in every town.

As Augustine's powers in Hippo grew over the next several years, he conducted an unrelenting campaign to reunite the Donatists with the universal Church, first by persuasion and then by force. His arguments for unity rested on the basic belief that because the Church was the embodiment of the one and final redemptive act of God, there was no salvation outside the Church. Against the Donatists, he argued that the sacraments were valid by virtue of the authority of the Church, without regard to the moral quality of the priest. The Donatists' insistence on clerical purity seemed to Augustine to be incompatible with the maintenance of the authority of the Church, for if the efficacy of the sacraments depends only on the worthiness of the one who administers them, then any good man, whether of the Church or not, might perform the mass and administer baptism.

These arguments on behalf of the institutional Church led Augustine into a position which is an excellent illustration of the dilemmas inherent in the institutionalization of religion.

The pressure of institutionalism . . . forced Augustine to affirm the special, indeed the unique, status of the Church, its hierarchy, and its sacraments. . . . From this point of view the [Church] is a very complex structure, very different from the simple and direct relationship in which, when Augustine was thinking mystically, he conceived each soul to stand to God.

There is no way to bring these two conceptions of man's relation to God into accord. On the one hand, the requirements of institutionalism committed Augustine to holding that

[32] See pp. 158–159.

[33] Peter Brown, *Augustine of Hippo: A Biography* (Berkeley, Calif.: University of California Press, 1967), p. 214.

the only way and the only hope are the sacraments administered by regularly ordained priests of the Church. On the other hand, his mysticism and his predestinationism explicitly denied this. To take the latter first: if we are predestined for salvation (or for damnation, as the case may be) what we do or leave undone is obviously inconsequential. And as regards his mysticism, the central fact of his experience at Milan was direct communion with God, unmediated by any of the Church's sacraments. From this point of view, where mysticism and predestinationism come together, salvation is a private and individual affair. . . . Here the Church and its sacraments are unimportant: the Church, because all the various lines of authority and all the various relationships it involves are irrelevant to the simple, unambiguous relationship in which each saved soul stands to God; the sacraments, because if the soul has not turned they cannot help, while if it *has* turned they are unnecessary.

The result is that there is a striking ambivalence about everything Augustine said on this subject. At times, when he was thinking ecclesiastically, he could write of baptism as "Thy life-giving sacrament," imputing to it some sort of magical effect like that of similar rites in the earlier mystery cults. And this, of course, is the obvious implication of the position he adopted against the Donatists. It is the rite itself (providing, of course, that it is administered by the Church) which is efficacious: it operates automatically regardless of who in particular administers it. In this connection we should note his belief that heretics and schismatics who dared to partake of the sacraments were hurt thereby.

At other times, when he was thinking mystically and forgot his responsibilities as a churchman, the sacraments tended to drop out of the picture. Thus we are assured that certain Old Testament figures are saved, though they could have known nothing of the sacraments. Though they lived before the Christian revelation, they had had hints of its meaning: they were saved "by faith in this mystery and by godliness of life." And the same applies to us, except, of course, that whereas those pre-crucifixion saints had only the barest of hints to guide and instruct them, we have the wonderful example, the obvious instruction, of Jesus's life, death, and resurrection.

Sometimes the two divergent points of view get expressed together. Thus, in one passage, he tells us that his soul was "changed by faith and Thy sacrament." Augustine never succeeded in resolving the contradiction that lurks in this "and." [34]

Nevertheless, he was convinced that the Donatists must be firmly dealt with. Believing as he did that Christian conversion must of necessity be voluntary, he first tried to combat the heresy through preaching and writing, but when that failed he came around to the view being urged on him by many of his colleagues that stronger methods were necessary. The cooperation of the imperial court at Ravenna was obtained, and in 405 the Donatists were outlawed and actively persecuted. Augustine found scriptural warrant in the Gospel according to St. Luke for this use of physical compulsion.

> For those who make hedges, their object is to make divisions. Let them be drawn away from the hedges, let them be plucked up from among the thorns. They have stuck fast in the hedges, they are unwilling to be compelled. Let us come in, they say, of their own good will. This is not the Lord's order, "Compel them," saith He, "to come in." Let compulsion be found outside, the will will arise within. [35]

[34] From *A History of Western Philosophy* by W. T. Jones. Copyright 1952 by Harcourt, Brace & World, Inc., and reprinted with their permission.

[35] *Sermon* CXII, 8 in Herbert A. Deane, *The Political and Social Ideas of St. Augustine* (New York: Columbia University Press, 1963), pp. 201–202. Reprinted by permission of the publisher.

Compulsion cannot make a true believer out of a heretic, but it can, Augustine believed, force him out of the "hedges" of heresy where he is lost and into the unity of the Catholic Church. Inside the Church, he will hear true doctrine preached and will receive valid sacraments and will have at least the chance of repentance and the reception of God's grace.

The use by the Church of the coercive power of the state to suppress heresy implied a relationship between Church and state not foreseen in earlier Christian writings.

Ever since the conversion of Constantine, Emperors had issued decrees against enemies of the Church; especially during the reigns of Theodosius I and his sons there had been a steady steam of imperial laws and edicts against heretics and schismatics. However, Augustine made an important contribution to this development. He not only recognized and accepted the fact that rulers were using their power to defend the Church, but he set forth, by argument and appeal to the Scriptures, a thoroughgoing defense of these activities. Perhaps without clearly recognizing the full and final consequences of his teachings, he moved in the direction of a theocratic theory of the State, a theory which was to be fully developed in the Middle Ages by a series of great Popes, from Gregory VII to Boniface VIII, and by their supporters.

The theocratic element in Augustine's teachings about the nature and functions of state power—and it is always only an element of his doctrine, which co-exists with many other different elements—is a direct consequence of the view that the State ought to punish those who are guilty of heresy or schism. For heresy and schism are religious questions—questions of doctrine and of ecclesiastical organization—and it is the bishops of the Church who decide what is orthodox doctrine and correct organization and discipline within the Church and what, on the other hand, constitutes heresy and schism. No strong church, least of all the vigorous Catholic Church of the Western Empire in the fifth century, would permit secular rulers to decide for themselves these issues of doctrine and organization. In this area, at least, the State and its officials become, therefore, auxiliaries of the Church and its officers. The leaders of the Church, by their own procedures and deliberations, determine what is orthodox and what is unorthodox. The political authorities are reduced to the status of "the secular arm," the coercive instrument by which ecclesiastical decisions are enforced upon dissident and recalcitrant members. Even when the officials of the State cooperate willingly with the Church authorities, they are obviously subordinate to the Church which sets the ends that they implement. Furthermore, it is the Church as the higher authority which will decide what other matters of state activity have so close a tie with religious or moral issues that they, too, must be dealt with by the State under the direction of ecclesiastical authority.[36]

Augustine's Philosophy of History

Despite the theocratic implications of his writings against the Donatists, Augustine maintained a radical distinction between Church and state. The basis of this distinction is made clear in the context of his philosophy of history. The Church owed its superiority to the temporal state not by virtue of its superior organization, not even by its identification with the divine power, but by virtue of the role assigned to it by God in the unfolding of His divine purpose in history. This cosmic drama of creation, earthly progress, and final judgment Augustine sketched out in the greatest of his later works, *The City of God*.

The occasion for the composition of *The City of God* was the sack of Rome in 410 by Alaric the Visigoth. While not important in a military sense, this event impressed the imagination of contemporaries. Eternal Rome, the founder of

[36] Deane, *The Political and Social Ideas of St. Augustine*, pp. 215–216. Reprinted by permission.

the Empire, untouched by foreign invaders for nearly a thousand years, had fallen. Saint Jerome, living in his hermitage in Bethlehem, recorded his shock at hearing the news: "When the brightest light on the whole earth was extinguished, when the Roman empire was deprived of its head and when, to speak more correctly, the whole world perished in one city, then 'I was dumb with silence, I held my peace, even from good, and my sorrow was stirred' (Ps. 39:2)."[37] Had Rome fallen because the ancient gods were offended by the recent triumph of Christianity? Did the fall of Rome prefigure, as Jerome suggested, the end of the world? It was to counter these claims that Saint Augustine wrote *The City of God.*

The work was begun in 413 and took over thirteen years to complete. It is made up of twenty-two books and follows a careful plan. The first ten books are divided into two parts. In the first part, Saint Augustine argues against the belief that human welfare depends upon the worship of any god or gods, for the true God sends blessings and ills upon the just and unjust alike. This argument was directed both against those who blamed the Christian religion for the fall of Rome and against earlier Christian apologists who had advanced the idea that the advent of Christ had led to a general improvement of the material conditions of the world. Saint Augustine reviews Greek and Roman history in considerable detail in these books to show that moral depravity and physical calamities had been the lot of mankind before as well as after the beginning of the Christian era. Yet he also recognizes the greatness of Rome and the benefits which her rule has brought to the provinces. These he attributes to the providential purpose of God by whose power and judgment alone earthly kingdoms are formed and maintained. Thus Augustine deprives the Roman Empire of all independent significance. It is neither God's chosen instrument for man's salvation and thus

[37] Theodor E. Mommsen, "St. Augustine and the Christian Idea of Progress: The Background of the City of God," *Journal of the History of Ideas,* 12 (1951), pp. 346–347.

not justified by natural law, nor is it an evil force working against God's purposes.

In a second five books, Saint Augustine reviews pagan religions and judges them harshly as leading to immorality. In this judgment, he recognizes his concurrence with Socrates and Plato. Here Augustine reviews much of what he had written in the *Confessions* and other works concerning the merits and shortcomings of Platonism.

Having in the first two parts set forth his arguments against the pagans, Augustine turns in the remainder of his work to an exposition of his own doctrines. He begins by affirming a linear view of historical development. The world was created in time and will come to an end at another definite moment in time known only to God. Indeed, time itself, as we experience it, is a product of creation and stands in contrast to the timeless constancy of God. He explicitly rejects the classical notion of an external world without beginning and end in which the passage of time can be conceived of only as recurring cycles. Such a notion was contrary to the account of creation in Genesis and the prophetic promise of a final judgment and redemption. The linear view of history implies that each event, from creation to apocalypse, is unique, deriving its significance from the providential purposes of God rather than, for instance, from its place in a causal sequence. Nothing happens but what God knows and plans it. There is no place for the classical notion of chance or *fortuna*. The historical process is ordered and purposeful, but its precise duration is not known to men. Augustine refutes those millennialists who attempted to calculate the date of the final judgment or tried to find clues to its coming in historical phenomena.

In vain, then, do we attempt to compute definitely the years that may remain to this world, when we may hear from the mouth of the Truth that it is not for us to know this. Yet some have said that four hundred, some five hundred, others a thousand years, may be completed from the ascension of the Lord up to His final coming. But to point out how each of them supports his own opinion would take too long, and is not necessary; for indeed they use human conjectures, and bring forward nothing certain from the authority of the canonical Scriptures. But on this subject He puts aside the figures of the calculators, and orders silence, who says, "It is not for you to know the times, which the Father hath put in His own power."[38]

What really matters in history is not its chronological extent nor the rise and fall of empires, but the drama of salvation and damnation in a world to come. Profane history has meaning only in the context of sacred history.

Accordingly, only four books out of twenty-two deal in part with what we would call "history," the meaning of which depends on the prehistory and posthistory in heaven, on the transcendent beginning and end. Only by this reference to an absolute beginning and end has history as a whole a meaning. On the other hand, beginning and end are also not meaningful in themselves but with reference to the story which they begin and end, and the central happening of this history is Jesus Christ's advent, the eschatological event.[39]

The story begins with Adam's sin and the expulsion of man from paradise. It ends with the final judgment when the elect will reign eternally with God, and the rest of Adam's progeny will suffer eternal punishment in hell. The whole course of this drama is expressed by Saint Augustine as the history of two communities of men, the sons of Cain who live according to man and the sons of Abel who live according to God, or, alternatively as this history of two cities, the earthly and the heavenly.

. . . Two cities have been formed by two loves: the earthly by the love of self, even to the contempt of God; the heavenly by the love of God, even to the contempt of self. The former, in a word, glories in itself, the latter in the Lord. For the one seeks glory from men; but the greatest glory of the other is God, the witness of conscience. The one lifts up its head in its own glory; the other says to its God, "Thou art my glory, and the lifter up of mine head." In the one, the princes and the nations it subdues are ruled by the love of ruling; in the other, the princes and the subjects serve one another in love, the latter obeying, while the former take thought for all. The one delights in its own strength, represented in the persons of its rulers; the other says to its God, "I will love Thee, O Lord, my strength." And therefore the wise men of the one city, living according to man, have sought for profit to their own bodies or souls, or both, and those who have known God "glorified Him not as God, neither were thankful, but became vain in their imaginations, and their foolish heart was darkened; professing themselves to be wise"—that is, glorying in their own wisdom, and being possessed by pride—"they became fools, and changed the glory of the incorruptible God into an image made like to corruptible man, and to birds, and four-footed beasts, and creeping things." For they were either leaders or followers of the people in adoring images, "and worshipped and served the creature more than the Creator, who is blessed for ever." But in the other city there is no human wisdom, but only godliness, which offers due worship to the true God, and looks for its reward in the society of the saints, of holy angels as well as holy men, "that God may be all in all." [40]

The city of God and the earthly city are not intended to be synonymous with the institutional Church and the state. They are rather two mystical societies representing the opposite tendencies of human life. The historical community existing in time between creation and judgment

[38] *The City of God*, XVIII, 53.

[39] Karl Löwith, *Meaning in History: The Theological Implications of the Philosophy of History* (Chicago: The University of Chicago Press, 1949), p. 169.

[40] *The City of God*, XIV, 28.

is a temporary state in which the city of God and the earthly city are "commingled" together. The visible Church bears a special relationship to the eternal city as the embodiment of God's revelation in Christ which orients men toward salvation. Thus, for the Christian man, life in the historical dimension is a pilgrimage toward God; indeed the entire historical process derives its meaning from that journey.

It was in the context of this supernatural drama that the political order derived its meaning. Just as the measure of a good act was to be determined by the disposition of the individual soul, so the value of human society depended upon its disposition, that is, the degree to which it served the divine purpose. In Book Nineteen of the *City of God,* after tracing the history of the two cities from Adam to the advent of Christ, Augustine arrives at a discussion of the meaning of secular society in the light of divine purpose. In doing so, he sets the framework within which political thought would operate for centuries.

THE CITY OF GOD
Saint Augustine[41]

BOOK NINETEEN

v. Of the social life, which, though most desirable, is frequently disturbed by many distresses

. . . The life of the wise man must be social. For how could the city of God (concerning which we are already writing no less than the nineteenth book of this work) either take a beginning or be developed, or attain its proper destiny, if the life of the saints were not a social life? But who can enumerate all the great grievances with which human society abounds in the misery of this mortal state? Who can weigh them? . . . Who ought to be, or who are

[41] Saint Augustine, *The City of God,* trans. Marcus Dods, 1899.

more friendly than those who live in the same family? And yet who can rely even upon this friendship, seeing that secret treachery has often broken it up, and produced enmity as bitter as the amity was sweet, or seemed sweet by the most perfect dissimulation? It is on this account that the words of Cicero so move the heart of every one, and provoke a sigh: "There are no snares more dangerous than those which lurk under the guise of duty or the name of relationship. For the man who is your declared foe you can easily baffle by precaution; but this hidden, intestine, and domestic danger not merely exists, but overwhelms you before you can foresee and examine it. . . . If, then, home, the natural refuge from the ills of life, is itself not safe, what shall we say of the city, which, as it is larger, is so much the more filled with lawsuits civil and criminal, and is never free from the fear, if sometimes from the actual outbreak, of disturbing and bloody insurrections and civil wars?

xii. That even the fierceness of war and all the disquietude of men make towards this one end of peace, which every nature desires

Whoever gives even moderate attention to human affairs and to our common nature, will recognize that if there is no man who does not wish to be joyful, neither is there any one who does not wish to have peace. For even they who make war desire nothing but victory—desire, that is to say, to attain to peace with glory. For what else is victory than the conquest of those who resist us? and when this is done there is peace. . . . In his own home, too, he makes it his aim to be at peace with his wife and children, and any other members of his household; for unquestionably their prompt obedience to his every look is a source of pleasure to him. And if this be not rendered, he is angry, he chides and punishes; and even by his storm he secures the calm peace of his own home, as occasion demands. For he sees that peace cannot be maintained unless all the members of the same domestic circle be subject to one head, such as he himself is in his own house. . . .

xiii. Of the universal peace which the law of nature preserves through all disturbances, and by which every one reaches his desert in a way regulated by the just Judge

The peace of the body. . . consists in the duly proportioned arrangement of its parts. The peace of the irrational soul is the harmonious repose of the appetites, and that of the rational soul and the harmony of knowledge and action. The peace of body and soul is the well-ordered and harmonious life and health of the living creature. Peace between man and God is the well-ordered obedience of faith to eternal law. Peace between man and man is well-ordered concord. Domestic peace is the well-ordered concord between those of the family who rule and those who obey. Civil peace is a similar concord among the citizens. The peace of the celestial city is the perfectly ordered and harmonious enjoyment of God, and of one another in God. The peace of all things is the tranquillity of order. Order is the distribution which allots things equal and unequal, each to its own place. . . .

. . . God, then, the most wise Creator and most just Ordainer of all natures, who placed the human race upon earth as its greatest ornament, imparted to men some good things adapted to this life, to wit, temporal peace, such as we can enjoy in this life from health and safety and human fellowship, and all things needful for the preservation and recovery of this peace, such as the objects which are accommodated to our outward senses, light, night, the air, and waters suitable for us, and everything the body requires to sustain, shelter, heal, or beautify it: and all under this most equitable condition, that every man who made a good use of these advantages suited to the peace of his mortal condition, should receive ampler and better blessings, namely, the peace of immortality, accompanied by glory and honour in an endless life made fit for the enjoyment of God and of one another in God; but that he who used the present blessings badly should both lose them and should not receive the others.

xvii. What produces peace, and what discord, between the heavenly and earthly cities

The families which do not live by faith seek their peace in the earthly advantages of this life; while the families which live by faith look for those eternal blessings which are promised, and use as pilgrims such advantages of time and of earth as do not fascinate and divert them from God, but rather aid them to endure with greater ease, and to keep down the number of those burdens of the corruptible body which weigh upon the soul. Thus the things necessary for this mortal life are used by both kinds of men and families alike, but each has its own peculiar and widely different aim in using them. The earthly city, which does not live by faith, seeks an earthly peace, and the end it proposes, in the well-ordered concord of civic obedience and rule, is the combination of men's wills to attain the things which are helpful to this life. The heavenly city, or rather the part of it which sojourns on earth and lives by faith, makes use of this peace only because it must, until this mortal condition which necessitates it shall pass away. Consequently, so long as it lives like a captive and a stranger in the earthly city, though it has already received the promise of redemption, and the gift of the Spirit as the earnest of it, it makes no scruple to obey the laws of the earthly city, whereby the things necessary for the maintenance of this mortal life are administered; and thus, as this life is common to both cities, so there is a harmony between them in regard to what belongs to it. But, as the earthly city has had some philosophers whose doctrine is condemned by the divine teaching, and who, being deceived either by their own conjectures or by demons, supposed that many gods must be invited to take an interest in human affairs, and assigned to each a separate function and a separate department . . . it has come to pass that the two cities could not have common laws of religion, and that the heavenly city has been compelled in this matter to dissent, and to become obnoxious to those who think differently, and to stand the brunt of their anger and hatred and persecutions, except in so far as the minds of their enemies have been alarmed by the multitude of the Christians and quelled by the manifest protection of God accorded to them. This heavenly city, then, while it sojourns on earth, calls citizens out of all nations, and gathers together a society of pilgrims of all languages, not scrupling about diversities in the manners, laws, and institutions whereby earthly peace is secured and maintained, but recognising that, however various these are, they all tend to one and the same end of earthly peace. It therefore is so far from rescinding and abolishing these diversities, that it even preserves and adapts them, so

long only as no hindrance to the worship of the one supreme and true God is thus introduced. Even the heavenly city, therefore, while in its state of pilgrimage, avails itself of the peace of earth, and, so far as it can without injuring faith and godliness, desires and maintains a common agreement among men regarding the acquisiton of the necessaries of life, and makes this earthly peace bear upon the peace of heaven; for this alone can be truly called and esteemed the peace of the reasonable creatures, consisting as it does in the perfectly ordered and harmonious enjoyment of God and of one another in God. . . .

xxi. Whether there ever was a Roman republic answering to the definitions of Scipio in Cicero's dialogue

This, then, is the place where I should fulfil the promise I gave in the second book of this work, and explain as briefly and clearly as possible that if we are to accept the definitions laid down by Scipio in Cicero's *De Republica,* there never was a Roman republic; for he briefly defines a republic as the weal of the people. And if this definition be true, there never was a Roman republic, for the people's weal was never attained among the Romans. For the people, according to his definition, is an assemblage associated by a common acknowledgment of right and by a community of interests. And what he means by a common acknowledgment of right he explains at large, showing that a republic cannot be administered without justice. Where, therefore, there is no true justice there can be no right. For that which is done by right is justly done, and what is unjustly done cannot be done by right. For the unjust inventions of men are neither to be considered nor spoken of as rights; for even they themselves say that right is that which flows from the fountain of justice, and deny the definition which is commonly given by those who misconceive the matter, that right is that which is useful to the stronger party. Thus, where there is not true justice there can be no assemblage of men associated by a common acknowledgment of right, and therefore there can be no people, as defined by Scipio or Cicero; and if no people, then no weal of the people, but only of some promiscuous multitude unworthy of the name of people. Consequently, if the republic is the weal of the people, and there is no people if it be not associated by a common acknowledgment of right, and if there is no right where there is no justice, then most certainly it follows that there is no republic where there is no justice. Further, justice is that virtue which gives every one his due. Where, then, is the justice of man, when he deserts the true God and yields himself to impure demons? Is this to give every one his due? Or is he who keeps back a piece of ground from the purchaser, and gives it to a man who has no right to it, unjust, while he who keeps back himself from the God who made him, and serves wicked spirits, is just?

xxiv. The definition which must be given of a people and a republic, in order to vindicate the assumption of these titles by the Romans and by other kingdoms

But if we discard this definition of a people, and, assuming another, say that a people is an assemblage of reasonable beings bound together by a common agreement as to the objects of their love, then, in order to discover the character of any people, we have only to observe what they love. Yet whatever it loves, if only it is an assemblage of reasonable beings and not of beasts, and is bound together by an agreement as to the objects of love, it is reasonably called a people; and it will be a superior people in proportion as it is bound together by higher interests, inferior in proportion as it is bound together by lower. According to this definition of ours, the Roman people is a people, and its weal is without doubt a commonwealth or republic. But what its tastes were in its early and subsequent days, and how it declined into sanguinary seditions and then to social and civil wars, and so burst asunder or rotted off the bond of concord in which the health of a people consists, history shows, and in the preceding books I have related at large. And yet I would not on this account say either that it was not a people, or that its administration was not a republic, so long as there remains an assemblage of reasonable beings bound together by a common agreement as to the objects of love. But what I say of this people and of this republic I must be understood to think and say of the Athenians or any Greek state, of the Egyptians, of the early Assyrian Babylon, and of every other nation, great or small, which had a public government. For, in general, the city of the ungodly, which did not obey the command of God that it should offer no sacrifice save to Him alone, and which, therefore, could not give to the soul its proper command over the body, nor to the reason its just authority over the vices, is void of true justice.

xxvi. Of the peace which is enjoyed by the people that are alienated from God, and the use made of it by the people of God in the time of its pilgrimage

Wherefore, as the life of the flesh is the soul, so the blessed life of man is God, of whom the sacred writings of the Hebrews say, "Blessed is the people whose God is the Lord." Miserable, therefore, is the people which is alienated from God. Yet even this people has a peace of its own which is not to be lightly esteemed, though, indeed, it shall not in the end enjoy it, because it makes no good use of it before the end. But it is our interest that it enjoy this peace meanwhile in this life; for as long as the two cities are commingled, we also enjoy the peace of Babylon. For from Babylon the people of God is so freed that it meanwhile sojourns in its company. And therefore the apostle also admonished the Church to pray for kings and those in authority, assigning as the reason, "that we may live a quiet and tranquil life in all godliness and love." And the prophet Jeremiah, when predicting the captivity that was to befall the ancient people of God, and giving them the divine command to go obediently to Babylonia, and thus serve their God, counselled them also to pray for Babylonia, saying, "In the peace thereof shall ye have peace"—the temporal peace which the good and the wicked together enjoy.

xxvii. That the peace of those who serve God cannot in this mortal life be apprehended in its perfection

But the peace which is peculiar to ourselves we enjoy now with God by faith, and shall hereafter enjoy eternally with Him by sight. But the peace which we enjoy in this life, whether common to all or peculiar to ourselves, is rather the solace of our misery than the positive enjoyment of felicity . . . but, in that final peace to which all our righteousness has reference, and for the sake of which it is maintained, as our nature shall enjoy a sound immortality and incorruption, and shall have no more vices, and as we shall experience no resistance either from ourselves or from

others, it will not be necessary that reason should rule vices which no longer exist, but God shall rule the man, and the soul shall rule the body, with a sweetness and facility suitable to the felicity of a life which is done with bondage. And this condition shall there be eternal, and we shall be assured of its eternity; and thus the peace of this blessedness and the blessedness of this peace shall be the supreme good.

xxviii. The end of the wicked

But, on the other hand, they who do not belong to this city of God shall inherit eternal misery, which is also called the second death, because the soul shall then be separated from God its life, and therefore cannot be said to live, and the body shall be subjected to eternal pains. And consequently this second death shall be the more severe, because no death shall terminate it. But war being contrary to peace, as misery to happiness, and life to death, it is not without reason asked what kind of war can be found in the end of the wicked answering to the peace which is declared to be the end of the righteous? The person who puts this question has only to observe what it is in war that is hurtful and destructive, and he shall see that it is nothing else than the mutual opposition and conflict of things. And can he conceive a more grievous and bitter war than that in which the will is so opposed to passion, and passion to the will, that their hostility can never be terminated by the victory of either, and in which the violence of pain so conflicts with the nature of the body, that neither yields to the other? For in this life, when this conflict has arisen, either pain conquers and death expels the feeling of it, or nature conquers and health expels the pain. But in the world to come the pain continues that it may torment, and the nature endures that it may be sensible of it; and neither ceases to exist, lest punishment also should cease. . . .

BOOK TWENTY-TWO

xxix. Of the beatific vision

And now let us consider, with such ability as God may vouchsafe, how the saints shall be employed when they are clothed in immortal and spiritual bodies, and when the flesh shall live no longer in a fleshly but a spiritual fashion. And indeed, to tell the truth, I am at a loss to understand the nature of that employment, or, shall I rather say, repose and ease, for it has never come within the range of my bodily senses. And if I should speak of my mind or understanding, what is our understanding in comparison of its excellence? For then shall be that "peace of God which," as the apostle says, "passeth all understanding"— that is to say, all human, and perhaps all angelic understanding, but certainly not the divine.

xxx. Of the eternal felicity of the city of God, and of the perpetual Sabbath

How great shall be that felicity, which shall be tainted with no evil, which shall lack no good, and which shall afford leisure for the praises of God, who shall be all in all! For I know not what other employment there can be where no lassitude shall slacken activity, nor any want stimulate to labour. I am admonished also by the sacred song, in which I read or hear the words, "Blessed are they that dwell in Thy house, O Lord; they will be still praising Thee." All the members and organs of the incorruptible body, which now we see to be suited to various necessary uses, shall contribute to the praises of God; for in that

life necessity shall have no place, but full, certain, secure, everlasting felicity. For all those parts of the bodily harmony, which are distributed through the whole body, within and without, and of which I have just been saying that they at present elude our observation, shall then be discerned; and, along with the other great and marvellous discoveries which shall then kindle rational minds in praise of the great Artificer, there shall be the enjoyment of a beauty which appeals to the reason. What power of movement such bodies shall possess, I have not the audacity rashly to define, as I have not the ability to conceive. Nevertheless I will say that in any case, both in motion and at rest, they shall be, as in their appearance, seemly; for into that state nothing which is unseemly shall be admitted. One thing is certain, the body shall forthwith be wherever the spirit wills, and the spirit shall will nothing which is unbecoming either to the spirit or to the body. True honour shall be there, for it shall be denied to none who is worthy, nor yielded to any unworthy; neither shall any unworthy person so much as sue for it, for none but the worthy shall be there. True peace shall be there, where no one shall suffer opposition either from himself or any other. God Himself, who is the Author of virtue, shall there be its reward for as there is nothing greater or better, He has promised Himself. What else was meant by His word, through the prophet, "I will be your God, and ye shall be my people," then, I shall be their satisfaction, I shall be all that men honourably desire—life, and health, and nourishment, and plenty, and glory, and honour, and peace, and all good things? This, too, is the right interpretation of the saying of the apostle, "That God may be all in all." He shall be the end of our desires who shall be seen without end, loved without cloy, praised without weariness. This outgoing of affection, this employment, shall certainly be, like eternal life itself, common to all.

But who can conceive, not to say describe, what degrees of honour and glory shall be awarded to the various degrees of merit? Yet it cannot be doubted that there shall be degrees. And in that blessed city there shall be this great blessing, that no inferior shall envy any superior, as now the archangels are not envied by the angels, because no one will wish to be what he has not received, though bound in strictest concord with him who has received; as in the body the finger does not seek to be the eye, though both members are harmoniously included in the complete structure of the body. And thus, along with this gift, greater or less, each shall receive this further gift of contentment to desire no more than he has.

Neither are we to suppose that because sin shall have no power to delight them, free will must be withdrawn. It will, on the contrary, be all the more truly free, because set free from delight in sinning to take unfailing delight in not sinning. For the first freedom of will which man received when he was created upright consisted in an ability not to sin, but also in an ability to sin; whereas this last freedom of will shall be superior, inasmuch as it shall not be able to sin. This, indeed, shall not be a natural ability, but the gift of God. . . . In that city, then, there shall be free will, one in all the citizens, and indivisible in each, delivered from all ill, filled with all good, enjoying indefeasibly the delights of eternal joys, oblivious of sins, oblivious of sufferings, and yet not so oblivious of its deliverance as to be ungrateful to its Deliverer.

. . . There shall be the great Sabbath which has no evening, which God celebrated among His first works, as it is written, "And God rested on the seventh day from all His works which He had made. And God blessed the seventh day, and sanctified it; because that in it He had rested from all His work which God began to make." For we shall ourselves be the seventh day, when we shall be filled and replenished with God's blessing and sanctification. There shall we be still, and know that He is God; that He is that which we ourselves aspired to be when we fell away from Him, and listened to the voice of the seducer, "Ye shall be as gods," and so abandoned God, who would have made us as gods, not by deserting Him, but by participating in Him. For without Him what have we accomplished, save to perish in His anger? But when we are restored by Him, and perfected with greater grace, we shall have eternal leisure to see that He is God, for we shall be full of Him when He shall be all in all. For even our good works, when they are understood to be rather His than ours, are imputed to us that we may enjoy this Sabbath rest. For if we attribute them to ourselves, they shall be servile; for it is said of the Sabbath, "Ye shall do no servile work in it." Wherefore also it is said by Ezekiel the prophet, "And I gave them my Sabbaths to be a sign between me and them, that they might know that I am the Lord who sanctify them." This knowledge shall be perfected when we shall be perfectly at rest, and shall perfectly know that He is God.

This Sabbath shall appear still more clearly if we count the ages as days, in accordance with the periods of time defined in Scripture, for that period will be found to be the seventh. The first age, as the first day, extends from Adam to the deluge;

the second from the deluge to Abraham, equalling the first, not in length of time, but in the number of generations, there being ten in each. From Abraham to the advent of Christ there are, as the evangelist Matthew calculates, three periods, in each of which are fourteen generations—one period from Abraham to David, a second from David to the captivity, a third from the captivity to the birth of Christ in the flesh. There are thus five ages in all. The sixth is now passing, and cannot be measured by any number of generations, as it has been said, "It is not for you to know the times, which the Father hath put in His own power." After this period God shall rest as on the seventh day, when He shall give us (who shall be the seventh day) rest in Himself. But there is not now space to treat of these ages; suffice it to say

that the seventh shall be our Sabbath, which shall be brought to a close, not by an evening, but by the Lord's day, as an eighth and eternal day, consecrated by the resurrection of Christ, and prefiguring the eternal repose not only of the spirit, but also of the body. There we shall rest and see, see and love, love and praise. This is what shall be in the end without end. For what other end do we propose to ourselves than to attain to the kingdom of which there is no end?

I think I have now, by God's help, discharged my obligation in writing this large work. Let those who think I have said too little, or those who think I have said too much, forgive me; and let those who think I have said just enough join me in giving thanks to God.

Amen.

SUGGESTIONS FOR FURTHER READING

The following select bibliography is intended for the student who wishes to follow up points raised by his reading. It does not include all of the works cited in the text. Therefore students should also consult the footnotes. Much more comprehensive bibliographies are included in the general historical works cited below. Books available in paperback are marked with an asterisk.

General Works of Reference
The Encyclopedia of Philosophy, Paul Edwards, ed. New York, The Macmillan Company, 1967.
Encyclopedia of the Social Sciences, E. R. Seligman, ed. New York, The Macmillan Company, 1930.
International Encyclopedia of the Social Sciences, David L. Sills, ed. New York, The Macmillan Company, 1968.
New Catholic Encyclopedia, Catholic University of America, eds. New York, McGraw-Hill, Inc., 1967.
The Oxford Classical Dictionary, M. Cary and others, eds. New York, Oxford University Press, 1949.

Some Useful Introductory Works on Social Institutions
Eisenstadt, S. N., *The Decline of Empires.* Englewood Cliffs, N. J., Prentice-Hall, Inc., 1967.
Friedrich, C. J., ed., *Authority.* Cambridge, Mass. Harvard University Press, 1958.
——, *Community.* Indianapolis, Liberal Arts Press, 1959.
* Goode, W. J., *The Family.* Englewood Cliffs, N. J., Prentice-Hall, Inc., 1964.
Hart, H. L. A., *The Concept of Law.* New York, Oxford University Press, 1961.
*Inkeles, A., *What Is Sociology?: An Introduction to the Discipline and Profession.* Englewood Cliffs, N. J., Prentice-Hall, Inc., 1964.
MacIver, R. M., *The Modern State.* New York, Oxford University Press, 1926.
* O'Dea, T. F., *The Sociology of Religion.* Englewood Cliffs, N. J., Prentice-Hall, Inc., 1966.
* Parsons, T., *Societies: Evolutionary and Comparative Perspectives.* Englewood Cliffs, N. J., Prentice-Hall, Inc., 1966.
Stone, J., *The Social Dimensions of Law and Justice.* Stanford, Stanford University Press, 1966.

General Works on Roman History

Alföldi, A., *Early Rome and the Latins*. Ann Arbor, University of Michigan Press, 1964.

Balsdon, J. P. V. D., *Life and Leisure in Ancient Rome*. New York, Mc-Graw-Hill, Inc., 1969.

* Barrow, R. H., *The Romans*. Baltimore, Penguin Books, Inc., 1949.

Bloch, R., *Origins of Rome*. New York, Frederick A. Praeger, Inc., 1960.

Boak, A. E. and W. G. Sinnigen, *A History of Rome to 565 A.D*. New York, The Macmillan Company, 1965.

Bourne, F. C., *A History of the Romans*. Indianapolis, D. C. Heath & Company, 1966.

The Cambridge Ancient History, Vols. VII–XII, J. B. Bury, F. E. Adcock, and others, eds. New York, Cambridge University Press, 1923–1939.

Cary, M., *The Geographic Background of Greek and Roman History*. New York, Oxford University Press, 1949.

* Carcopino, J., *Daily Life in Ancient Rome*. H. T. Rowell, ed., E. O. Lorimer, tr. New Haven, Yale University Press, 1940.

* Dill, S., *Roman Society from Nero to Marcus Aurelius*. Cleveland, World Publishing Company, 1956.

* Dudley, D. R., *The Civilization of Rome*. New York, New American Library, 1960.

Frank, T., *An Economic History of Rome*, 2d rev. ed. Baltimore, Johns Hopkins University Press, 1927.

Grant, M., *The Climax of Rome*. Boston, Little, Brown & Co., 1968.

Grimal, P., *The Civilization of Rome*. New York, Simon & Schuster, Inc., 1963.

* Hadas, M., *A History of Rome*. New York, Doubleday & Company, Inc., 1956.

Jones, A. H. M., *The Decline of the Ancient World*. New York, Holt, Rinehart and Winston, Inc., 1966.

———, *The Later Roman Empire, 284–602*. Norman, Okla., University of Oklahoma Press, 1964.

* Lewis, N., and M. Reinhold, eds., *Roman Civilization*, 2 vols. New York, Harper & Row, Publishers, 1951.

* Lot, F., *The End of the Ancient World and the Beginnings of the Middle Ages*, P. and M. Leon, trs. New York, Barnes & Noble, Inc.; Harper & Row, Publishers, 1961.

McDonald, A. H., *Republican Rome*. New York, Frederick A. Praeger, Inc., 1966.

Rostovtzeff, M. I., *The Social and Economic History of the Roman Empire*, 2d rev. ed. (2 vols.), P. M. Frazer, ed. New York, Oxford University Press, 1957.

Rowell, H. T., *Rome in the Augustan Age*. Norman, Okla.: University of Oklahoma Press, 1962.

* Syme, R., *The Roman Revolution*. New York, Oxford University Press, 1960.
* Taylor, L. R., *Party Politics in the Age of Caesar*. Berkeley, University of California Press, 1949.

Van der Heyden, A. A. M. and H. H. Scullard, eds., *Atlas of the Classical World*. Camden, N.J. Thomas Nelson & Sons, 1960.

Roman Institutions

Crook, J. A., *Law and Life of Rome, 90 B.C.–A.D. 212*. Ithaca, N. Y., Cornell University Press, 1957.

Homo, L., *Roman Political Institutions from City to State,* M. R. Dobie, tr. New York, Barnes & Noble, Inc., 1965.

Jones, A. H. M., *Studies in Roman Government and Law*. New York, Barnes & Noble, Inc., 1960.

Larsen, J. A. O., *Representative Government in Greek and Roman History*. Berkeley, University of California Press, 1955.

* Levi, M. A., *Political Power in the Ancient World*. New York, New American Library, 1965.

Nicholas, B., *An Introduction to Roman Law*. New York, Oxford University Press, 1962.

Sherwin-White, A. N., *Roman Citizenship*. New York, Oxford University Press, 1939.

Taylor, L. R., *Roman Voting Assemblies: From the Hannibalic War to the Dictatorship of Caesar*. Ann Arbor, University of Michigan Press, 1966.

Watson, G. R., *The Roman Soldier*. Ithaca, N. Y., Cornell University Press, 1969.

Westerman, W. L., *The Slave Systems of Greek and Roman Antiquity*. Philadelphia, American Philosophical Society, 1955.

Roman Culture

Arnold, E. V., *Roman Stoicism*. New York, The Macmillan Company, 1911.

* Cairns, H., *Legal Philosophy from Plato to Hegel*. Baltimore, Johns Hopkins Press, 1950.

Clarke, M. L., *Rhetoric at Rome*. New York, Barnes & Noble, Inc., 1953.

* ———, *The Roman Mind: Studies in the History of Thought from Cicero to Marcus Aurelius*. Cambridge, Mass., Harvard University Press, 1956.

* Cowell, F. R., *Cicero and the Roman Republic*. Baltimore, Penguin Books, Inc., 1956.

Earl, D. A., *The Moral and Political Tradition of Rome*. Ithaca, Cornell University Press, 1967.

Ferguson, J., *Moral Values in the Ancient World*. New York, Barnes & Noble, Inc., 1958.

Fowler, W. W., *The Religious Experience of the Roman People*. New York, The Macmillan Company, 1911.

Fritz, K. von, *The Theory of the Mixed Constitution in Antiquity*. New York, Columbia University Press, 1954.

* Grant, M., *Roman Literature*, rev. ed. Baltimore, Penguin Books, Inc., 1958.

* Gwynn, A. O., *Roman Education from Cicero to Quintilian*. New York, Russell & Russell, Publishers, 1926.

Hunt, H. A. K., *The Humanism of Cicero*. New York, Cambridge University Press, 1954.

Lintott, A. W., *Violence in Republican Rome*. New York, Oxford University Press, 1968.

L'Orange, H. P., *Art Forms and Civic Life in the Late Roman Empire*. Princeton, Princeton University Press, 1965.

MacDonald, W. L., *The Architecture of the Roman Empire*, 2 vols. New Haven, Yale University Press, 1965.

* Marrou, H. I., *A History of Education in Antiquity*. New York, New American Library, 1956.

Palmer, L. R., *The Latin Language*, 3d ed. New York, Barnes & Noble, Inc., 1954.

Christianity and the Roman Empire

Baynes, N. H., *Constantine the Great and the Conversion of Europe*. New York, Oxford University Press, 1931.

Brown, P., *Augustine of Hippo*. Berkeley, University of California Press, 1967.

* Cochrane, C. N., *Christianity and Classical Culture: A Study of Thought and Action from Augustus to Augustine*. New York, Oxford University Press, 1940.

* D'Arcy, M. C. and others, *St. Augustine: His Age, Life and Thought*. Cleveland, World Publishing Company, 1957.

*Deane, H. A., *Political and Social Ideas of St. Augustine*. New York, Columbia University Press, 1963.

Dodds, E. R., *Pagan and Christian in an Age of Anxiety*. New York, Cambridge University Press, 1965.

Frend, W. H., *The Early Church*. Philadelphia, J. B. Lippincott Company, 1966.

Goodenough, E. R., *The Church in the Roman Empire*. New York, Holt, Rinehart and Winston, 1931.

Greenslade, S. L., *Church and State from Constantine to Theodosius*. Naperville, Ill., Allenson, 1954.

Jones, A. H. M., *Contsantine and the Conversion of Europe*. New York, The Macmillan Company, 1948.

Momigliano, A., *Paganism and Christianity in the Fourth Century*. New York, Oxford University Press, 1963.

* Nock, A. D., *Conversion: The Old and the New in Religion from Alexander the Great to Augustine of Hippo*. New York, Oxford University Press, 1952.

* Van der Meer, F., *Augustine the Bishop: Church and Society at the Dawn of the Middle Ages*. New York, Sheed & Ward, Inc., 1961.